Quicken 4 for W[indows] Answers: Certified Tech Support

**Mary Campbell &
David Campbell, CPA**

Osborne **McGraw-Hill**
Berkeley • New York • St. Louis
San Francisco • Auckland • Bogotá
Hamburg • London • Madrid • Mexico
City • Milan • Montreal • New Delhi
Panama City • Paris • São Paulo
Singapore • Sydney • Tokyo • Toronto

Osborne **McGraw-Hill**
2600 Tenth Street, Berkeley, California 94710, USA

For information on software, translations, or book distributors outside of the U.S.A., please write to Osborne McGraw-Hill at the above address.

Quicken 4 for Windows Answers: Certified Tech Support

Copyright © 1995 by McGraw-Hill, Inc. All rights reserved. Printed in the United States of America. Except as permitted under the Copyright Act of 1976, no part of this publication may be reproduced or distributed in any form or by any means, or stored in a database or retrieval system, without the prior written permission of the publisher, with the exception that the program listings may be entered, stored, and executed in a computer system, but they may not be reproduced for publication.

1234567890 DOC 998765

ISBN 0-07-882129-0

Publisher
Larry Levitsky

Acquisitions Editor
Joanne Cuthbertson

Project Editor
Mark Karmendy

Copy Editor
Vicki Van Ausdall

Computer Designer
Roberta Steele

Series Design and Illustrator
Marla Shelasky

Quality Control Specialist
Joe Scuderi

Cover Design
Ted Mader Associates

Information has been obtained by Osborne **McGraw-Hill** and Corporate Software Inc. from sources believed to be reliable. However, because of the possibility of human or mechanical error by our sources, Osborne **McGraw-Hill**, Corporate Software Inc., or others, Osborne **McGraw-Hill** and Corporate Software Inc. do not guarantee the accuracy, adequacy, or completeness of any information and is not responsible for any errors or omissions or the results obtained from use of such information. Because tax regulations are complex and constantly changing, you will want to check with your tax attorney or accountant to select strategies that are within the framework of the law and most advantageous to your situation.

About the Authors

Software expert Mary Campbell is the author of *Quicken 4 for Windows Made Easy* and has written four other books in the Certified Tech Support series covering DOS, WordPerfect for Windows, Excel for Windows, and Microsoft Access. She has also written best-selling books on Lotus 1-2-3, dBASE, and Harvard Graphics. As an experienced corporate trainer and president of her own computer training company, she has taught thousands of people to use these and many other popular software programs.

David Campbell, co-author of all the editions of *Quicken Made Easy*, which has been revised for every new software release, and *Quickbooks for Profit: Making the Numbers Work* (DOS version), is chairman of the Accounting Department at Case Western Reserve University, where he is also a professor of accounting. In addition, he is a CPA and has published widely on accounting systems methods. Professor Campbell holds a Ph.D. in accounting from the University of Georgia.

Contents

Foreword	xv
Acknowledgments	xvii
Introduction	xix

1
Top Ten Tech Terrors   1

The transaction that I just entered disappeared. How do I get it back?   2

Why does my Portfolio View show all securities instead of just the ones in the investment account displayed at the top of the window?   3

Why do I see a message that Windows cannot find BILLMNDW.EXE when I start Windows?   4

When installing Quicken I get the message "Unable to Decompress Application Files." What is causing the problem?   5

Why do I have a negative balance in my investment account?   5

Why don't I see any subcategories in my Budget window?   6

How can I alphabetize my stocks so I can find them faster in the Portfolio View window?   6

I just updated my stock prices and a lot of stocks that I didn't change show some of the stock prices that I just entered. Why?   7

Why won't Quicken let me transfer money to my investment account from my checking account?   7

Why won't Quicken remember to use the Standard check style that I keep selecting?   8

2
Starting Out and Setting Up   11

Setup Requirements   13

Hardware requirements   13

Using old Quicken files	14
Backwards compatibility	14
Finding old Quicken files	15
Finding existing files in Quicken	15
Eliminating Quicken reminders	16
Saving a minimized window	17
Printing checks versus reports	17
Virus checker messages	17

Transferring Quicken Files Between Computers — 17

Moving Quicken files from one computer to another	17
Getting Mac files onto DOS platform	18

Backups — 19

BACKUP directory files	19
Approaches to backing up files	20

Startup and File Options — 21

Automatically starting up Quicken	21
Opening the right file	21
Renaming files	22

Setting Up a Communications Link — 23

Setting up a modem	23
Call waiting	25
IntelliCharge connection	25
IntelliCharge account errors	26

Standard Categories — 26

Identifying standard home categories	26
Identifying standard business categories	28
Changing categories	28

Transferring Data Between Files — 30

Moving data to another file	30
Copying data between files	32

Custom Categories — 34

Creating a category	34
Tax categories	35
Deleting a subcategory	36
Transferring categories	37

Historical Data — 37

Entering old transactions	37
Re-entering old data	37
Repetitive entries from the past	40
Deleting last year's transactions	42

Protecting Data — 43

Preventing others from accessing data	43
Accidentally changing data	44

3
Registers and Transactions — 45

Changing the Register's Appearance — 46

Showing more entries	46
Register buttons	47
Account selectors	47

Accounts Versus Categories — 48

Difference between accounts and categories	48
Entering a transaction	49

Creating Subcategories — 50
Subdividing existing categories — 50

Switching Categories and Accounts — 50
Moving entries — 50
Switching between accounts — 51

Basic Transactions — 51
Undeleting a transaction — 51
Searching for entries — 52
Finding particular transactions — 52
Fixing misspellings — 54
Fast way to enter dates — 55
Difference between Xs in Clr field — 56
Printing transactions — 56
Ordering transactions in a list — 57
Printing transactions by order — 57
Transferring transactions — 59
Changing a split transaction — 60
Storing addresses with payments — 60
Entering ATM transactions — 60

Adjusting Account Register Balances — 62
Reconciling account register — 62
Reconciling credit card register — 62

Hiding Account Balances — 63
Viewing bank balance — 63
Hiding minimum checking amount — 63

Credit Cards — 64
Credit card interest rates — 64
Credit card limit changes — 65
Tracking credit card purchases — 65

Monitoring Cash — 66
Tracking spending — 66
Recording weekly spending — 66

Sales Tax and Reminders — 67
Allocating sales tax to categories — 67
Reminders to paying bills — 68

Memorized Transactions — 70
Use of transactions as templates — 70
Individual use of memorized transaction feature — 71
Using percentages rather than numbers — 72
Fixing errors — 74
Deleting a memorized transaction — 74
Deleting a group of memorized transactions — 75
Using constants as entries — 75

Scheduled Transactions — 76
Entering transactions before they occur — 76
Use of repeating transactions — 76
Normal transaction to scheduled one — 79

Scheduled Transaction Groups — 79
How to schedule transactions at once — 79
Changing transactions in a group — 81
Getting rid of transaction groups — 82

4
Checks and Reconciliation — 83

Writing and Voiding Checks — 85
How to void a check — 85

Writing a postdated check	86
Combination check/cash payments	86
Hiding text in the Payee field	87
Fixing check writing mistakes	87
Locating an address on an old check	88

Joint Checking Accounts — 89

Setting up a joint checking account	89
Showing only the transactions of half of a joint checking account	90

Scheduled Payments — 90

Scheduled transactions for checks	90
Loan payments	91

Printing Checks — 91

Check printing test	91
How to align checks in the printer	91
Printing additional checks on a partially used page	95
Misprinted checks	95
When Quicken doesn't print checks after clicking Print Checks icon	95

Changing a Check's Appearance — 96

Logos on checks	96
Check background changes	97

Reconciliation Problems — 97

Adding interest and service charges	97
Reconciling uncleared transactions	99
Checks and deposits not entered into Quicken	99
Incorrect beginning balance	100
Opening balance doesn't match ending balance	100
Reconciling bank statements with errors	101
Savings goals and reconciliation	101
Canceling unfinished reconciliations	101
Checks with bank discrepencies	102

CheckFree — 102

What CheckFree is and why use it	102
Making payments with CheckFree	103
Paying a loan with CheckFree	106
Listing my CheckFree transactions	107
Contacting CheckFree	108
Difference between electronic payment and electronic funds transfer	108
Stopping electronic payments once sent	109
Stopping a series of fixed electronic payments	109
Confirming a CheckFree payment	111
Transmission problems with OS/2	111

5
Taxes — 113

Tax Planning — 115

Estimating taxes owed	115
Showing withholding amounts	116
TurboTax versus Tax Planner	117

Tax Form Assignments — 117

Correct tax lines to use	117
Adding categories to tax form lines for use in the Tax Planner	118
Not including categories in the Tax Planner's tax forms	118
Categories marked as tax-related	119
Including expenses and income in the Tax Planner	119

Importing Quicken Data into the Tax Planner	120
Previewing taxes	120
Missing transactions in Tax Planner	121
Selecting data year to import	121

Tax Reports	122
Finding necessary numbers for tax forms	122
Difference between Tax Summary and Tax Schedule report	122
Source of Tax Planner's numbers	123
Printing Tax Planner results	124

Entering Income into the Tax Planner	126
Matching up W-2 with Tax Planner	126
Annual income estimate after job change	128
Calculating taxes with paycheck's net amount	128
Keeping tax-deferred income from showing up in the tax forms	130

IRA Deduction in the Tax Planner	130
Calculating IRA deduction	130
Entering IRA contributions after the fact	131

Itemizing	131
Quicken itemizing recommendations	131
Medical and dental bills	132
Local income taxes in Tax Planner	133
Refund checks	133
Points on my home mortgage	133
Recording home improvements	134

Schedules B, C, and D	135
Schedule B list of payers	135
Separate business concerns	137
Getting Schedule C information	137
Preparing Schedule D	137

Self Employment Taxes and Tax Credits	138
Calculating self-employment taxes	138
Spouse's business income appearing as yours	139
Calculating credits in the Tax Planner	139

Withheld, Estimating, and Estimated Taxes	140
Last year's taxes versus this year's withholding	140
Estimating remaining year's tax	140
Entering taxes already paid	141

Updating the Tax Planner	142
Taxes if rates change	142
Quicken's updates if tax changes	142

Planning	142
After current year	142
Testing changes temporarily	143

6
Investments 145

Setting Up Investment Accounts	147
When to use investment accounts	147
When to add a new account	148
Different investment actions	148

Stock Symbols and Names	149
Stock symbol meanings	149

Company name changes	150	**Stock Dividend**	**175**
Investment Goals	**150**	Recording a dividend	175
When to use investment goals	150	Recording fractional shares	175
Seeing what I own	151	**Tax-deferred Transactions,**	
Seeing investment earnings	153	**Gifts, and Inheritances**	**176**
Stock Options and Stock		Entering tax-deferred information	176
Rights	**154**	Recording gifts of stock	176
Recording buying and selling options	154	Recording inherited investments	177
Soon-to-expire options	158	**Bonds and Treasury Bills**	**177**
Stock rights versus stocks	158	Entering accrued interest	177
Employee Stock Options	**159**	Handling interest checks	179
Qualified employee stock options	159	Handling treasury bills	180
Nonqualified employee stock options	161	1099-OID on zero-coupon bonds	180
Individual Retirement		Entering Series EE bond	181
Accounts	**164**	**Limited Partnerships**	**182**
Keeping track of IRAs	164	Recording receivings	182
IRA's and mutual fund's annual fee	165	**Capital Gains and**	
401(k) Plans	**165**	**Investment Values**	**182**
Entering 401(k) information	165	Listing capital gains	182
Paycheck's 401(k) contributions	166	Finding out current worth	183
Company contributions to 401(k)	168	**Brokerage Accounts**	**184**
Check Writing from an		Transferring shares	184
Investment Account	**169**	Adding money	185
Writing a check	169	Recording additions and deletions	185
		Recording interest after stock is sold	186
		Different Security Prices	**186**
		How Quicken tracks	186
		Working in the Portfolio	
		View Window	**188**
		Register versus Portfolio View window	188
Buyouts, Spin-offs and		Showing more than one account	189
Return of Capital	**170**	Combining different views	189
Converting stocks	170	Showing already sold stock	190
Entering spin-off shares	171	**Investment Graphs**	**191**
Adding capital returns	174	Differing IRR	191

Showing missing securities	191

Scheduled Investment Transactions — 193

Creating for investments	193

Storing Prices and Portfolio Price Update — 194

Historical prices of stock	194
Using the Portfolio Price Update	194
Paying to use Portfolio Price Update	195
Current prices	195
Stock indexes	195

7
Business — 197

Setting Up Quicken for Business — 199

Changing categories for business	199
A separate business budget	200

Using Quicken for Business Versus Personal Finances — 200

Using the same Quicken file	200
Part personal/part business expenses	201

Payroll — 202

Kinds of categories and accounts	202
Employee wages	203
Employee withholdings	203
Entering separate payroll tax amounts	206
Generating W-2 numbers	208
Getting numbers for payroll taxes	209
Numbers for Forms 940 and 941	209
Payroll tax reminder	209

Sales Tax — 210

Tracking sales tax	210

Job Costing — 210

Job order costing in Quicken	210
Expenses by store or department	211
Rental income and expenses	211

Depreciation — 213

Recording depreciation in Quicken	213
Recording Section 179 deductions	214

Owner Withdrawals and Keogh Contributions — 214

Tracking personal expenditures from a business account	214
Recording Keogh contributions	215

Business Deductions — 216

Business mileage in Quicken	216
Meal and entertainment deductions	218

Accounts Receivable and Accounts Payable — 218

Recording accounts receivable	218
Creating accounts receivable report	220
How to keep track of bills	221
Listing who you need to pay	223

8
Budgeting — 225

Budget Reports — 227

Planned versus actual spending	227
Where recent budget is	228
Missing beginning characters in title	228

Sideways printing 229

Creating Budget Entries 229

Using existing data 229
Using last year's numbers 231
Applying January's numbers to rest of year's budget 231
Repeat category budget 232
Savings budget 232
Two versus three paychecks a month 234
Use of underscore in categories 234

Hiding Budget Numbers 235

Non-budget items 235
Non-budgeted expenditures 236

Supercategories 236

Parent category for regular category 236
Organization by supercategories 237
Supercategory assignments to non-budget categories 238

Budget Differences 238

Non-matching numbers 238
Problems with Autocreate feature 239

Budget Window 240

When a deleted account is displayed 240
Viewing subcategories 240
Time periods other than months 241

Exporting Budget Data 241

To word processor or spreadsheet 241

Creating Multiple Budgets 243

How to create more than one budget 243

9
Reports and Graphs 245

Types of Reports 247

Viewing expenditures 247
Monthly spending report 250
Missing last year's data for Comparison report 250
Show/hide transfers between accounts in Cash Flow Report 252

Targeting Reports 252

Limit reports to business transactions 252
Setting dates for report 253
Fiscal year versus calendar year 254
Showing amounts for each month 255
Missing entries 255

Layout and Format 256

Using descriptions versus names 256
Shortened report entries 257
Customize Report dialog box options 258
Text fonts 258
Changing text in Report window 258
Changing report's margins 259

Printing Reports 260

Fitting in more columns 260
Different look after printing 260
Print button in iconbar versus in button bar 261
Printing on different sized paper 262

QuickZoom Reports 262

Finding origin of a given number 262
Fixing wrong entry 263
Different mouse pointer displays 263

Quicken Reports in Word Processors 264

Copying to word processor 264

Fixing bad columns	265	**10**		
Report Windows	**265**	**Financial Planning**	**283**	
Disappearing reports	265			
Saving reports	266	**Savings Planner**	**285**	
Keeping same dates	266	Estimating CD earnings	285	
Filtering Reports	**267**	Estimating mutual fund value	287	
Ignoring zero amount transactions	267	Focus on today's dollars	288	
Filtering to include multiple items	269	**Retirement Planner**	**289**	
Using filters to find missing entries	269	How much to withdraw when retired	289	
Deleting uncategorized transactions	269	**Refinance Planner**	**290**	
Other Report Settings	**270**	Making the loan calculations	290	
Cash flow versus income & expense	270	**Savings Goals**	**292**	
Differing balance amounts	271	Earmarking dollars	292	
Graphs	**271**	Checking goals	293	
Showing savings	271	Recording spending of savings	294	
Bar or slice values	272	**Forecasting**	**296**	
Using same numbers as in reports	273	Forcasting savings	296	
Changing Graphs	**276**	Forecasting versus budgeting	296	
Hiding a category	276	Forecasted income and expenses	297	
Changing accounts	276	When buying a house	297	
Viewing more detail	277	When dealing with other expenses that will change	299	
Graphs into separate windows	277	When using this year's data	299	
Making graphs faster	278	Changing time period	299	
Printing Graphs	**278**	From budget numbers	300	
Graphs with patterns versus colors	278	Comparing to the budget	300	
Speeding up printing time	279	Using forecast numbers for budget	302	
Using color	280			
Printing problems in Quicken	280	**Index**	**303**	

Foreword

Few things are as frustrating as having a computer problem that you can't solve. Computer users often spend hours trying to find the answer to a *single* software question! That's why the tech support experts at Corporate Software Incorporated (CSI) have teamed up with Osborne/McGraw-Hill to bring you the **Certified Tech Support Series**—books designed to give you all the solutions you need to fix even the most difficult software glitches.

At Corporate Software, we have a dedicated support staff that handles over 200,000 software questions every month. These experts use the latest hardware and software technology to provide answers to every sort of software problem. CSI takes full advantage of the partnerships that we have forged with all major software publishers. Our staff frequently receives the same training that publishers offer their own support representatives and has access to vendor technical resources that are not generally available to the public.

Thus, this series is based on actual *empirical* data. We've drawn on our support expertise and sorted through our vast database of software solutions to find the most important and frequently asked questions for Quicken. These questions have also been checked and rechecked for technical accuracy and are organized in a way that will let you find the answer you need quickly—providing you with a one-stop tech support solution to your software problems.

No longer do you have to spend hours on the phone waiting for someone to answer your tech support question! You are holding the single, most authoritative collection of answers to your software questions available—the next best thing to having a tech support expert by your side.

We've helped millions of people solve their software problems. Let us help you.

Randy Burkhart
Senior Vice President, Technology
Corporate Software Inc

Acknowledgments

I would like to thank all the staff at Corporate Software who enthusiastically committed so much time and knowledge to this effort. So many of them spent time on weekends and after hours to search their data banks for the best questions and answers. They also spent untold hours reviewing manuscript and pages and responding to all of our requests for help. Without all of their hard work, this book would not exist. I would like to personally thank each of the following people for their assistance: Kim A., Brian A., Pam M., Linda S., Gary D., Micheal H., Andre O., Lenny B., K.C.C., David S., John C., Delores B., Eric H., Gary H., Peter D., Penny G., Merv N., Calvin S., Howard H., Curtis G., and Neal S.

The staff at Osborne was also an important part of this book. Without exception, everyone did more than their share to insure that we met all the important deadlines. I would like to extend special thanks to Larry Levitsky, Publisher, for the idea to do the series and all of his work with Corporate Software to make the idea a reality; Joanne Cuthbertson, Acquisitions Editor, who took the time to read each chapter and made excellent suggestions for improvements; Kelly Vogel, Editorial Assistant, who helped to organize all the components of the project; Mark Karmendy, Project Editor, whose handling of this project was as flawless as ever; and all of the Production staff, who each did everything possible to make this book the best source of technical support available.

I would also like to especially thank my assistant, Gabrielle Lawrence. She contributed extensively to the book's contents and art work. She also proofread the final manuscript to help catch technical and grammatical errors.

Introduction

There is no good time to have a problem with your computer or the software you are using. You are anxious to complete the task you started and do not have time to fumble through a manual looking for an answer that is probably not there anyway. You can forget about the option of a free support call solving your problems since most software vendors now charge as much as $25 to answer a single question. *Quicken 4 for Windows Answers: Certified Tech Support* can provide the solution to all of your Quicken problems. It contains the most frequently asked Quicken questions along with the solutions to get you back on track quickly. The questions and answers have been put together from our extensive use of Quicken as well as extracted from the data banks of Corporate Software, the world's largest supplier of third-party support. Since they answer over 200,000 calls a month from users just like you, odds are high that your problem has plagued others in the past and is already part of their data bank. *Quicken 4 for Windows Answers: Certified Tech Support* is the next best thing to having a Corporate Software expert at the desk right next to you. The help you need is available seven days a week, any time you have a problem.

Quicken Answers is organized into ten chapters. Each chapter contains questions and answers on a specific area of Quicken. Within each chapter, you will find the questions organized by features of that Quicken topic. With this organization, you can read through questions and answers on particular topics to familiarize yourself with them before the troubles actually occur. An excellent index makes it easy for you to find what you need even if you are uncertain which chapter would cover the solution.

Throughout the book you will also find the following elements to help you sail smoothly through your Quicken tasks, whether you are a novice or a veteran user:

- **Frustration Busters:** Special coverage of Quicken topics that have proven confusing to many users. A few minutes spent reading each of these boxes can help you avoid problems in the first place.
- **Tech Tips and Notes:** Short technical helps that provide additional insight to a topic addressed in one of the questions.
- **Tech Terrors:** Pitfalls you will want to steer clear of.
- **Tech Acct:** Financial hints that are not necessarily a Quicken feature.

Top Ten Tech Terrors

Every computer user experiences technical difficulties at one time or another. We've tapped the data banks and consultant expertise at Corporate Software to identify and provide step-by-step solutions to ten of the most common Quicken for Windows problems. These are problems encountered by *thousands* of users. These users have turned to the consultant expertise at Corporate Software for help, and so can you!

In fact, you can probably avoid these common problems altogether simply by reviewing this list. If for some reason, however, you still run into any of them, you'll know just what to do.

Quicken 4 for Windows Answers: *Certified Tech Support*

The transaction that I just entered disappeared. How do I get it back?

Quicken organizes your register transactions by date. The transaction's date that you just entered probably is out of range of the dates that appear in the section of the register you are viewing. The best way to find the entry is to search your register for the transaction's payee or some other unique feature of the entry. To search for a particular payee in a register:

1. Click the Find button in the Register window's button bar. This button performs the same function as choosing Find in the Edit menu. You will see a dialog box like this:

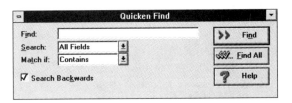

2. Type the payee that you want to locate in the Find text box.
3. Select Payee from the Search drop-down list box.
4. Keep selecting Find until Quicken shows the transaction that you just entered.
5. Press ESC or double-click the Control menu box to put the Quicken Find dialog box away.

Tech Terror: For investment accounts, you can choose Find in the Edit menu when you want to search for a particular investment. Investment registers have different buttons in the button bar; you won't see Find in the button bar. Investment transactions also do not have a Payee field, so you will need to select a different field to search.

2 Why does my Portfolio View show all securities instead of just the ones in the investment account displayed at the top of the window?

Your Portfolio View window is set to show all securities that you have set up rather than the ones that you have in the account. You can tell this because several of the securities have nothing in the Shares column, as the Portfolio View window shows in Figure 1-1. You can change this window to have the list of securities only include the ones that you own with the chosen account. To do this:

1. Choose the Custom button from the Portfolio View window.
2. Select the Securities tab.
3. Select the Hide Securities You Do Not Own check box.
4. Select OK.

If you still have this problem, the security that you do not want to see has its display status changed. To adjust this security, perform the first two steps above. Then, highlight the security

FIGURE 1-1   Portfolio View window showing securities you have set up

you think that you should not see in the list and select the Default button. When you select OK, that security will disappear if the selected investment accounts do not have any of that security. You have two other possible display status settings: Hide Always and Show Always. Hide Always removes the security from the Portfolio View window. Show Always displays the security in the Portfolio View window, even when you are hiding ones that you do not own and the investment account does not include any of that security.

Why do I see a message that Windows cannot find BILLMNDW.EXE when I start Windows?

This message appears because Windows is set to run the BILLMNDW.EXE program and it cannot find the program file. This occurs for two reasons. One reason is that you moved or deleted the BILLMNDW.EXE file. If you moved BILLMNDW.EXE, you need to change the properties of the Billminder icon in the Startup group of the Program Manager, or edit your WIN.INI file and change the Load= line that loads Billminder. If you deleted BILLMNDW.EXE, you will also want to delete the Billminder icon from the Startup group of the Program Manager, or delete the Load= line in WIN.INI.

The second reason has to do with the number of characters in the load line. This is the line that loads Windows and other programs once Windows starts. When C:\QUICKENW\BILLMNDW.EXE makes the load line too long, the extra characters are dropped off; Windows is therefore looking for a file such as C:\QUICKENW\BILLMNDW.E, which it cannot find. When you shorten the load line, you can run Billminder. To shorten the load line, you need to edit the batch file that you use to start Windows and remove some of the items on the line that loads Windows.

Chapter 1 *Top Ten Tech Terrors*

4 When installing Quicken I get the message "Unable to Decompress Application Files." What is causing the problem?

This error message is most often caused by not having enough free disk space available when you install Quicken. Clear some space and reinstall. Most virus detection software also results in this message.

5 Why do I have a negative balance in my investment account?

One of your early transactions is a Buy action that should be a BuyX or ShrsIn. The investment account shown below is an example of where this has happened. BuyX adds shares and expects an account to supply the funds for the transaction. ShrsIn adds shares without requiring an account to supply the funds. ShrsIn works well for adding earlier transactions and gifts where you do not want to select an account to supply the funds. With the Buy action, Quicken is assuming that you use money in the account. A negative balance to Quicken means that you borrowed money from your broker to buy the investments. To fix this problem, move to the Buy transaction. You can replace Buy with ShrsIn or you can select BuyX and a transfer account. Select Re*c*ord to complete the change.

6. Why don't I see any subcategories in my Budget window?

If you don't see your subcategories, they are condensed into their parent category. For example, when the Auto category hides its subcategories, you do not see the Fuel, Loan, and Service subcategories. You may notice that the - button in front of Auto has changed to a + as you can see here:

Click this button and the subcategories appear. The + button changes to the - button again as you can see here:

[−] Auto

The Auto - Other row is for what is budgeted to the Auto category that is not budgeted to a specific subcategory.

7. How can I alphabetize my stocks so I can find them faster in the Portfolio View window?

The Portfolio View window automatically alphabetizes the stocks. However, they are first grouped according to the security type. This means that you see bonds, then CD, then mutual funds, then stocks with the securities in each group listed in alphabetical order. You cannot change this order.

Tech Tip: You can find your investments faster by hiding the ones that are not in the investment account selected at the top of the Portfolio View window. The steps for this are described earlier in this chapter.

Chapter 1 *Top Ten Tech Terrors*

I just updated my stock prices and a lot of stocks that I didn't change show some of the stock prices that I just entered. Why?

Quicken uses the security symbols to match prices with particular stocks. For example, if you have two stocks that have the symbol INVST, updating the price for one of them updates both of their prices. This means that you should only have the same symbol for more than one security if you want them to have the same price. This can happen if you track different batches of securities separately, such as stock in a company that you bought through a broker versus that same company's stock bought through an employee stock plan. If the stocks are not the same, change the symbol that you use for one of them with these steps:

1. Choose Security from the Lists menu. You will notice in the Security List window that more than one stock has the same entry in the Symbol column.
2. Highlight the security that you want to change and select Edit from the button bar.
3. Type a new symbol in the Symbol text box and select OK.
4. Choose Close from the button bar to put the window away.

Why won't Quicken let me transfer money to my investment account from my checking account?

When you transfer money to your investment account, you don't want to use the Transfer button in the bank account's Register window button bar. If you try, you will find that Quicken will not let you select an investment account for where you are transferring money to. Instead, enter the transaction as you would for any payment. For the Category field, select the investment account. For example, suppose you transfer $1,000 from the Checking account to the Broker investment account. The transaction looks like this:

Date	Num	Payee		Payment	Clr	Deposit	Balance	
		Category	Memo					
12/21/95	867	Merrill Lynch		1,000 00			10,613 36	
		[Brokerage Acct]	Adding Money to buy more					
1/ 9/96		Mauseo Opt by Mar		1,015 00			9,598 36	
		[Brokerage Acct]	Purchased options for Mau					
2/18/96		Mauseo Corp		7,500 00			2,098 36	
		[Brokerage Acct]						

You can quickly see how this transaction appears in the investment account by moving to the transaction and selecting Go To Transfer from the Edit menu. This command has a shortcut of CTRL+X. You will see this transaction in the investment account like the one here:

Date	Action	Security	Price	Shares	Amount	Clr	Cash Bal	
	Memo		Xfer Acct	Xfer Amt	Comm Fee			
12/21/95	XIn	Merrill Lynch			1,000 00		3,126 75	
	Adding Money to buy more stoc		[Checking]					
1/ 9/96	BuyX	Mauseo Opt by Mar	2	500	1,015 00		3,126 75	
	Purchased options for Mauseo		[Checking]	1,015.00	15 00			
2/18/96	Sell	Mauseo Opt by Mar	2	500	1,000 00		4,126 75	
	Used Mauseo options to buy							
2/18/96	BuyX	Mauseo Corp	15	500	8,500 00		3,126 75	
	Bought Mauseo stock w/option		[Checking]	7,500.00	1,000 00			

Tech Tip: You can also enter this transfer as an XIn transfer from the investment account's Register window. Chapter 6, "Investments," has more questions about this and other investment transactions.

10. Why won't Quicken remember to use the Standard check style that I keep selecting?

What is probably happening is that even after you change the check style to Standard, when you return to the Check Printer Setup dialog box, Quicken still shows the last selection. You probably also have noticed that Quicken is not saving other printer settings. To fix this problem, you will want to rename the WPR.DAT file that Quicken created to store your printer settings.

Then, the next time that you use Quicken, Quicken re-creates this file to start your printer settings from scratch. At this point, the WPR.DAT file will save and remember your printer settings. To rename your WPR.DAT file:

1. Exit Quicken.
2. Open the File Manager. This program's icon is in the Main program group in the Program Manager.
3. Find and highlight the WPR.DAT file, which is in the same drive and directory as your other Quicken program files.
4. Choose Re_n_ame from the _F_ile menu.
5. Type a new name for this file, such as **OLD_WPR.DAT**, in the _T_o text box and select OK.
6. Choose E_x_it from the _F_ile menu to leave the File Manager.
7. Start Quicken again. Quicken re-creates the WPR.DAT file.

Tech Tip: Renaming the WPR.DAT file sets all printer setup data to defaults; you will have to reset *all* of the printer setup options.

Starting Out and Setting Up

Getting up and running with Quicken is easy—just let Quicken's Install program do it for you! All you have to do is insert the first Quicken disk into your A drive (substitute another letter for A, if appropriate), choose Run from the Program Manager's File menu, type **a:\install** in the Command Line box, and click OK. The Install program takes it from there! Once installed, you can start Quicken by simply double-clicking its program-item icon in the Program Manager. If you have used an older version of Quicken, check out Quicken's new features in the Frustration Busters box.

Quicken 4 for Windows can read data files created with earlier versions of Quicken. If you are a new Quicken user, it will guide you through the start-up process and help you to create the accounts that form the basis of your new data files.

FRUSTRATION BUSTERS!

Quicken 4 for Windows has many new features. If you have used a previous version of Quicken, check out these features to familiarize yourself with all the new options. If you are new to Quicken, these are just a few of the features that make Quicken an extraordinary financial management package.

- HomeBase—This window provides a table of contents displaying most popular features.

- Snapshots—Snapshots display an instant graphic overview of your finances. Just click the SnpShts button in the iconbar and you'll see six summaries of your financial information.

- Forecasting—Quicken can create graphs to show how your expenses and income will change over time. You can also change the items included in the forecast to give you an idea of how a change in earning or spending will affect your savings.

- Tax Planner—The Tax Planner creates a sample tax return that estimates your tax liability at the end of the year. You can use actual Quicken data to make your projections and plan how changes will alter your tax bill.

- Budgeting—A new supercategory feature can group existing categories for budgeting. This can save time by allowing you to plan your budget with just the level of detailed breakdown that you need.

- Savings goals—Savings goals make it easier to keep track of money that you set aside for important goals. You don't have to put your savings into a separate account to keep from spending it.

- Progress bar—Whether you want to know how far you have to go to reach a savings goal or whether you are spending too much in a specific category, the Progress bars provide you with a monitoring tool.

- Account register—Quicken 4 for Windows provides new features for switching between accounts and categorizing groups of transactions. Other new options include changing the register

Chapter 2 *Starting Out and Setting Up*

appearance and entering amounts and dates with a calculator or calendar.

- Financial Calendar—The Financial Calendar shows your financial transactions one month at a time. You can display your account balances, add reminder notes, and print this calendar.

- Reminders—Quicken can let you know that you have checks to print, scheduled transactions to record, investment transactions to perform, and notes every time you start Quicken.

- Reports—You can now preview reports before you print them. Businesses can compare earnings between months or years with the new Profit and Loss Comparison report.

- Graphs—Now you can memorize and recall your favorite graphs.

- Online services—Quicken can utilize your modem to update stock prices with Portfolio Price Update. You can use the CheckFree service to pay bills electronically without ever writing a check. With Intuit Marketplace, you can order Intuit supplies electronically. You can even register your copy of Quicken without leaving your computer.

Setup Requirements

What kind of a computer do I need to run Quicken?

Quicken 4 for Windows requires that your computer be equipped as follows:

- A 386 or higher IBM compatible computer with 4 MB of RAM
- At least 8 MB of free disk space

- VGA or higher resolution monitor
- DOS 3.3 or higher
- Windows 3.1 running in standard or enhanced mode (enhanced mode is needed for most functions)
- A printer that is set up to print output from Windows applications

For Quicken Deluxe, you need an additional 1 MB of RAM and an additional 4 MB of free hard disk space. You may also want a modem to provide access to the online services. A system equipped with more than the minimum requirements provides better performance for Quicken.

Can I use my old Quicken files on the new version of Quicken?

Yes. Quicken automatically converts files in an older format into the format that Quicken 4 for Windows uses. This includes files from earlier versions of Quicken for Windows and files from Quicken for DOS for versions 5 and later. If you have a Quicken 3 or 4 for DOS file, follow these steps:

1. Choose Open from the File menu.
2. Enter the name of the file in the File Name box. If Quicken is not looking for the file in the correct location, include the directory path before the filename.
3. Select OK.

Can I use my new Quicken files on older versions of Quicken?

No. Older versions of Quicken do not understand Quicken 4 for Windows files. This includes DOS versions 5, 6, and 7; however, there are conversion disks available from Intuit.

Chapter 2 *Starting Out and Setting Up*

Where are my old Quicken data files?

The first time you start Quicken 4 after installing it, you may not find your old Quicken data at once or you may even see a message that Quicken is not able to open the files. The reasons for this are

- During Quicken's installation, when Quicken found existing Quicken data files and asked if you wanted to move them, you chose not to.
- Quicken didn't find existing Quicken data files during installation and they are not in the same directory as Quicken's program files.

Don't worry. In both of these cases, your files aren't lost; you just need to tell Quicken where to find them. To locate your data:

1. Choose Open from the File menu. The Drives drop-down list box displays the drive that Quicken checks for files. The Directories list box highlights the directory on this drive. You need to change these selections to tell Quicken where to find your data.
2. Select the drive containing your Quicken data files in the Drives drop-down list box.
3. Select the directory containing your Quicken data files in the Directories list box. You can double-click any directory that you see in the list box in order to switch to that directory.
4. Select the Quicken file to open from the File Name list box or type its name in the File Name text box.
5. Select OK.

When I started Quicken, the Quicken New User Setup dialog box appeared. How do I get to my existing files?

Because Quicken couldn't find the file it wanted to open, it displayed the Quicken New User Setup dialog box shown in Figure 2-1. Close this dialog box by pressing ALT+F4 or

Quicken 4 for Windows Answers: *Certified Tech Support*

FIGURE 2-1 Quicken New User Setup dialog box

double-clicking the Control box in the dialog box's upper-left corner. Select Yes when prompted about closing Setup. Next, choose Open from the File menu. Select the file you want to work with and select OK.

Can I eliminate the Quicken reminders I see every time I start Quicken?

You have the option of turning off Quicken's reminders. To make this change:

1. Click the Options button in the iconbar, then click the Reminders button.
2. Clear the Show Reminders on Startup check box and select OK.
3. Select Close.

Now, you won't automatically see the Quicken Reminders window. If you ever want to see this box, just select Reminders from the Activities menu.

Chapter 2 *Starting Out and Setting Up*

How can I see as little as possible when I open Quicken?

If you attempt to save an empty desktop, Quicken will save whatever was on it before you emptied it since Quicken needs something to save. However, if you really want to see as little as possible, open an account, minimize the window, and exit Quicken. Quicken will save the minimized window; the next time you open Quicken, this small icon is all you see. Having a window open is a good idea since it is a quick reminder of which data file you have open.

Do I need a separate printer for checks versus reports since I have separate setups for each?

No. The only reason that you have two printer setups is that you probably want to use different settings for your printer when you print reports or graphs versus when you print checks. For most people, the two setups are for the same printer.

When I install Quicken, my virus checker displays messages. Are my Quicken disks bad?

No, your Quicken disks are fine. Most virus protection programs interfere with Quicken's installation program. To solve this problem, disable your virus protection, install Quicken, and then restore the virus protection.

Transferring Quicken Files Between Computers

How do I move my Quicken files from one computer to another?

Quicken's backup and restore feature can transfer data files to a different computer as follows:

1. Open the file in Quicken that you want to transfer.

2. Put a disk in drive A.

3. Choose Backup from the File menu and then OK. If the backup will not fit on one disk, you will have an extra dialog box so you can choose to back up on multiple disks. Quicken will prompt you to insert additional disks as they are needed, since its backups can require several disks. This process creates a backup copy of the current Quicken file on the disk in drive A.

4. Select OK when you see the message that the file was backed up successfully.

5. Start Quicken on the computer on which you want the copy of the file to reside.

6. Put the disk onto which you backed up your data into this computer's disk drive.

7. Choose Restore from the File menu.

8. Enter the Quicken file name in the File Name text box and select OK. This computer now has a copy of the Quicken file that you copied from the original computer.

9. Select OK when you see the message that the file was restored successfully. Quicken opens this file for you.

Tech Tip: If your file is small, the backup copy is identical to what you would get if you copied the file with the File Manager. If your file is large (that is, it has more data than will fit on one disk), the file will be different; you can only restore it to the original one by choosing Restore from the File menu.

How do I get my Quicken for the Mac files onto my IBM-compatible computer?

Use Apple's File Exchange to copy the Quicken file to a DOS formatted disk. Put the disk in the drive on your PC and open the file in Quicken for Windows.

Chapter 2 *Starting Out and Setting Up*

Backups

Why do I have files in a BACKUP directory when I haven't made backups?

Quicken automatically backs up your data files to this directory every seven days. Quicken also keeps several of these historical backups. Unless you've changed the settings, you will see several copies of your data file in this BACKUP directory. To indicate the order of the different backups, Quicken uses up to the first seven letters of the data file's name, then adds a number—1 through the highest backup number. If your data is in a file called QDATA, after a while, your BACKUP directory may have the following filenames:

QDATA1—Contains a backup made within the last week

QDATA2—Contains a backup made over a week ago

QDATA3—Contains a backup made over two weeks ago

QDATA4—Contains a backup made over three weeks ago

QDATA5—Contains a backup made over four weeks ago

Quicken renames the existing files each week as it creates a new backup. This means that last week, the contents of QDATA2 were named QDATA1.

You can decide the number of backups Quicken makes. To do this:

1. Quit Quicken.
2. Find the Notepad program icon in the Program Manager and double-click it to start the Notepad application. The Notepad icon is normally in the Accessories group window.
3. Choose Open from the File menu to open a file in Notepad.

Quicken 4 for Windows Answers: *Certified Tech Support*

4. Type **C:\WINDOWS\QUICKEN.INI** in the File Name text box and select OK. If your Windows files are in a different drive or directory, replace C or WINDOWS with the correct information.

5. Move to the line containing AutoCopy=.

6. Change the number after AutoCopy= to a number from 0 to 9. When this number is 0, Quicken doesn't copy your data to the BACKUP directory.

7. Choose Exit from the File menu and select Yes when prompted for whether you want to save this file.

8. Start Quicken with the new setting for how many backup copies Quicken makes.

If you need to return to an earlier copy, choose Restore from the File menu, then select the file you want to restore from the BACKUP directory.

Tech Note: Quicken performs two types of backups. The backup created with the Backup command in the File menu copies the Quicken file to a disk other than the hard drive. The backup that Quicken automatically performs to the BACKUP directory backs up your data to another directory on the same drive. Although this backup is often faster, if anything happens to the hard drive, your automatic backups will not be usable. Make sure that you frequently make backups onto other diskettes.

What's the difference between backing up my files when I leave Quicken and backing them up with the Backup command in the File menu?

None. The prompt that you see when you leave Quicken is just a reminder to create backups.

Chapter 2 *Starting Out and Setting Up*

Startup and File Options

 Can I set my computer to automatically start Quicken every time I start my computer?

You can set your system to start Quicken every time you start Windows. All you have to do is add Quicken in your Startup program group. To do this:

1. Switch to the Program Manager within Windows.
2. Highlight the Quicken icon in the Quicken group window.
3. Choose Copy from the File menu.
4. Select Startup from the To Group drop-down list box and select OK.

Now, the next time you start Windows, Quicken starts too.

Tech Tip: If you want to start Windows every time you turn on your computer, just add Win to the end of the AUTOEXEC.BAT file. Your computer performs the instructions in this file every time it starts or is rebooted.

 How do I tell Quicken which file I want opened?

You can switch from one open Quicken file to another using the Open command in the File menu. From the Open Quicken File dialog box, select the file you want to open and select OK. You need to switch between files when, for example, you create separate ones for business and personal finances.

Another option is to create separate Program Manager icons and let each one open a different Quicken data file. All you have to do is copy the Quicken program icon using the steps from the previous answer. You can copy a program icon to the same or a different program group. Then, highlight the icon and press ALT+ENTER or choose Properties from the File menu. At the end of the entry in the Command Line text box, add the name of the data file, as in **C:\QUICKENW\qw.exe HOME**. You may also want to alter what is in the Description text box to describe the data file you will open. The Program Item Properties dialog box shown here displays these settings, which were made for one of the icons. Then, to open Quicken using that data file, double-click its icon. However, the program icon only works when Quicken is not already running.

Program Item Properties	
Description:	Home Quicken data file
Command Line:	C:\QUICKENW\qw.exe HOME
Working Directory:	C:\QUICKENW
Shortcut Key:	None
	☐ Run Minimized

Buttons: OK, Cancel, Browse..., Change Icon..., Help

How do I give my Quicken files a different name?

Since a Quicken "file" actually consists of five or six different files, you should use Quicken rather than the File Manager to rename them. Quicken renames all files in the set with one request. To rename files in Quicken:

1. Choose File Operations from the File menu and select Rename.

2. Select the .QDT file of your Quicken data that you want to rename in the File Name text and list box.

3. Enter the new name for your Quicken data in the New name for Quicken file text box.

4. Select OK.

Chapter 2 *Starting Out and Setting Up*

Quicken renames the files. These file types are distinguished by their extensions. They and the general type of data they contain are described in Table 2-1.

Setting Up a Communications Link

How do I set up my modem to use it with Quicken?

When you choose Set Up Modem from the Online menu for the first time, Quicken will automatically configure itself for your modem. If you normally have to dial any extra numbers to make phone calls (such as dialing a 9 to get an outside line) you will need to enter these numbers when Quicken prompts for a dialing prefix. You can also use this prefix to enter special numbers that turn off phone line features such as call waiting. After the autoconfigure is complete, you can connect with Intuit for such services as IntelliCharge, Intuit Marketplace, Portfolio Price Update, or Software Registration; however, you will need to take a special action before using CheckFree.

If you cannot connect to Intuit, you should choose Set Up Modem from the Online menu again and make the necessary

File Extension	Type of Data the Files Contain
QDT	All of your transactions
QNX	Index of your transactions
QMT	Everything you memorized
QDI	The dictionary that includes addresses for unprinted checks and descriptions for split transactions
QST	Other information including investment prices, custom icons, Financial Calendar notes, additional account information, and loan information
QTX	Tax information when you use the Tax Planner

TABLE 2-1   File Extensions and the Type of Data Each One Stores

changes. The appropriate settings depend on your modem, how the modem connects to the computer, and any appropriate phone number prefix. You can test that the modem's settings are correct when you register your copy of the software by modem. Just select Software Registration from the Online menu. Enter the information in the Quicken 4 for Windows Software Registration dialog box. After you select OK, you can answer the survey questions and select Register. After the registration is complete, you can no longer select Software Registration in the Online menu; this will remind you that you have already registered.

CheckFree requires a special setup entry even if you have already used another online service with Quicken. To set up the modem for CheckFree, select CheckFree from the Activities menu and then Set Up Modem. From the Set Up Modem - CheckFree dialog box, enter the dial type, port, speed, and the CompuServe ID number and initialization string you obtain from CheckFree when you initiate the service. This dialog box might look like the one shown here. When you select OK, Quicken is ready to connect to CheckFree.

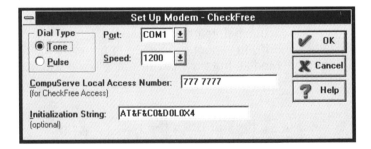

Tech Terror: If the modem is not turned on the first time you choose Set Up Modem from the Online menu, autoconfigure does not work because it gets no response from the modem. After you turn on your modem, choose Set Up Modem from the Online menu and select Autoconfigure. You may also need to do this if you begin using a different modem and need to reapply the automatic configuration.

Chapter 2 *Starting Out and Setting Up*

Will call waiting interfere with my using my modem with Quicken?

Call waiting works by adding a signal to the phone lines when it indicates that you have another incoming call. This signal can interfere with any messages sent by phone, such as when you use Quicken's online services. To prevent this problem, you need to temporarily disable call waiting. Your telephone company can tell you the phone number to dial for this. Common ones are *70 for pulse phones and 1170 for rotary phones. Check with your local phone company to obtain the correct code for your area. To add this prefix:

1. Choose S̲et Up Modem from the Online menu.
2. Enter the numbers after D̲ialing Prefix or select one of the ones from the drop-down list box.
3. Select OK.

I can't get through to IntelliCharge. What is the problem?

Most connection problems are simple to fix:

- The line could be busy. Try again in a few minutes.
- Your modem needs to dial a prefix, such as dialing a 9 to get an outside line. Select S̲et Up Modem from the Online menu and enter the correct prefix after D̲ialing Prefix. Select OK, then try again.
- Your modem needs one of the settings changed. Select S̲et Up Modem from the Online menu and select Auto̲configure. Then try again.
- Your modem is not turned on. Turn it on and try it again.

Tech Tip: A simple test that your modem is working correctly is to try it with other applications, such as connecting to your favorite bulletin board.

Quicken found an error when it configured my IntelliCharge account. How do I fix it?

The error probably occurred because IntelliCharge was unable to send or receive information when Quicken set up your new account. Most likely a modem problem occurred that can be resolved with the suggestions in the previous question. Noise on your phone line from high winds or an electrical storm is another possibility. If you have a special feature such as call waiting, you may need to disable it temporarily to prevent the signals it generates from being interpreted as noise. You can use the steps described earlier in the chapter to disable it by adding a special dialing prefix.

Standard Categories

What categories do I get when I select Quicken's standard home categories?

When you create a Quicken data file with the H<u>o</u>me check box selected, you will have all the categories listed in Table 2-2.

Category	Description	Type	Tax Related
Bonus	Bonus Income	Income	Yes
CPP	Canadian Pension Plan	Income	Yes
Div Income	Dividend Income	Income	Yes
Gift Received	Gift Received	Income	Yes
Int Inc	Interest Income	Income	Yes
Invest Inc	Investment Income	Income	Yes
Old Age Pension	Old Age Pension	Income	Yes
Other Inc	Other Income	Income	Yes
Salary	Salary Income	Income	Yes
Salary Spouse	Spouse's Salary Income	Income	Yes
Auto	Automobile Expenses	Expense	No
Fuel	Auto Fuel	Subcategory	No

TABLE 2-2   Standard Categories for Home Use

Chapter 2 Starting Out and Setting Up

Category	Description	Type	Tax Related
Loan	Auto Loan Payment	Subcategory	No
Service	Auto Service	Subcategory	No
Bank Chrg	Bank Charge	Expense	No
Charity	Charitable Donations	Expense	Yes
Cash Contrib.	Cash Contributions	Subcategory	Yes
Non-Cash	Non-Cash Contributions	Subcategory	Yes
Childcare	Childcare Expense	Expense	No
Christmas	Christmas Expenses	Expense	No
Clothing	Clothing	Expense	No
Dining	Dining Out	Expense	No
Dues	Dues	Expense	No
Education	Education	Expense	No
Entertain	Entertainment	Expense	No
Gifts	Gift Expenses	Expense	Yes
Groceries	Groceries	Expense	No
GST	Goods and Services Tax	Expense	Yes
Home Repair	Home Repair & Maint	Expense	No
Household	Household Misc. Exp	Expense	No
Housing	Housing	Expense	No
Insurance	Insurance	Expense	No
Int Exp	Interest Expense	Expense	Yes
Invest Exp	Investment Expense	Expense	Yes
Medical	Medical Expense	Expense	Yes
Doctor	Doctor & Dental Visits	Subcategory	Yes
Medicine	Medicine & Drugs	Subcategory	Yes
Misc	Miscellaneous	Expense	No
Mort Int	Mortgage Interest Exp	Expense	Yes
Other Exp	Other Expenses	Expense	Yes
PST	Provincial Sales Tax	Expense	Yes
Recreation	Recreation Expense	Expense	No
RRSP	Reg Retirement Sav Plan	Expense	No
Subscriptions	Subscriptions	Expense	No
Supplies	Supplies	Expense	No
Tax	Taxes	Expense	Yes
Fed	Federal Tax	Subcategory	Yes
Medicare	Medicare Tax	Subcategory	Yes

TABLE 2-2   Standard Categories for Home Use *(continued)*

Category	Description	Type	Tax Related
Other	Misc. Taxes	Subcategory	Yes
Prop	Property Tax	Subcategory	Yes
Soc Sec	Soc Sec Tax	Subcategory	Yes
State	State Tax	Subcategory	Yes
Tax Spouse	Spouse's Taxes	Expense	Yes
Fed	Federal Tax	Subcategory	Yes
Medicare	Medicare Tax	Subcategory	Yes
Soc Sec	Soc Sec Tax	Subcategory	Yes
State	State Tax	Subcategory	Yes
Telephone	Telephone Expense	Expense	No
UIC	Unemploy. Ins. Commission	Expense	Yes
Utilities	Water, Gas, Electric	Expense	No
Gas & Electric	Gas and Electricity	Subcategory	No
Water	Water	Subcategory	No

TABLE 2-2   Standard Categories for Home Use *(continued)*

What categories do I get when I select Quicken's standard business categories?

When you create a Quicken data file with the Business check box selected, your Quicken data file includes all the categories listed in Table 2-3.

I selected the wrong type of categories when I created my Quicken file. How do I fix it now?

When you create a new Quicken file, you can choose whether the file starts off with predefined categories for home, business, or both. If you wanted to include the categories for home or business but didn't select the check box, you can add the second set of categories afterwards. To add these categories:

1. Choose Import from the File menu.

Category	Description	Type	Tax Related
Gr Sales	Gross Sales	Income	Yes
Other Inc	Other Income	Income	Yes
Rent Income	Rent Income	Income	Yes
Ads	Advertising	Expense	Yes
Bus. Insurance	Insurance (not health)	Expense	Yes
Bus. Utilities	Water, Gas, Electric	Expense	Yes
Business Tax	Taxes & Licenses	Expense	Yes
Car	Car & Truck	Expense	Yes
Commission	Commissions	Expense	Yes
Freight	Freight	Expense	Yes
GST	Goods and Services Tax	Expense	Yes
Int Paid	Interest Paid	Expense	Yes
L&P Fees	Legal & Prof. Fees	Expense	Yes
Late Fees	Late Payment Fees	Expense	Yes
Meals & Entertn	Meals & Entertainment	Expense	Yes
Office	Office Expenses	Expense	Yes
PST	Provincial Sales Tax	Expense	Yes
Rent on Equip	Rent-Vehicle,mach,equip	Expense	Yes
Rent Paid	Rent Paid	Expense	Yes
Repairs	Repairs	Expense	Yes
Returns	Returns & Allowances	Expense	Yes
Supplies, bus.	Supplies	Expense	Yes
Travel	Travel Expenses	Expense	Yes
Wages	Wages & Job Credits	Expense	Yes

TABLE 2-3 Standard Categories for Business

2. Type **Home** or **Business** in the QIF File to Import field depending on which categories you want to add.

3. Select the Category List check box and select OK.

The HOME.QIF and BUSINESS.QIF files contain the predefined categories for home and business. Importing these categories has no effect on the transactions you have already entered.

Quicken 4 for Windows Answers: *Certified Tech Support*

You may also have categories that you no longer want. To remove any category:

1. Choose Category & Transfer from the Lists menu to show the Category & Transfer List window that displays all the available categories.
2. Highlight any category that you do not want and select the Delete button in the button bar. You can select this button by clicking it or pressing ALT+D.
3. Select the Close button to put the window away when you are done.

Transferring Data Between Files

I added an account to the wrong file. How do I move it to the correct one?

To move an account from one file to another requires a sequence of steps. You need to export the account's transactions from the wrong file. Next, you import the account and its transactions

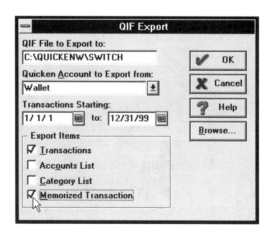

FIGURE 2-2   QIF Export dialog box

Chapter 2 *Starting Out and Setting Up*

into the correct one. Finally, you remove the account that is in the wrong file. Here are the steps.

1. Open the file containing the account you want to move.
2. Choose Export from the File menu to open the QIF Export dialog box. The QIF Export dialog box shown in Figure 2-2 has some entries completed.
3. Type the path and filename for where you want to put the data you will export. For example, you can type **C:\QUICKENW\SWITCH** to create a file named SWITCH.QIF in C:\QUICKENW that contains the data you export.
4. Select the account that is in the wrong file from the Quicken Account to Export from drop-down list box.
5. Check that the dates under Transactions Starting are correct. Leave the original entries of 1/1/1 and 12/31/99 intact when you want to transfer all the entries.
6. Select the Transactions check box.
7. Select the Memorized Transactions check box when you want the memorized transactions for the account included in the QIF file.
8. Select OK to export the file. You now have a file that has a copy of the transaction information. Exporting has no effect on the original entries.
9. Open the file where you want to add the account.
10. Choose Create New Account from the Activities menu.
11. Create a new account that has the same account type as the one you are importing with a zero balance. When the account is created, you can see the account's Register window.
12. Choose Import from the File menu to display the QIF Import dialog box. This dialog box looks very similar to the QIF Export dialog box in Figure 2-2. The QIF File to Import field already shows the file containing the exported data.
13. Select the account you created in steps 10 and 11 in the Quicken Account to Import into drop-down list box. This is the account where you want the transactions added. For example, if you are transferring your credit card

account and it is called Credit Card in the correct file, select Credit Card. Quicken doesn't care if the account name that supplied these transactions is different.

14. Select OK. Quicken imports the transactions and other information from the QIF file into this newly created account in the correct file. If the imported transactions include categories that are not already in the correct data file, you will see a prompt about creating them. Select Yes to create these new categories or No to remove the categories from the transactions when the category does not exist.

15. Check that the data you have imported is correct.

16. Switch to the Quicken data file that incorrectly contained the account and delete the account you no longer need.

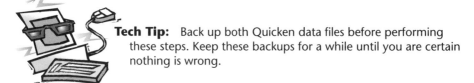

Tech Tip: Back up both Quicken data files before performing these steps. Keep these backups for a while until you are certain nothing is wrong.

How do I copy data between files?

You copy data between Quicken data files using QIF files. QIF, or Quicken Interchange Format, represents a file format specially designed for transferring between Quicken files. QIF is the only file format Quicken accepts to import data. Using QIF files, you can transfer account transactions, categories, accounts, and memorized transactions between files. To copy information between files:

1. Open the file containing the information you want to copy.

2. Choose Export from the File menu to show the QIF Export dialog box.

3. Type the path and filename that will store the data you are exporting. For example, if you type **C:\QUICKENW\TRANSFER**, Quicken creates a file

Chapter 2 *Starting Out and Setting Up*

named TRANSFER.QIF in C:\QUICKENW that contains the copy of the data.

4. Select what you want to copy. Your choices include

   - Transactions to copy the transactions in one of the accounts. Make sure to select which account from the Quicken Account to Export from drop-down list.
   - Accounts List to copy the accounts that are in the current data file. Importing accounts into another data file only adds the accounts that are not already in that file. Accounts that are already in the other file will not be affected.
   - Category List to copy the categories from the file. When you import them into another file, categories that are not already in the other file are added and categories that are already there do not change.
   - Memorized Transactions to copy the memorized transactions from the file. You can import them into another file to add them to the memorized transactions already in that other file.

5. Check that the dates under Transactions Starting are what you want. Leave the original entries of 1/1/1 and 12/31/99 intact when you want to transfer all the entries. You can change either date to limit the copied transactions to ones before or after a specific date.

6. Select OK to export the file.

7. Open the file where you want the information copied.

8. Back it up so that you can restore the prior copy if you don't like the results.

9. Choose Import from the File menu to display the QIF Import dialog box. The QIF File to Import text box already shows the correct file name.

10. Select what you want copied into this file. Your choices include

    - Transactions to add the transactions in the QIF file to an account in the currently opened file. Make sure to select the account in the current data file into which you want these transactions added from the Quicken Account to Import into drop-down list. This is not necessarily the same account that they were copied from when you exported the data.

- Acc**o**unts List to add the accounts in the QIF file that are not in the current data file. Accounts that are already in this file are not affected.
- **C**ategory List to add categories from the QIF file to the current data file. Categories that match ones in the QIF file are not changed.
- **M**emorized Transaction to add memorized transactions from the QIF file to the current data file.

11. Select OK. Quicken imports the information from the QIF file and adds it to the current data file.

12. Check that the data you have imported is correct.

Custom Categories

I can't find the category I want. How do I make my own?

Quicken includes many preset categories, but you can also add your own to meet specific needs. To add a new category:

1. Start the process for creating a new category, which can be done in either of the following ways:

- Edit a transaction and enter the name of the new category in the Category field and select Re**c**ord.
- Choose **C**ategory & Transfer from the **L**ists menu and select **N**ew in the window's button bar.

Either method opens the Set Up Category dialog box.

2. Add or modify the entry in the **N**ame text box for the name that you want for this category.

3. Enter a longer description in the **D**escription text box.

4. Select **I**ncome, **E**xpense, or S**u**bcategory for the type of category you are creating. If you select S**u**bcategory, select the parent category from the adjoining drop-down list box.

Chapter 2 *Starting Out and Setting Up*

5. If the entries affect your taxes, select the Tax-related check box, then select where this category's expenses appear on your tax forms in the Form drop-down list box. A completed dialog box might look like this:

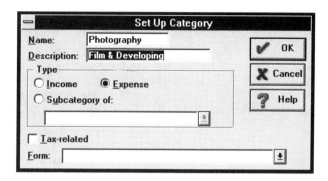

6. Select OK to create this category.

At this point, you can continue entering transactions or close the Category & Transfer List window.

What categories should I set up to help me with my taxes?

Quicken has already set up categories to provide tax information. If you have added categories or want to customize them to meet special needs, you might need to change some of the assignments. The tax features already in place for existing categories are

- Marking categories as tax-related. You can summarize the entries that you have assigned to tax-related categories by creating a Tax Summary report. Create this report choosing Home from the Reports menu and then Tax Summary. When you select OK, Quicken creates the report. You can also change which categories are tax-related by displaying a list of categories. Choose Category & Transfer from the Lists menu, then highlight the category and select Edit. You can select or clear the Tax-related check box to add or remove it from your Tax Summary reports.

Tech Note:
Categories can be tax-related without assigning them to specific tax form entries.

- Assigning categories to specific tax form entries. For example, the Prop subcategory of Taxes is assigned to Schedule A:Real estate taxes. You can create a Tax Schedule report that groups transactions according to tax form entries. Create this report by choosing Home from the Reports menu and then Tax Schedule. Select OK to create this report. Besides this Tax Schedule report, Quicken's Tax Planner can create sample tax returns that predict what your tax return looks like with the entries you have made. The procedure to change the tax form entry for any category is similar to the one described above for setting the tax-related status. Display a list of categories by choosing Category & Transfer from the Lists menu, then highlight the category and select Edit. Select the Tax-related check box, then select the tax form entry from the Form drop-down list box.

Can I delete a subcategory without deleting the parent category?

Yes, you can remove a subcategory without removing the parent category. All the transactions that you assigned to the subcategory now are assigned to the parent category. Deleting a subcategory works the same way as deleting any category. To delete a category:

1. Choose Category & Transfer from the Lists menu.
2. Highlight the category that you no longer want.
3. Select Delete in the window's button bar.
4. Respond to the prompt about deleting a category or subcategory. When you delete a subcategory, select Yes to have the transactions assigned to the subcategory reassigned to the parent category. When you delete a category, select OK to confirm that you want to delete it.

When you delete a category that has transactions assigned to it, the transactions have the category assignment removed. Quicken doesn't let you delete a category that has subcategories. You must delete the subcategories first.

Chapter 2 *Starting Out and Setting Up*

How do I get categories from one file into another?

You can copy categories from one file to another. All you have to do is export the categories to a QIF file—Quicken's standard file format for transferring data. Then you can import this file into another Quicken data file. To do this:

1. Open the file with the categories that you want to see in another file.
2. Export the categories. Choose Export from the File menu and type a file name in the QIF File to Export to text box.
3. Select the Category List check box so that the QIF file includes all categories in the current file and select OK.
4. Open the Quicken data file where you want the categories added.
5. Bring the categories from the QIF file into this one. Choose Import from the File menu. The name of the file already appears after QIF File to Import. Select OK.
6. Select Category & Transfer from the Lists menu. You can see the new categories interspersed through this list.

Historical Data

How far back should I go for entering transactions into my Quicken registers?

As far back as you want to use Quicken to review your financial data.

Do I have to enter all my old data when I start using Quicken?

Your Quicken data can only provide analysis for the time period of transactions that you enter. Therefore, make your decision of when to start recording entries in Quicken based on the time periods that you want Quicken to give you information about.

Here is a way to add old checkbook entries to your checking account:

1. Back up your real data file. If you do something wrong, you can always return to the backup copy.
2. Create a new file in Quicken.
3. Create a checking account in this new file. Don't worry about the opening balance amount.
4. Add the old transactions to this account. While you have to add them one-by-one, you can take advantage of QuickFill features to supply categories and payee names.
5. Reconcile the account in this new file. The ending balance is the beginning account balance of the bank statement you used to start the real account (the one that you want to add these older transactions to). Don't put in the interest and service charges if you already entered these transactions into the register. After you mark all the transactions in the Reconcile Bank Statement window and select Done, you will see the dialog box for adjusting the balance. Type a date before the first date of the entries you made and select Adjust Balance. Then you can choose if you want a reconciliation report. A transaction report for this account might look like the one in Figure 2-3.
6. Export the checkbook entries. Choose Export from the File menu and type a name for the file in the QIF File to Export to text box. You may want to select the Category List and Memorized Transactions check boxes so any new categories that you created or memorized transactions that you will want to continue to use are available in the other file. Select OK. Since the Transactions check box is selected, this export file contains all the transactions in the register.
7. Open the real Quicken data file and show the Register window where you want the old transactions added. Notice the ending balance at this point. When you are done, the account will have the same balance but it will also have the older entries.

```
                              Transaction Report
                             1/95 Through 11/28/95
11/28/95                                                                          Page 1
OLDCHECK-Checking
   Date     Num     Description           Memo              Category        Clr     Amount

           BALANCE 12/31/94                                                           0.00

  1/1/95          Opening Balance                         [Checking]         x        0.00
  1/1/95          Balance Adjustment                                         x      682.00
  7/16/95   ATM   Spending Money      Groceries, Gas & Stuff    Misc         x      -50.00
  7/21/95   ATM   Spending Money      Groceries, Gas & Stuff    Misc         x     -100.00
  7/22/95   ATM   Deposit Paycheck                         Salary            x      420.37
  7/29/95   ATM   Spending Money      Groceries, Gas & Stuff    Misc         x      -50.00
  7/29/95   ATM   Deposit Paycheck                         Salary            x      420.37
  7/31/95   341   Properties Development                  Housing            x     -375.41
  8/3/95    342   Sam's Club          Juice for rafting trip   Vacation      x       -8.00
  8/5/95    ATM   Money for rafting trip                                     x      -50.00
  8/5/95    ATM   Deposit Paycheck                         Salary            x      420.37
  8/11/95   343   Ameritech                                Telephone         x      -91.38
  8/11/95   344   Citibank Mastercard                      Misc              x     -620.44
  8/12/95   ATM   Spending Money                           Vacation          x     -150.00
  8/12/95   ATM   Deposit Paycheck                         Salary            X      420.37
  8/14/95   351   Washington Insurance                     Insurance         x      -45.00
  8/15/95         Interest                                 Int Inc           x        1.76
  8/17/95   345   Gene Ford Books     Books                Misc              x      -50.88
  8/20/95   346   Gypsy Peddler                            Misc              x      -24.00
  8/26/95   ATM   Deposit Paycheck                         Salary            x      420.37
  9/1/95    349   Properties Development                   Housing           x     -375.41
  9/2/95    ATM   Deposit Paycheck                         Salary            x      420.37
  9/7/95    347   The Illuminating Company                 Utilities:Gas & Electric  x  -55.12
  9/7/95    348   Citibank Mastercard                      Misc              x     -548.11

           TOTAL 1/1/95 - 11/28/95                                                  612.23

           BALANCE 11/28/95                                                         612.23

           TOTAL INFLOWS                                                          3,205.98
           TOTAL OUTFLOWS                                                        -2,593.75

           NET TOTAL                                                                612.23
```

FIGURE 2-3   Transaction report showing old entries in a separate data file

8. Delete the transaction for this checking account's opening balance. Highlight it and select Delete in the Register window's button bar.

9. Bring the checkbook entries from the other file into this one. Choose <u>I</u>mport from the <u>F</u>ile menu. The name of the file already appears after QIF File to Import. Select OK. The balance has returned to the same amount it was in step 7.

Tech Tip: Make entering the older transactions easier. Export the memorized transactions from the primary data file and import them into the new data file for your old transactions. Earlier in the chapter, we described how you can copy these entries. Having the memorized transactions available makes entering the older transactions easier and makes sure that the entries are consistent.

Tech Terror: Make finding entry errors easier. When you are entering your checkbook, add one page at a time.

How can I add repetitive entries from the past?

When you are adding old transactions, you may often have some like paychecks, rent, or loan payments that are the same each time. You can easily add them for a whole year following these simple steps:

1. Create a scheduled transaction for the regularly occurring transaction you need to enter. Choose Sc<u>h</u>eduled Transaction from the <u>L</u>ists menu to open the Scheduled Transaction List window and select <u>N</u>ew. Enter the information for the transaction in the dialog box.

2. Set <u>N</u>ext Scheduled to the date of the first transaction that you want Quicken to add for you. For example, for rent that you pay on the first of the month, you can enter **1/1/95**.

3. Set <u>F</u>requency to how often the transaction is made.
4. Set Re<u>g</u>ister entry to Automatically enter.
5. Select OK to leave this dialog box.
6. Exit Quicken.

Chapter 2 *Starting Out and Setting Up*

7. Restart Quicken and open this file. Quicken automatically made all the transactions for you between the date you entered in step 2 and the current date.

At this point, you may want to edit the scheduled transaction so that when the next scheduled date comes up, Quicken prompts you about recording it, instead of doing it automatically. To see these transactions that Quicken automatically added:

1. Open the Register window for the account where these transactions are entered.
2. Select the F_ind button in the register's button bar.
3. Enter the payee name in the Find text box and select F_ind All. The Quicken Find window expands to list all the transactions for this payee. You can see how the scheduled transactions are added like the one for rent in Figure 2-4.

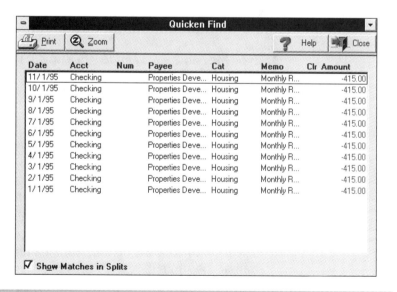

FIGURE 2-4   Adding repetitive transactions at once

Quicken 4 for Windows Answers: *Certified Tech Support*

After the end of the year, can I just delete all of last year's transactions?

You could try, but you probably wouldn't like the results since it is time consuming and makes account balances incorrect. A better solution is to create an archive of the current file following these steps:

1. Choose Year-End Copy from the File menu.

2. Select Start New Year and OK. Quicken shows the Start New Year dialog box. The one shown below shows this box after some entries are made.

3. Type the name you want for the copy of the current file in the Copy All Transactions to File text box. This is the one you want to later back up and keep with your records since it contains last year's transactions.

4. Set the date for transactions that you want to keep in the current file in the Delete Transactions From Current File Older Than text box. Usually, you would use a date like 1/1/95 to remove transactions from 1994.

5. If you want the current file moved to a different directory, enter the name of that directory in the Move Current File to text box.

6. Select OK to copy the current file, then remove old transactions from it.

7. Select which file you want to use and select OK. Choose Use old file to open the file named in step 3 that has all the transactions or choose Use file for new year to open the file that has the older transactions removed.

Chapter 2 *Starting Out and Setting Up*

Now the file you were working on has last year's transactions removed. When you look at this current file, most of last year's transactions are removed and condensed into the Opening Balance transaction at the top of the register for each account. Quicken does not remove all old transactions, however. The current data file still has the old transactions in your investment account. You need these transactions in your current file since sales and stock splits in the current year are affected by the prior year's transactions and not just the opening balance. The file also keeps uncleared transactions. This way you can correctly reconcile your checking account.

Protecting Data

How do I prevent my kids from accessing my data?

You can add a password to your Quicken data file. Then no one can open the file without first knowing the correct password. To add this password:

1. Choose P<u>a</u>sswords from the <u>F</u>ile menu and then choose <u>F</u>ile.
2. Type the password in the <u>P</u>assword text box and select OK.
3. Type the password a second time so Quicken knows that you correctly entered the password the first time and select OK.

Now when you try to open the data file, Quicken prompts for the password as shown below. If you cannot enter the correct password, you cannot open the file.

How do I prevent myself from accidentally changing last year's data?

You can do this two ways depending on whether you want to see last year's data. You can add a password that you must supply when you try to change entries before a certain date. To add this password protection to the open file:

1. Choose Passwords from the File menu and then choose Transaction.
2. Type the password in the Password text box.
3. Type the date in the Required For Dates Through text box that selects the transactions that require a password to change when they occur before or up to this date. For example, to limit changes to 1995's transactions, type **12/31/94**.
4. Select OK.
5. Type the password a second time so Quicken knows that you correctly entered the password the first time and select OK.

Now when you try to modify a transaction that occurred before the cutoff date, you can try to change it. However, when you select Record, if you cannot enter the correct password when prompted, the transaction does not change.

Another possibility for preventing changes to last year's data is to remove it from the file. Rather than deleting the transactions, follow the directions provided earlier in this chapter, in the section "Historical Data."

Registers and Transactions

Transactions are the backbone of your financial information. Every financial event—from paying a bill to receiving a quarterly dividend check—represents a transaction. With the exception of checks, you enter transactions in a Register window. Here, you record what you've spent and received, just as if you were writing on a paper check register. Just as a paper check register organizes information in one easy to access location, your Quicken register keeps an historical record of all your transactions. If you create separate accounts for checking, saving, and investments, you will have three different Quicken registers.

Recording transactions with Quicken is simple. Two especially useful features, scheduled and memorized transactions, are described in the Frustration Busters box.

Quicken 4 for Windows Answers: *Certified Tech Support*

Quicken has two features that make register entries and paying bills easier. If you haven't used them, try them out to find out what they can offer you.

- Scheduled Transactions—These are transactions that Quicken reminds you of or makes for you. They can record automatic payments and deposits. They provide reminders for you to pay bills as they become due.

- Memorized Transactions—These are transactions that supply the complete payee name, amount, category, and memo once you select a payee.

If you are unfamiliar with these types of transactions, look at the questions for these topics discussed later in the chapter since they include the steps you perform for these transactions.

Changing the Register's Appearance

How can I show more entries in the register?

You have a couple of options for showing more entries in the register. Here is what you can do

- Hide the button bar by clicking the Hide/Show button at the top of the vertical scroll shown below. When you click this button, the button bar disappears to leave more room for showing transactions. When you want the button bar to appear again, click the Hide/Show button again.

Chapter 3 *Registers and Transactions*

Hide/Show button

[Screenshot of Checking - Home Federal Checking: Bank register window showing transactions from 6/13/95 to 6/25/95, with 1-Line Display checkbox selected and Ending Balance of 1,935.92]

- Show only one line from each transaction. Click the 1-Line Display check box and the transactions only use one line as you can see above. While the Memo field does not appear, entries already in this field will reappear once you clear the 1-Line Display check box and return to two lines for each transaction.

- Click the Maximize button in the window's upper-right corner. Then the Register window fills all the available area.

The buttons at the top of the register disappeared. How do I get them back?

The button bar for the window is hidden. All you have to do is click the Hide/Show button again and these buttons will reappear.

Why don't I see account selectors for all accounts in the Register window?

Investment Register windows have different features than the Register windows for other types of accounts. Therefore, Investment Register windows only show the account selectors for investment accounts and other Register windows show only the account selectors for non-investment accounts.

Accounts Versus Categories

What is the difference between accounts and categories?

An account records transactions that affect the value of your assets and liabilities. You might have a checking account, an investment account, or a loan account. A category defines a transaction by describing what type of expense was incurred or what type of income was earned.

You use categories to maintain more meaningful information about your finances. Figure 3-1 shows a report with several ATM withdrawals labeled "Spending Money" and no category assignments. You can't tell from these entries whether this money went to food, gas, or entertainment. On the other hand, compare these transactions with the report in Figure 3-2 showing the same transactions after categories are added. You can create reports that tell you how much you spent on gas, how much you spent on food, and so on if you use categories in your

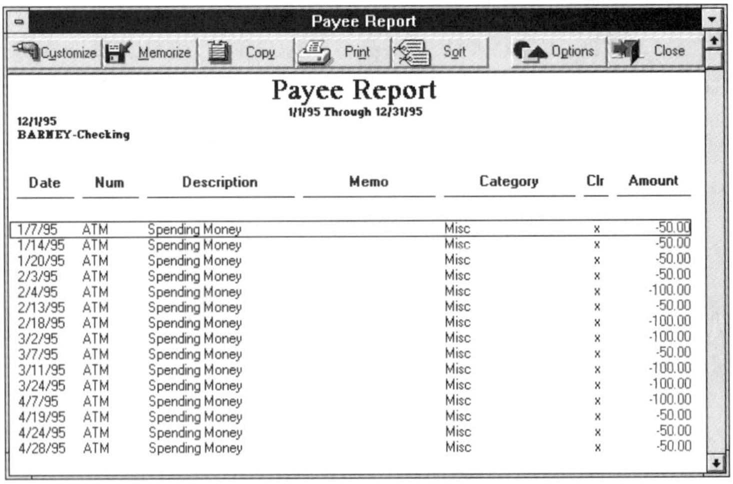

Payee Report
1/1/95 Through 12/31/95

12/1/95
BARNEY-Checking

Date	Num	Description	Memo	Category	Clr	Amount
1/7/95	ATM	Spending Money		Misc	x	-50.00
1/14/95	ATM	Spending Money		Misc	x	-50.00
1/20/95	ATM	Spending Money		Misc	x	-50.00
2/3/95	ATM	Spending Money		Misc	x	-50.00
2/4/95	ATM	Spending Money		Misc	x	-100.00
2/13/95	ATM	Spending Money		Misc	x	-50.00
2/18/95	ATM	Spending Money		Misc	x	-100.00
3/2/95	ATM	Spending Money		Misc	x	-100.00
3/7/95	ATM	Spending Money		Misc	x	-50.00
3/11/95	ATM	Spending Money		Misc	x	-100.00
3/24/95	ATM	Spending Money		Misc	x	-100.00
4/7/95	ATM	Spending Money		Misc	x	-100.00
4/19/95	ATM	Spending Money		Misc	x	-50.00
4/24/95	ATM	Spending Money		Misc	x	-50.00
4/28/95	ATM	Spending Money		Misc	x	-50.00

FIGURE 3-1 Register Report showing transactions not broken down by categories

Chapter 3 *Registers and Transactions*

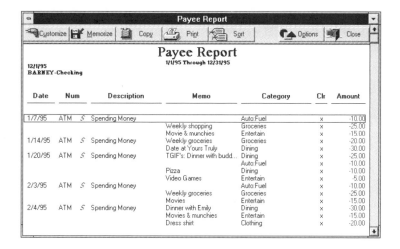

FIGURE 3-2   Register Report using categories to give more information on where money is spent

transactions. These modified transactions with the S after the ATM in the Num field are split transactions. The transaction's total is split to include multiple category and memo field entries for each of the amounts that make up the total.

Can I enter a transaction without a category?

Yes, you can omit the category entry in transactions. However, remember that, without categories, you cannot take advantage of many of Quicken's report features, budget features, and the Tax Planner.

However, if you prefer to enter many transactions without categories, you can turn off Quicken's warning when you record a transaction without a category. To do this:

1. Open a non-investment account Register window.
2. Select Options in the button bar, then the Miscellaneous tab.
3. Clear the Warn Before Recording Uncategorized Transactions check box and select OK.

Creating Subcategories

Is there any way to subdivide existing categories?

You can use subcategories to further divide the transactions assigned to an income or expense category. Quicken already includes some subcategories. For example, one of Quicken's standard home categories, the Utilities category, has subcategories of Gas & Electric and Water that further divide where your money for utilities is spent.

You can create your own subcategories just as you would create regular categories using the steps listed in Chapter 2, "Starting Out and Setting Up." The only difference is that instead of selecting Income or Expense as the category type, you select Subcategory. Next, select the parent income or expense category from the adjoining drop-down list box.

Switching Categories and Accounts

I assigned entries to the wrong category. How do I shift the entries to the correct category?

Quicken has a special command just for reassigning categories in entries. To use this feature:

1. Select Recategorize in the Activities menu.

2. Using the Search Category drop-down list box, select the category that contains the misplaced entries.

3. Select Find All to show all the matching transactions in the bottom half of the Recategorize window.

4. Select which of the listed transactions you want to change so they have check marks. The ones with check marks are the categories that will change and the ones without will not. You can also select all them quickly by selecting the Mark All button.

Chapter 3 *Registers and Transactions*

5. Select the correct category in the Replace With drop-down list box.
6. Select Replace and select OK for confirmation so that Quicken can make the replacements.
7. Select OK after Quicken makes the replacements.
8. Select Close to put this window away.

This feature only works for non-investment accounts.

Is there an easy way to switch between accounts in my Register window?

Quicken makes it easy to switch between accounts. If you look below the transactions in a Register window, you will see small buttons with your account names on them. You can change which account appears in that Register window with the click of a button. You may also notice a change in color that each transaction row uses since registers use different colors for the different account types.

Also, you can open a separate Register window to show a different account. To open a new Register window for any account, open the Account List window by choosing Account from the Lists menu or by pressing CTRL+A. Highlight the account you want and select Open. This has the same effect as double-clicking the account name or highlighting it and pressing ENTER.

Quicken also supports pressing CTRL+R or selecting the Register button in the iconbar to open a register. This opens or switches to the most recently used register. This has the same effect as choosing Use Register in the Activities menu.

Basic Transactions

I deleted the wrong transaction. How do I get it back?

Unfortunately, you'll need to reenter it.

Can I search for entries in a register's Category field?

You can search for a register entry in a Category field, Date field, or any other field in the transaction. To do this:

1. Display an account's Register window.
2. Click the Find button in the Register window's button bar. This button performs the same function as choosing Find in the Edit menu.
3. Type what you want to locate in the Find text box.
4. Select from the Search drop-down list box the field in the register that contains the entry. You can leave it as All Fields if you do not know or the entry might be in more than one field.
5. Select from the Match if drop-down list box how Quicken limits the search. Matching options can find transactions that include the Find entry in a longer entry or as the entire entry. Other matching options compare the entry in the Find text box with the transactions to match ones that are greater than or less than the Find text box entry.
6. Select Find All to alter the Quicken Find window to show all the matching transactions.

   As an example, Figure 3-3 shows this window after searching for Hobbies in the Category field. Notice how the list includes transactions from several accounts.

Tech Terror: You can choose Find in the Edit menu of an investment account's Register window when you want to search for a particular investment. You won't see Find in the button bar because investment registers have different buttons in their Register windows.

How can I find all transactions paid to a particular company or person?

You have two options for showing transactions made to a specific company or person. One possibility is using the Find button as described in the previous question. This method can find specific payees by selecting the Payee field as the field you

Chapter 3 *Registers and Transactions*

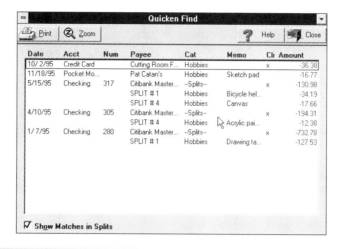

FIGURE 3-3 Quicken Find window showing transactions with a specific entry in the Category field

want to match. You have another option that is available only for the Payee field. You can create a report on transactions for a specific payee by following these steps:

1. Highlight the payee that you want to find in the account's Register window.

2. Choose the Rep<u>o</u>rt button in the Register window's button bar. Quicken creates a Payee Report like the one shown in Figure 3-4. You can also create this report by choosing <u>O</u>ther from the <u>R</u>eports menu, then choosing <u>T</u>ransaction and customizing the report to change the title and limit the matching transactions to the desired payee.

Tech Tip: This method only works with one account at a time. This means that if you make payments to Finast with both checks and credit cards, you would have to create a Payee Report for each account. However, you can have multiple accounts on one Payee Report. Create the Payee Report for one of the accounts. Then, select C<u>u</u>stomize and the <u>A</u>ccounts option button. Select the accounts you want included in the report and select OK.

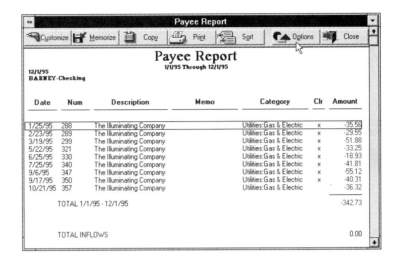

FIGURE 3-4   Payee Report showing payments to a specific payee

I misspelled a store's name for the last six months. How can I fix the name in all the transactions?

Quicken's Find and Replace feature can fix an error in transactions. To try out this feature:

1. Switch to a Register window.
2. Select Find/Replace in the Edit menu.
3. Type the incorrect entry in the Find text box.
4. Select from the Search drop-down list box the field in the register that contains the entry. You can leave it as All Fields but if your data file is large, Quicken may find the misspellings slowly.
5. Select a matching option from the Match if drop-down list box.
6. Select Find All so the bottom half of the Find and Replace window shows all the matching transactions.
7. Select which of the listed transactions you want to change. The ones with check marks will change and the ones without will not. You can select a group of them by

Chapter 3 *Registers and Transactions*

clicking the first one, holding down SHIFT, then clicking the last one in the group.

8. Select in the Replace drop-down list box the field in the register that will contain the new entry.
9. Make the new entry in the With drop-down list box. If the transaction is memorized, you can use the drop-down arrow to show memorized transactions and select one from the list.
10. Select the Replace button and select OK for confirmation so Quicken can make the replacements.
11. Select OK after Quicken makes the replacements.
12. Select Close to put this window away.

If the transaction is memorized, remember to edit the memorized transaction. If your data file includes both the old memorized transaction and the new one, make sure to delete the old one so you don't accidentally use it again.

Is there a fast way to enter dates?

Quicken has lots of shortcuts for entering dates. The following table shows the keys you can type to quickly change the date. The Effect column shows some of the letters italicized as a mnemonic device, to help you recall each key's function.

Key	Effect
+	Increase day by 1
–	Decrease day by 1
t	Set to *t*oday's date
m	First day of *m*onth
h	Last day of mont*h*
y	First day of *y*ear
r	Last day of yea*r*

Besides these keys, you can also select dates with a calendar. Whenever you see a small calendar next to a field, the Date icon, you can click it to show a calendar like the one shown next.

While the full month appears, you can click any date to select it and click the << and >> buttons to change the month shown.

What's the difference between the two types of Xs in the Clr field of a register?

The x or X distinguishes how the account was cleared. The larger X marks transactions cleared by Quicken as when you reconcile the account. The smaller x marks transactions that you cleared by clicking the Clr field. Usually, you let Quicken clear transactions for you; however, when you first set up Quicken, you may need to clear some of the transactions.

Tech Tip: You can change the smaller x to the larger one by clicking the Clr field again.

Can I print the transactions in the register?

You can create a Register Report that lists all the transactions in a register. To create this report, move to an empty transaction in the Register window and select the Report button in the window's button bar. Figure 3-5 shows a sample of such a report.

Tech Tip: Once you create the Register Report, take advantage of Quicken's report options. These report options can select the date range, the accounts, and the categories as well as other available options. Chapter 9, "Reports and Graphs," has more frequently asked questions about how you can change your reports.

Chapter 3 *Registers and Transactions*

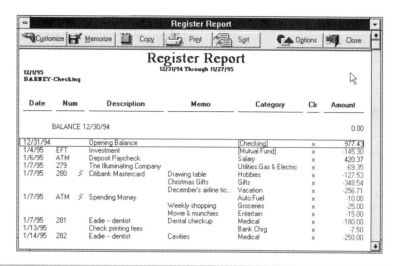

FIGURE 3-5   Register Report showing the account's transactions

Can I list register transactions in an order other than date?

A Register Report can list its entries sorted according to any field except the Memo field. To create such a report:

1. Move to an empty transaction in the Register window and select the Rep<u>o</u>rt button in the window's button bar.
2. When you see the report, select S<u>o</u>rt in the Report window's button bar.
3. Select the field that sorts the records, then select OK. Now the report lists the account's transactions sorted by the chosen field.

How can I print register transactions organized by category?

Besides sorting a Register Report by the category, you can also group the transactions by category. You can create an Itemized Category Report by selecting <u>H</u>ome from the <u>R</u>eports menu and then <u>I</u>temized Categories. When you select OK, Quicken creates

Tech Tip: Selecting which accounts and categories appear in a report is an option for most of Quicken's reports. The steps are the same regardless of which report you create.

a report like the one in Figure 3-6. This report shows all accounts combined. You can further limit this report to specific categories and accounts. Just click the Customize button in the button bar. Next select Accounts or Categories/Classes depending on which you want to limit. After selecting one, you see a list of the accounts or categories and classes. Click the ones you want to add to or remove from the report. The accounts, categories, or classes that have check marks appear in the report. Ones without a check mark do not.

Quicken creates an Itemized Category Report out of a Register Report by customizing the report and selecting Category from the Subtotal By drop-down list box. You can use this same drop-down list box to alter other reports when you want them grouped by categories.

In an Itemized Category Report, you can sort the transactions within each group using the same Sort button in the Report window's button bar. This was described in the previous question.

FIGURE 3-6   Itemized Category Report showing transactions grouped by category

Chapter 3 *Registers and Transactions*

 I put transactions into the wrong account. How do I transfer them?

If you just have one or two, deleting the wrong entries then entering them in the correct account is the quickest solution. When you have a lot of them, you want a different solution. You can perform these steps to transfer them:

1. Back up your data file. In case anything goes wrong, you can return to your backup.
2. Show the Register window for the account in which the transactions were mistakenly entered.
3. Choose Export from the File menu to show the QIF Export dialog box.
4. Type the path and filename where Quicken will store the data you are exporting, as in **C:\QUICKENW\SWITCH**.
5. Select the account with the incorrect transactions from the Quicken Account to Export from drop-down list.
6. Change the dates under Transactions Starting to include the transactions that are in the wrong account. Ideally, the transactions in the wrong account are contained in a data range that does not include correctly entered transactions. Otherwise, you will export both the transactions that you want to move and other transactions that correctly belong in the first account. After you add the misplaced transactions to the correct account, you will have to delete the transactions that you entered correctly into the first account from the second account.
7. Select the Transactions check box and clear the others so the QIF file contains the transactions in this date range.
8. Select OK to export the file.
9. Choose Import from the File menu to display the QIF Import dialog box.
10. Select the account where you want the transactions correctly placed in the Quicken Account to Import into drop-down list box.
11. Select OK. Quicken imports the transactions from the QIF file into the account you selected.

12. Check that the data you have imported is correct in the new account.
13. Switch to the account that incorrectly contained the transactions and delete the transactions you no longer need.

How do I change a split transaction to affect only one category?

Open the Splits window to show the existing categories and amounts. Then select Clear All and Yes to Quicken's confirmation prompt. All splits disappear. Now enter the category, memo, and amount. When you select OK, the single category that you entered now appears in place of —Splits—.

Can I store addresses with payments the way I can with check transactions?

Only check transactions can store addresses; payments cannot. You can see the address of a check transaction if it is a memorized or scheduled transaction. Just highlight the transaction in the Scheduled Transaction List or Memorized Transaction List window and select Edit, then Address. In the Memorized Transaction List window, these check transactions have Chk in the Type column.

How do I enter ATM transactions?

An ATM withdrawal or deposit is just like any other withdrawal or deposit that you make. Just enter ATM in the Num field. Since you still have this cash available, you may want to set up a separate account for this cash. The ATM withdrawals are recorded as transfers to this account. Figure 3-7 shows a register entry for an ATM deposit. In this case, the category is Pocket Money. This transaction means that you took $50 out of your checking

Chapter 3 *Registers and Transactions*

account with your ATM card and put it in your pocket. You can also see part of the Pocket Money account that shows how this money was spent. If you didn't record the ATM withdrawal as a transfer, you would want to assign it to a category describing where you spent the money.

Tech Acct: If you don't keep track of where you spend the cash in your wallet, you will find it slipping through your fingers. Set up an account like the Pocket Money one above to track those miscellaneous amounts.

 **Tech Acct:** Don't forget that your bank may charge usage fees for the ATM. Record these amounts either when you reconcile the statement or when you use the ATM. The standard home categories includes a Bank Chrg category that you can assign these charges to.

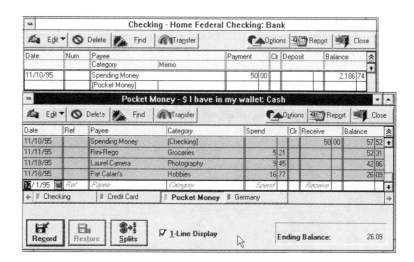

FIGURE 3-7 Recording ATM withdrawals as transfers to a separate account

Adjusting Account Register Balances

How do I adjust my bank account register to agree with my account statement?

You may find that the balance does not agree due to an incorrect opening balance, missing transactions, or errors in transactions. You can adjust the account's balance when you reconcile the account. When you reconcile your account and select Done from the Reconcile Bank Statement dialog box, the Adjust Balance dialog box prompts that Quicken will add an Adjust Balance transaction to this register. You can enter the date for the adjusting entry and select Adjust Balance.

Tech Acct: Adjusting your balance this way is, ideally, the last resort. Your Quicken data file has better information about your finances when you take the time to find out which payment or charge you need to adjust. Look at some of the questions in Chapter 4, "Checks and Reconciliation."

How do I adjust my credit card's register to agree with my credit card statement?

Like the problem described in the previous question, a credit card statement that does not match your register usually is caused by missing entries. As the first step, select the Cancel button when you see the Adjusting Register to Agree with Statement dialog box. Then, compare the entries in the Pay Credit Card Bill dialog box with the entries in your credit card statement. Reconcile it as much as possible. Select Done. When the Adjusting Register to Agree with Statement dialog box reappears, select a category to assign to the adjusting transaction. This assigns the amount to the category just like the other credit card entries have been assigned to categories. Select Adjust Balance to enter this adjusting balance transaction and continue with the credit card payment.

Hiding Account Balances

How do I see my actual bank balance if I put money aside for a savings goal?

Savings Goals let you hide money from yourself without removing the actual money from your accounts. Savings goals appear as withdrawals and transfers to a Savings Goal account. Your register can hide these amounts as if the transfers were never made by selecting the Hide Sav. Goal check box at the bottom of the Register window. If you don't see this check box, the account shown in the register doesn't have any amount set aside. When you clear this check box again, the amount set aside for the savings goal appears and your bank balance goes down.

How can I hide the minimum amount that I have to keep in my checking account?

When you have to keep a minimum balance in your account, you may not want to show it in your account balance. You can hide it from yourself by creating a Savings Goal for the minimum balance and contributing the minimum balance to this Savings Goal. To do this:

1. Choose Savings Goals from the Plan menu.
2. Select New to create the new savings goal.
3. Type a savings goal name, like **Minimum Balance**, in the Goal Name text box.
4. Type the checking account's minimum balance in the Goal Amount text box and select OK. You now have a savings goal for your checking account's minimum balance. You can ignore the finish date and projected monthly contribution.
5. Select the Contribute button.

6. Select the checking account in the From Account drop-down list box.

7. Type the checking account's minimum balance in the text box after the $ sign and select OK. You just set aside the checking account's minimum balance.

8. Select Close to put the Savings Goals window away.

9. Return to the account's Register window. The transaction you have made looks like this:

Date	Num	Payee		Payment	Clr	Deposit	Balance
		Category	Memo				
12/1/95		Contribution towards goal		1,000 00			935 92
		[Minimum Balance]					

Now your bank balance doesn't include the minimum balance, which would remind you to not write checks below the minimum. If you want to see what the balance really is, select the Hide Sav. Goal check box. Quicken then treats the account as if you had no savings goals and the minimum balance is included in the account's balance.

Credit Cards

Can Quicken remember my credit cards' interest rates so I remember to pay the highest rate card off first?

When you have unpaid credit balances, you want to pay off the credit card with the highest interest rate. To make sure that you can tell which one this is, include the interest rate in the credit card information. To add this interest rate, show the Account List window by choosing Account from the Lists menu. Then for each credit card, highlight the account and select Info. Add the percentage to the Interest Rate text box and select OK. Then, you can go through the information for your credit card accounts with outstanding balances to see which one should be paid off first.

Tech Tip: If you frequently need to know the credit card interest rate, change the credit card account's description so it includes the percentage. For example, change the description of Mastercard to Mastercard 16%. Then, when you open that account's Register window, the interest rate appears in the title bar.

Chapter 3 *Registers and Transactions*

How do I change my credit card limit?

To change your credit card limit:

1. Click the Accounts button in the iconbar or press CTRL+A to show the Account List window.
2. Highlight the credit card account and select the Edit button in the window's button bar.
3. Type the new limit in the Credit Limit text box and select OK.

I don't want a separate credit card account. How can I tell Quicken what my credit card purchases are for?

Instead of having a separate register that tracks all your credit card purchases, you can enter the purchases when you pay the credit card bill. In this case, you record your credit card payment just as you would record any other payment. Select Splits and here is where you divide the credit card bill into the different categories. The Register window in Figure 3-8 shows both the recorded transaction and the Splits window that shows the categories assigned to different amounts of the transaction.

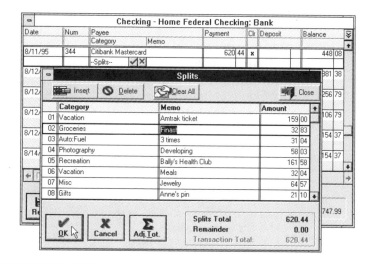

FIGURE 3-8   Credit card purchases divided into categories when the bill is paid

Monitoring Cash

How can I get a report on my income and the bills that I paid, to learn whether I've spent more than I saved?

A Cash Flow Report lists your income and expenses during any period of time. To create a Cash Flow Report, choose <u>H</u>ome from the <u>R</u>eports menu and then Cash <u>F</u>low. Select OK to create this report.

You can also have it broken out by month or another period. Just select C<u>u</u>stomize in the button bar, then Month in the Col<u>u</u>mn drop-down list box. You can also select the date range for this cash flow by entering dates in the To and From text boxes. Figure 3-9 shows a Cash Flow Report that shows the total as well as the individual amounts for three months.

How can I record what I've spend during the week without keeping receipts?

When you record what you withdraw for spending, you can treat the withdrawal as a transfer to a cash account. For example, in Figure 3-10, you can see the Pocket Money account Register window. As you make withdrawals, they appear as transfers from the Checking account to this account. At the end of each week, create a transaction that records the difference between what you had and what you currently have. These transactions appear in Figure 3-10 as the ones with the payee of "Pocket Money Spent Last Week."

Tech Acct: Don't be surprised if you start tracking how you spend your money! The "Spent" amounts can add up and it is frustrating at the end of the year to have no idea where hundreds or even thousands of dollars have gone.

```
                         Cash Flow Report by Month
                              1/1/95 Through 3/31/95
12/1/95                                                                              Page 1
BARNEY-Bank,Cash,CC Accounts
                                                                        OVERALL
          Category Description    1/1/95       2/1/95       3/1/95       TOTAL

          INFLOWS
            Int Inc                 3.81         3.39         4.20         11.40
            Salary              1,681.48     1,681.48     2,101.85      5,464.81

          TOTAL INFLOWS         1,685.29     1,684.87     2,106.05      5,476.21
          OUTFLOWS
            Auto:
              Fuel                 20.00        20.00        14.50         54.50
              Service              70.22         0.00        44.38        114.60

            Total Auto             90.22        20.00        58.88        169.10
            Bank Chrg               7.50         0.00         0.00          7.50
            Charity                 0.00         0.00        20.00         20.00
            Clothing                0.00        55.00         0.00         55.00
            Dining                 65.00        50.00         0.00        115.00
            Dues                   15.00         0.00         0.00         15.00
            Entertain              20.00        30.00         7.00         57.00
            Gifts                 348.54        20.00        31.16        399.70
            Groceries              93.77        60.10        84.03        237.90
            Hobbies               127.53         0.00         0.00        127.53
            Household               0.00         0.00        22.19         22.19
            Housing                 0.00       277.00         0.00        277.00
            Medical               430.00         0.00         0.00        430.00
            Misc                   45.00       100.00       350.00        495.00
            Photography             0.00         0.00        41.13         41.13
            Tax:
              Local               353.00         0.00         0.00        353.00

            Total Tax             353.00         0.00         0.00        353.00
            Telephone              29.22        25.04        31.60         85.86
            Utilities:
              Gas & Electric      104.91        19.55        45.11        169.57

            Total Utilities       104.91        19.55        45.11        169.57
            Vacation              256.71         0.00         0.00        256.71
            TO Personal Mutual Fund 145.30     116.24       116.24        377.78

          TOTAL OUTFLOWS        2,131.70       772.93       807.34      3,711.97

          OVERALL TOTAL          -446.41       911.94     1,298.71      1,764.24
```

FIGURE 3-9   Cash Flow Report to show what you have earned and spent

Sales Tax and Reminders

How do I allocate sales tax to categories?

When you have a split transaction, figuring out where sales tax goes may be a puzzle. This is an issue with purchases that affect

Quicken 4 for Windows Answers: Certified Tech Support

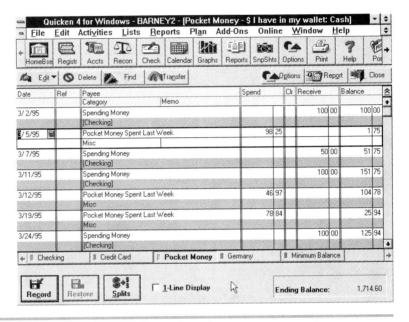

FIGURE 3-10 Recording each week how much pocket money was spent

multiple categories. You can create a Sales Tax category. Another possibility is to use the calculator in the Amount column. You want to multiply the amount for a category times 1 plus the sales tax rate. Then the amount includes the price plus its sales tax. You can see a receipt and the Splits window in Figure 3-11. The first item has the sales tax added with the entry of 27.99 * 1.06, assuming sales tax of six percent. Due to rounding errors, the last split in the dialog box will have a few extra cents of sales tax. The last item will automatically have the amount entered so you don't have to calculate the sales tax for the last item.

How do I tell Quicken to remind me about paying my bills?

Quicken's Billminder program can remind you of bills when you start Windows or DOS. Then you can decide at that point to go straight to Quicken to handle your finances or continue with other projects.

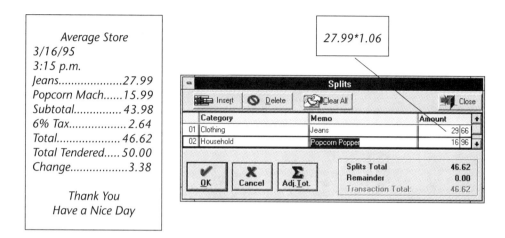

FIGURE 3-11 Allocating sales tax between different purchases

To turn Billminder off or on:

1. Choose the Options button in the iconbar and choose Reminders.

2. Select or clear the Turn on Billminder check box.

3. Select OK, then Close.

When Billminder is on, your reminder appears either when you start the computer or when you start Windows, depending on when Billminder is set to appear. This setting is made during installation. In Windows, you will see the Quicken Billminder icon as well as Quicken Billminder in Windows' Task List. When you select this icon or application name, Billminder shows a message that reminds you of the tasks to perform in Quicken. Selecting OK removes Billminder. When Billminder appears as part of the DOS boot process, you will see this message after you start your computer. You will see more detailed information about which data file needs attention, and so forth, when you go into Quicken. In fact, as soon as you open the data file with scheduled transactions, you see a dialog box like the one in Figure 3-12. At this point, you can select Record to record them or Done to skip recording them and save them for another time. If you have a different Quicken data file open, the

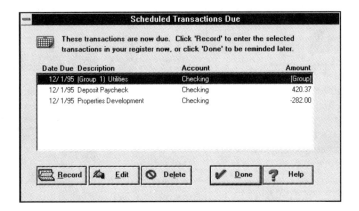

FIGURE 3-12   Window reminding you to pay bills

Quicken Reminders window will show which data file has scheduled transactions.

Memorized Transactions

Can I use a preexisting transaction as a template for another, similar transaction?

You can quickly enter transactions using existing transactions to supply most of their entries. For example, you can enter the check for this week's groceries using last week's check to supply many of this week's entries. Just make sure that you memorized the transactions that you want repeated. To use one of the memorized transactions, you can either select it from a list or take advantage of QuickFill. To recall a memorized transaction from a list:

1. Move to the next empty transaction in the Register window.
2. Choose Memorize Transaction from the Lists menu.
3. Highlight the transaction that you want recalled.

Chapter 3 *Registers and Transactions*

4. Select Use or double-click it. Quicken adds the memorized transaction's payee, amount, category, and memo to the empty transaction. The current date appears in the Date field.

5. Make any changes that you want to the transaction and select Record.

To recall a memorized transaction using Quicken's QuickFill feature:

1. Move to the next empty transaction in the Register window.

2. Enter the appropriate entries for the Date and Num field.

3. Select the payee for this field. You can type the beginning characters until Quicken supplies the rest of the entry. You can also select one of the listed payees from this field's drop-down list.

4. Move to the next field and make any appropriate changes to the transaction.

5. Select Record.

Can I use Quicken's memorized transactions feature for some, but not all, of my transactions?

You can select which transactions Quicken memorizes two ways. Your choices are

- You can individually memorize transactions. Move to them in a Register window and press CTRL+M. This has the same result as choosing Memorize Transaction from the Edit menu. When Quicken prompts that the transaction is about to be memorized, select OK.

- You can turn the automatic memorization feature off and on. Select the Options button in a Register window and the QuickFill tab. Select the Automatic Memorization of New Transactions check box to turn this feature on, or clear it to turn it off. Select OK to put this dialog box away.

Tech Tip: You may find that using the automatic memorize transactions feature when you first start is a good idea. After a while, you may want to turn off the automatic memorization feature since you yourself will have memorized most of the transactions that you repeatedly use.

Can memorized transactions remember percentages rather than numbers?

When you reuse a memorized transaction with multiple categories, its amount can be applied to the different categories in two ways:

- **As percentages** For example, suppose you memorize a $100 telephone bill that has $25 for the business phone category and $75 for the home phone category. When you recall this memorized transaction using percentages and the amount happens to be $200, $50 is assigned to the business phone category and $150 to the home phone category.

- **As dollar amounts** Using the same example as above, recalling this memorized transaction using $200 as the amount leaves $25 assigned to the business phone category and $75 to the home phone category. You can decide where the additional $100 goes.

The choice is made when you memorize the transaction. Automatically memorized transactions are memorized as amounts. When you manually memorize a transaction that has more than one category, Quicken asks if you want to memorize the splits as percentages. Selecting Yes memorizes the percentages and selecting No memorizes the amounts.

Chapter 3 *Registers and Transactions*

Memorized transactions remembered as percentages show %Spl in the Memorized Transaction window like the one shown here:

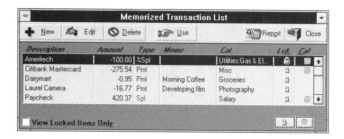

When you recall a transaction memorized as percentages, Quicken prompts with the following dialog box for you to enter the new transaction amount.

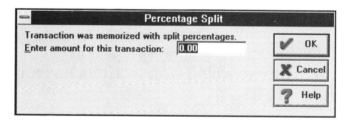

Once you enter the amount and select OK, you can select Record without making any entries in the Splits window.

When you memorize amounts, you can still allocate the amount by percentages but you will have to go through using the Splits window. When you type the new amount and you want to allocate the amount by percentages, select Record not Splits. Quicken displays this dialog box:

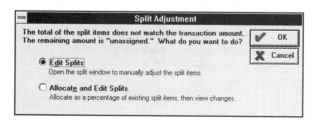

Choose the Allocate and Edit Splits option button. Then, the Splits window opens showing the percentages applied to the new amount. You can adjust these amounts or select OK and Record to record the transaction with the percentages applied to the amounts.

On the other hand, if you selected Edit Splits or selected Splits not Record, the amounts allocated to the categories do not change. The difference between the transaction amount and the amounts allocated in the Splits window appears at the bottom in the Remainder row.

Tech Tip: You can replace an automatically memorized transaction to use percentages. Just move to the transaction and press CTRL+M to rememorize it. Select Yes for the prompt for memorizing percentages, select OK to record the memorized transaction, and select Replace so the transaction now remembers the percentages instead of the amounts.

One of my memorized transactions has an error in it. How do I fix it?

Altering a memorized transaction is as easy as highlighting the memorized transaction and selecting Edit in the button bar. From the Edit Memorized Transaction dialog box, you can make any changes you want and then select OK when you are done.

Tech Terror: Fixing a memorized transaction only changes what Quicken remembers for the next time. You cannot fix the mistake in any previously recorded transactions this way. An earlier section, "Basic Transactions," contained information on changing widespread errors in your accounts.

How do I get rid of a memorized transaction?

After you use Quicken for a while, you will have some transactions that you'll never use again. For example, a purchase at a store's

Chapter 3 *Registers and Transactions*

going-out-of-business sale may never be repeated. You can delete these unneeded memorized transactions to make it easier to find the ones you do want. To remove the memorized transactions you no longer want:

1. Choose Memorized Transaction from the Lists menu or press CTRL+T.
2. Highlight the memorized transaction that you do not want.
3. Select Delete from the window's button bar.
4. Select OK to confirm that you want to delete a memorized transaction.
5. Repeat steps 2 through 4 for each memorized transaction you want to delete. Select Close when you are done.

Deleting memorized transactions has no effect on the original transactions that they were memorized from.

How do I delete a group of memorized transactions?

You can delete memorized transaction only one at a time from the Memorized Transaction List window. The answer to the previous question describes how you can delete a memorized transaction.

The amounts in my memorized transactions keep changing but I want them to use the same numbers. How do I do that?

You need to lock the transaction, so that every time you recall it, it will start off with the same amount. A *locked transaction*, therefore, is a memorized transaction where the amount does not change. For example, suppose that most movies that you see cost $14 for two tickets but sometimes you pay more or less. If this transaction is not locked, every time you enter going to a movie, Quicken enters whatever you spent the last time as the amount for this transaction. By locking this memorized transaction, the amount always stays at $14. You only change it for the times you spend a different amount. To lock memorized transactions:

1. Choose Memorized **T**ransaction from the **L**ists menu or press CTRL+T to show the Memorized Transaction List window.

2. Highlight the memorized transaction that you want to lock.

3. Click the Lock button or click the Lc**k** column where you want the lock to appear or be removed from.

Memorized transactions that have the little lock in the Lc**k** column of the Memorized Transaction List window are the ones whose amounts do not change.

Scheduled Transactions

Can I enter transactions that won't occur for a while so that I won't forget them?

You can create a scheduled transaction. Once the scheduled transaction becomes due, Quicken reminds you about it. Or, you can have Quicken automatically record the scheduled transaction for you. You may want to do this with automatic deposits and paychecks since these transactions frequently repeat. The following question contains information on creating repeating transactions. Creating a scheduled transaction for a single transaction follows the same steps.

How do I get Quicken to repeat transactions that occur on a regular basis?

You can repeat transactions by making them scheduled transactions. Scheduled transactions can record events that occur once or frequently, such as every other week, every month, or every year. The scheduled transaction can be entered automatically by Quicken or can remind you with a prompt that it needs to be recorded. To create a scheduled transaction:

1. Tell Quicken that you want to create a scheduled transaction. You can do this with either of these methods:

   - Select Scheduled Transaction from the Lists menu. Select New.
   - Double-click a date on the Financial Calendar window and select New. Make sure that the Scheduled Transaction option button is selected.

   Quicken shows the Create Scheduled Transaction or the Drag and Drop Transaction dialog box. The Create Scheduled Transaction dialog box looks like this after you complete some entries:

   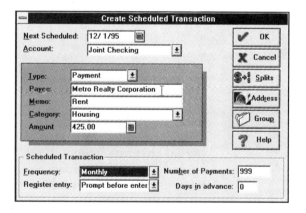

2. Enter the next date in the Next Scheduled text box for when you want this transaction recorded.

3. Select an account from the Account drop-down list box where this transaction will be recorded.

4. Select Payment, Deposit, Print Check, or Elec Payment (for CheckFree) from the Type drop-down list box. (See Chapter 4 for more information on CheckFree.)

5. Make entries in the Payee, Memo, Category, and Amount boxes just as if you were entering a transaction in a Register window. If the transaction has more than one

Tech Acct: Make all of your recurring transactions into scheduled transactions—even if the amount or date changes. Then, you will have reminders when they become due and you can see them in the Financial Calendar so that you have an idea of your upcoming cash flow.

category, select Splits and enter categories, memos, and amounts in the Splits window before selecting OK.

6. Select how often the transaction repeats in the Frequency text box.

7. Set how many times this transaction should be repeated in the Number of Payments box. If you leave this set to 999, Quicken continues to repeat this transaction indefinitely.

8. Select how you want this transaction recorded in the Register Entry drop-down list box. When it contains "Prompt before enter," Quicken prompts you about recording the transaction. When it contains "Automatically enter," Quicken records the transaction as soon as the scheduled date occurs.

9. Enter how many days ahead of time you want the transaction entered in the Days in advance text box. For instance, entering **3** records the scheduled transaction three days before the Next Scheduled entry. The register shows this entry as a postdated transaction.

10. Select OK. Quicken returns to the Scheduled Transaction List window or Financial Calendar. Quicken is now ready to remind you about upcoming scheduled transactions when the Register entry drop-down list box contains "Prompt before entering." If the Register entry drop-down list box contains "Automatically enter," Quicken records the transaction automatically.

11. Select Close to put the window away.

Remember that you can also have memorized transactions. Memorized transactions let you select your payee from the payee list, and then Quicken supplies the amounts, categories, and memo entries. Scheduled transactions work better for planning expenses since they appear on the Financial Calendar and they are reflected in the account balances.

Chapter 3 Registers and Transactions

Can I make a normal transaction into a scheduled one?

You can easily create scheduled transactions out of memorized transactions. You can do it from the Drag and Drop Transaction dialog box or the Create Scheduled Transaction dialog box that you use to enter a scheduled transaction.

As you complete either dialog box, QuickFill will complete your entries using the memorized transactions. This means that you can just start typing the payee's name and QuickFill supplies the rest of the name, an amount, a memo, and any categories.

The other method uses the memorized transactions listed in the Financial Calendar. When you drag a memorized transaction to a specific day, you see the Drag and Drop Transaction dialog box with many of the entries supplied from the memorized transaction's information. Once you select OK, you're done.

Tech Tip: The memorized transactions listed on the Financial Calendar are only the ones that have the Calendar icon in the Memorized Transaction List window. You can show this window by clicking Manage Lists in the Financial Calendar window. Then you can add the calendar or remove it from the Cal column by clicking that column or highlighting the transaction and selecting Cal.

Scheduled Transaction Groups

How can I schedule many transactions at once?

You can combine several transactions into a single scheduled transaction by combining those transactions into a group; however, only memorized transactions can be grouped. When you record the scheduled transaction, Quicken records all the transactions in that group. To create a scheduled transaction group:

1. Select Scheduled Transaction from the Lists menu.
2. Select New.
3. Select Group to display the Create Transaction Group dialog box. This dialog box looks like this after you have completed some entries:

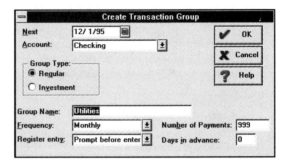

4. Enter the date in the Next text box for when Quicken should record the transactions in the group.
5. Select an account from the Account drop-down list box in which these transactions will be entered.
6. Type a name for the group in the Group Name text box.
7. Select how often the transactions repeat in the Frequency text box.
8. Set how many of these transactions should be made in the Number of Payments box. If you leave this set to 999, Quicken continues to enter these transactions indefinitely.
9. Select how you want these transactions recorded in the Register Entry drop-down list box. When it contains "Prompt before entering," Quicken prompts you about recording the transactions. When it contains "Automatically enter," Quicken records the transactions as soon as the scheduled date occurs.

Chapter 3 *Registers and Transactions*

10. Select OK. Quicken displays the Assign Transactions to Group dialog box, shown here:

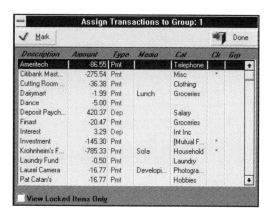

This dialog box lists all the memorized transactions in your data file.

11. Double-click the transactions that you want included in the group or highlight them and select <u>M</u>ark.

    A "1" appears in the Grp column for these transactions. The "1" indicates that the transaction is now a part of the first group.

12. Select Done when you are finished selecting transactions.

How do I change which transactions are in a scheduled transaction group?

You can change which transactions are part of a transaction group with these simple steps:

1. Select Sc<u>h</u>eduled Transaction from the <u>L</u>ists menu.
2. Highlight the transaction group and select Ed<u>i</u>t.
3. Select OK to finish with the Edit Transaction Group dialog box and display the Assign Transactions to Group dialog

box. The transactions with the same number in the Grp column as the number in the dialog box's title bar are part of the group you are editing. Transactions with different numbers in the Grp column are part of another transaction group.

4. Double-click the transactions that you want included in the group or highlight them and select <u>M</u>ark. You can even switch a transaction from another group into the current one by changing the group number to the current group's number.

5. Select Done when you finish changing which transactions are part of the scheduled transaction group.

How do I get rid of transaction groups?

You can delete scheduled transaction groups the same way you would delete scheduled transactions.

1. Select Sc<u>h</u>eduled Transaction from the <u>L</u>ists menu.

2. Highlight the transaction group you want and select <u>D</u>elete.

3. Select OK when prompted about deleting a scheduled transaction.

Checks and Reconciliation

Writing checks in Quicken requires no more effort than making a register entry. The process is especially simple when you use Intuit checks and then take advantage of Quicken's many check writing shortcuts.

Quicken also makes reconciling your account a breeze. The following Frustration Busters box has tips on reconciling your account.

Frustration Busters!

When you reconcile your checkbook, discovering why your checking account and bank statement differ can be frustrating and time consuming. Here are some tricks and tips that will help get things to balance:

- Double-check that all transactions in the statement appear in the register.

- Calculate the difference between the balance you want and the balance you have. Divide that number by 2 and look for a transaction equaling this amount. This will help you to find transactions where you entered the amount in the wrong column.

- Subtract the desired balance from the balance you have. Is the number evenly divisible by 9? If so, check the amounts. Chances are that you have two numbers transposed, such as 87 in place of 78.

- Check to see if you included a transaction twice.

- Check to see if you incorrectly marked a transaction as appearing on the statement.

- Check the amounts of each transaction, since one of them probably has an error in it.

- When you use an ATM with the account, remember to include any usage fees. Depending on your bank, they may be combined into one amount or separated and scattered throughout the statement.

Chapter 4 *Checks and Reconciliation*

Writing and Voiding Checks

How do I void a check?

To void a check, just move to that check's transaction in the Register window and choose <u>V</u>oid Transaction from the <u>E</u>dit menu. When you look at a voided transaction in a Register window, the Payee field includes ****VOID****, the Clr field contains an X, and the amount disappears. The following illustration shows a voided check transaction.

Date	Num	Payee		Payment	Clr	Deposit	Balance
		Category	Memo				
8/14/95	351	**VOID**Washington Insurance			x		1,247 09
		Insurance					

Tech Acct: Don't delete the transaction when you void a check. Voiding a check instead provides a reminder that you used that check.

Tech Tip: In a Write Checks window, you can also choose <u>V</u>oid Transaction from the <u>E</u>dit menu when you want to void a check that you haven't printed yet.

Tech Terror: Quicken does not prompt you before you void a check, nor does Quicken have an Undo feature. Make sure that you void the correct check. If you find out you did not, remove the X in the Clr field, remove **VOID** from the Payee name, and type the amount in the Payment or Deposit field.

Can I write a postdated check?

Yes, all you have to do is enter a date after the current date. When you write postdated checks, Quicken will show both how much is in the account as of today, as well as the total of all transactions (including the postdated ones) that you have entered. Writing a postdated check is just like writing any other check except that you are just putting a different date into the Date field.

I paid for something partially by check and partially by cash. How do I enter it?

When you pay using more than one account, enter the total transaction in only one account's register and indicate the amount that comes from the other account as a transfer. For example, suppose you paid for a new coat half with cash and half with a check. To enter this transaction:

1. Switch to the Register window for the checking account. Enter the date, check number, and payee for the check.
2. Enter the amount of the check in the Payment column.
3. Select Splits to open the Splits window.
4. Enter the account that supplied the funds for the purchase in the Category column.
5. Enter the amount that came from the other account as a negative number in the Amount column. Now the amount in the next line shows the total that you spent.
6. Add the categories and amounts for the purchase.

Chapter 4 *Checks and Reconciliation*

7. Select OK to finish the transaction, then Record to record it. A transaction and its Splits window made this way might look like this:

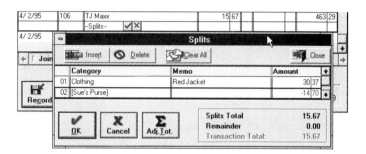

I want to add more information about a check's payee but I don't want the extra text printed. How do I hide text in a Payee field?

You can add text to the payee line inside brackets ({}) and Quicken won't print the brackets or what's inside them. For instance, if you write a check payable to Girl Scout Troop #415 {cookies}, the check only shows Girl Scout Troop #415. This bracket feature doesn't work for the Address or Memo field.

I wrote a check with an error on it. How do I fix it?

Hopefully, you discovered the error before you printed the check. To correct an unprinted check, switch to the Write Checks window, show the unprinted check, and make your corrections. You can change which check appears in the window with the scroll bar or with PGUP and PGDN. You can also select Find in the button bar to search for the check. Searching for an entry in a check is just like searching for a transaction entry from a Register window. You can also alter these checks by altering the transaction for the check in the Register window.

If you have printed the check, you can void it and then create a new one with the correct information. You cannot re-create that check since the check stock with that check's number is already used.

I need an address for a check I printed. Does Quicken remember the address?

Quicken does remember the address but seeing it again requires a few steps. The steps to perform depend on whether the transaction for the check is memorized. If it is

1. Choose Memorized Transaction from the Lists menu.
2. Highlight the transaction. This transaction has Chk in the Type column to remind you that this is paid by check.
3. Select Edit and Address to see the address.
4. Select OK twice.

If the transaction with the check's address is not memorized, you can still show it by following these steps:

1. Move to the transaction in the account's Register window.
2. Write down the check number on a piece of paper.
3. Replace the check number in the register with Print and select Record.
4. Switch to the Write Checks window.
5. Go through the checks until you find the one with the address that you want.
6. Switch back to the account's Register window.
7. Replace Print in the Num field with the check number in the register and select Record.

Joint Checking Accounts

 How do I set up a joint checking account?

A joint checking account is just like any other checking account to Quicken. However, with a joint checking account, you might want to separate the deposits and withdrawals of each person in the joint checking account. You can do this by adding classes to your transactions. Classes are nothing more than another way to divide transactions in addition to using categories. To set up a class for each person in the account:

1. Start the process for creating a new class. To start the process, you can do either one of the following:

   - Edit a transaction and type **/** and the name of the new class at the end of the Category field's entry, then select Re**c**ord.

   - Choose **C**lass from the **L**ists menu, then select **N**ew in the window's button bar.

   Either method opens the Set Up Class dialog box.

2. Add or modify the entry in the **N**ame text box for the name that you want for this class.

3. Enter a longer description in the **D**escription text box.

4. Select OK to create this class.

You can continue recording the transaction or close the Class List window. When you set up the joint checking account, edit the Opening Balance transaction and create a split that shows what each person contributed. After the category, type **/** and the class name, as in **/Kim** or **/Tom**. Figure 4-1 shows a Register Report with the opening balance split as well as other transactions with classes. As you create Quicken reports, you can create them to only include transactions with a specific class.

Quicken 4 for Windows Answers: *Certified Tech Support*

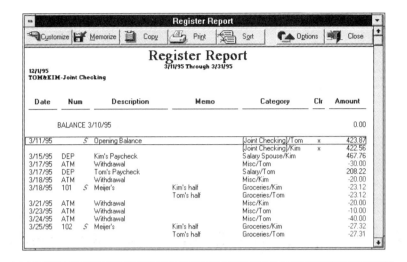

FIGURE 4-1   Register Report that shows classes added

How do my reports show only the transactions of my half of a joint checking account?

When you assign a class to each person's transactions in a joint checking account, you can limit the report to show only the transactions for that person. To make this change to any report, create the report you want. Then, choose Customize from the button bar and select the Matching option button. Select the class you created for the person from the Class Contains drop-down list box and select OK. Now the report that you created only shows what belongs to the person. For example, you can follow these steps on the report in Figure 4-1 to show only the transactions that apply to Kim by selecting Kim from the Class Contains drop-down list box.

Scheduled Payments

Can I create scheduled transactions for checks?

Yes, you can. Creating scheduled transactions that print checks is just like creating scheduled transactions for register entries,

Chapter 4 *Checks and Reconciliation*

which was covered in Chapter 3. The only difference is that in the Create Scheduled Transaction dialog box, you change Payment in the Type drop-down list box to Print Check. You can also create scheduled transaction groups that include printed checks. When you select the transactions that belong to a group, the ones that have Chk in the Type column are recorded as checks to print when you record the scheduled transaction group.

I have a loan payment automatically deducted from my checking account. Do I enter it into Quicken when it is paid or when I get my statement?

Enter the transaction when it is deducted from the account. Then your account reasonably represents your current balance. You probably want to create a scheduled transaction that automatically records the loan payment on the specific date. Chapter 3 has information about creating scheduled transactions.

Printing Checks

How do I test whether my checks will print correctly?

You can print sample checks first. These sample checks let you check the alignment of the print on the check. If it is wrong, read the following question for solutions.

How do I align checks in the printer?

Quicken can print sample checks to help you align checks correctly. The procedures for *page printers* and *continuous-feed printers* are different. Laser and ink jet printers that work with one page at a time are page printers; printers that work with a stream of pages, such as many dot matrix printers, are continuous-feed.

To print sample checks for a page printer:

Quicken 4 for Windows Answers: *Certified Tech Support*

Tech Note: After printing the sample, do not move the check up or down in the printer in order to align your text. Quicken adjusts where the printing is done so that you don't have to move the paper.

1. Insert the sample checks as you would any printer paper and make sure that the printer is on and ready to print.

2. Choose Printer Setup from the File menu and select Check Printer Setup to open the Check Printer Setup dialog box.

3. Check that the settings for Printer, Paper Feed, and Check Style match your printer, how the printer finds the paper, and your check style.

4. Select Align to show the Check Printer Alignment dialog box in Figure 4-2.

5. Make sure that the number of checks on each page is selected in the Checks on page area of the dialog box. Quicken remembers different settings for printing one, two, and three checks per page and can adjust accordingly.

6. Select Test. Quicken prints sample checks. Look at where the printed text appears relative to the text printed on the check, i.e., whether the Jane Doe prints in the correct location relative to the "Pay to the Order of." Decide whether Quicken needs to shift the printed text up or down or to the left or right.

FIGURE 4-2   Check Printer Alignment dialog box

Chapter 4 *Checks and Reconciliation*

7. If your sample check is properly aligned, select Done. If it did not align properly, continue with the following steps.

8. Drag the sample text for the check around on the sample check in the Check Printer Alignment dialog box to achieve the amount of the adjustment needed. As you drag the sample text, the Horiz and Vert text boxes change to show how far the text has shifted. You can also type entries in these text boxes when the adjustment is in small increments.

9. Select Test again to print another sample check. If your check is still misaligned, try steps 7 and 8 again, repeating them until the check is correctly aligned.

10. Select Done and then select OK when your sample check is properly aligned. You are now ready to print your checks.

When you print checks with a continuous-feed printer, you will want to order form leaders from Intuit. These form leaders make adjusting the printer each time you print checks easier so that you don't waste a check every time you start printing checks in Quicken. To test printing sample checks for a continuous-feed printer:

1. Insert the sample checks as you would any printer paper and make sure that your printer is turned on and ready to go.

2. Choose Printer Setup from the File menu and Check Printer Setup to open the Check Printer Setup dialog box.

3. Check that the settings for Printer, Paper Feed, and Check Style match your printer, how the printer finds the paper, and your check style.

4. Select Align.

5. Select Coarse or Fine for the amount of the adjustment that you want to make. You may want to select Coarse the first time for larger adjustments, then use Fine later for smaller ones. Fine can adjust text both up and down and side to side. Coarse can only adjust the text up and down, so you should make very large left and right adjustments by moving the paper in the printer. The directions for the rest of the procedure depend on whether you select Coarse or Fine.

Tech Note: When you print checks on a tractor-feed printer, align a specific object on the check stock with some part of the printer, like the top of the tractor feeds, and note that alignment somewhere, for future reference. Then you won't have to test your check's alignment each time you print checks.

6. If you select Coarse, then select OK. Quicken prints a sample check. Look at the printed sample for the text "Pointer Line" and an arrow. In the text box that Quicken displays, type the line number that the arrow points to on the paper. Select OK to print another sample. Repeat this step until Quicken shows the Please Note Position dialog box. Select OK to return to the Alignment for Continuous Printer dialog box.

7. If you select Fine, then select Test to print a sample. This Check Printer Alignment dialog box looks almost identical to the one shown in Figure 4-2. Then drag the sample text for the check around on the sample check in the Check Printer Alignment dialog box to achieve the amount of adjustment needed. As you drag the sample text, the Horiz and Vert text boxes change to indicate how far the text has shifted. You can also type entries in these text boxes when a small adjustment is needed. Repeat this step until the sample check prints correctly. Select Done to return to the Alignment for Continuous Printer dialog box.

8. Select Cancel to return to the Check Printer Setup dialog box and then select OK to finish with the printer setup.

Other possible check printing problems and their solutions appear in Table 4-1.

Print Problem	Problem Cause and Solution
Print lines are too close.	The printer is probably set to print eight lines to the inch. Change this to six.
Print lines wrap, and the date and amount are too far to the right.	The font selected is too large. Change to a smaller font size.
Print does not extend across the check, and the date and amount print too far to the left.	The font selected is too small and you need to switch to a larger font size.
Printer is spewing paper or producing illegible print.	The wrong printer is probably selected. Check which printer is selected.
Printer does not print.	The printer is probably not turned on, not on line, or not chosen in Quicken; or the cable may be loose.

TABLE 4-1   Correcting Printer Errors for Printing Checks

Chapter 4 *Checks and Reconciliation*

Tech Tip: When you print checks on a continuous-feed or ink jet printer, you can buy form feeders from Quicken. These form feeders prevent you from losing checks because you only printed a partial page or because continuous-feed printers require that the paper be beyond the printer head.

How do I print additional checks if I already printed some on that page?

You can print partial pages of checks. Continuous-feed printers do not distinguish between the top and middle of the page, so printing partial pages is no different from printing full pages. With page printers, such as laser and ink jet printers, Quicken needs some more information. You will need to tell Quicken which way you insert the checks into the printer. To do this, choose Printer Setup from the File menu and select Check Printer Setup. Select one of the options below Partial Page Printing Style. You can also use Align to set the alignment for a partial page of checks. After you select Align, you can select 1 or 2 to indicate whether you are making alignment settings for a partial page with one check or two. Otherwise the alignment process is exactly as described in the previous question.

How do you account for misprinted checks?

Since you cannot undo printing errors, you can void the check, then print a new one. If the problem is alignment, make sure to fix the alignment before printing any more.

Why doesn't Quicken print my checks when I click the Print Checks icon?

While the Print Checks icon, shown here, does not initially appear on the iconbar, you can add it as one of Quicken's many customization options. The Print Checks icon prints checks for a specific account. If the account that has checks to print is not the same account that the Print Checks icon uses, you will see the "You have no checks to print" message. You can either change the icon's account or add more than one Print Checks icon so each account has its own.

Changing a Check's Appearance

Can I print my logos on checks?

Yes, you can add a logo to your checks and have Quicken print them with the other check information. The logo must fit into a 1/2" square that will appear in the upper left corner of the check. Usually, for bitmaps that are 300 dpi, this means 150 pixels square in size. You can check the logo's size by opening it in Paintbrush, then choosing Image Attributes from the Options menu. Before you add the logo, save the logo in a BMP file with a square image size. If the image size is not square, your image may appear distorted. Once you have the logo in the BMP file, follow these steps to include the logo on your printed checks:

1. Choose Printer Setup from the File menu and then select Check Printer Setup.

2. Select the Logo button to open the Check Logo Artwork dialog box and choose File. The Open Artwork File dialog box is just like the dialog box that you use to open a Quicken file.

3. Set the drive and directory to the location of your BMP logo file.

4. Select the file in the File Name list box or type its name in the text box.

5. Select OK. You will see what the logo will look like in the Check Logo Artwork dialog box. Make sure you don't have a distortion problem.

Chapter 4 *Checks and Reconciliation*

6. Select OK to select this logo.
7. Select OK to complete the check printer setup. Now when you print the checks, Quicken prints the logo. You will not see the logo in the Write Checks window.

Tech Terror: If your printer only prints in one color, check how Quicken will print the logo. You don't want to print many checks only to discover that your logo doesn't look good in black and white.

Can I change the check's background?

You can change the check background on screen to use one of several interesting graphic designs. These graphics will never print on the checks themselves. All data files use the same check background. To change a check's background:

1. Select Options from the Write Checks window's button bar and the Checks tab.
2. Select the Artwork on Check Entry Screen check box to add a graphic to the checks.
3. Select which artwork you want to see from the adjoining drop-down list box.
4. Select OK. Figure 4-3 shows the Write Checks window after changing the background to Heartland.

Reconciliation Problems

How do I add interest and service charges?

When you start the reconciliation process, the Reconcile Bank Statement dialog box, shown here, has text boxes for service

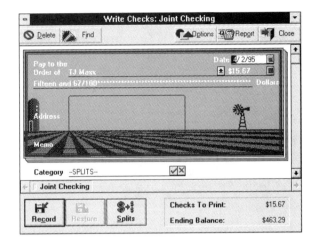

FIGURE 4-3   Heartland background added to the Write Checks window

charges and interest. Just enter the amounts, dates, and categories for these amounts in the text boxes.

Tech Acct: Don't forget to record service charges for ATM transactions. These charges can add up!

When I reconcile, can I select all transactions, then unselect only the few that haven't cleared?

You can see that the Reconcile Bank Statement dialog box in Figure 4-4 doesn't have a Mark All button but you can easily mark all the withdrawals and deposits. Click the first one in the list, then hold down SHIFT while you click the last one. All the transactions between the two are selected. You can also click one, then drag the mouse over the ones you want selected.

My bank statement has checks and deposits that I didn't enter into Quicken. How do I fix this?

Add these missing transactions. In the Reconcile Bank Statement window, select New to switch to the Register window for this account. Here you can add these transactions as you would any others. When you return to the Reconcile Bank Statement window, you will see the transactions that you just added.

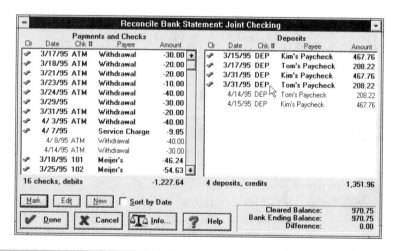

FIGURE 4-4 The Reconcile Bank Statement dialog box

The beginning balance is wrong when I reconcile my account. How do I fix this?

This problem is usually caused when your Quicken register doesn't include older transactions that only recently cleared. The opening balance amount is marked as cleared but it actually includes transactions that haven't cleared. You can adjust your account's balance during reconciliation. Then, the next time you reconcile the account, the beginning balance is correct. Doing the following takes care of the incorrect beginning balance immediately:

1. Reconcile the account. Leave the beginning balance alone. Use the ending balance you are given and reconcile the account as far as possible. You will end up with an amount after "Difference" in the Reconcile Bank Statement window. This is the amount for the transactions that are missing from the register because they are included in the opening balance transaction.

2. Select Done. You will see the dialog box for adjusting the balance. You probably want to set the date to the date of the beginning balance.

3. Select Adjust Balance.

4. Choose Yes or No for whether you want a reconciliation report.

My opening balance for reconciliation doesn't match the ending balance from the last reconciliation. How do I find out what caused the error?

What has happened is that the balance of the cleared transactions has changed since the last reconciliation. You might have changed the amount of a cleared transaction, marked a transaction as cleared, or unmarked a transaction as cleared. Once you find out where this transaction is, your problem is solved.

How do I reconcile my bank statement if I find an error in the statement?

You will need to change the bank statement's ending balance. If the bank error is a charge, add the amount of the charge to the bank's ending balance. If the bank error is a deposit, subtract the amount of the deposit from the bank's ending balance. If you notice the error before you start the reconciliation process, just enter the adjusted bank balance after you choose Reconcile from the Activities menu. If you do not realize it until you see the Reconcile Bank Statement window, select Info, enter the corrected ending balance in the Bank Statement Ending Balance text box, and select OK.

Tech Acct: When you find a bank error, notify the bank promptly. Most banks have as part of their account agreement that they only have to fix errors when they are notified within a reasonable time.

How do savings goals affect reconciliation?

They don't. Even though showing the savings goal contributions changes your account's balance, Quicken knows not to include them in the reconciliation.

Can I cancel reconciliation in the middle of the process?

When you are working in the Reconcile Bank Statement window, you can cancel the reconciliation process by selecting Cancel. Then select Don't Save so that you don't keep any clear markings for transactions that you marked as cleared. When you are ready to complete the reconciliation, start from the beginning.

What do I do about a check for which the bank charged an amount other than what I originally entered?

First, look at the check. If it is the bank's mistake, call the bank. If it is your mistake, you need to change the entry. Assuming that you discover this error while reconciling your account, follow these steps:

1. Highlight the transaction with the error in the Reconcile Bank Statement window.
2. Select Edit.
3. Change the amount for the check and select Record.
4. Select the Window menu and the entry in the menu for the Reconcile Bank Statement window. You can see that the changes you make are applied to the window's data.

CheckFree

I've heard about CheckFree. What is it and why would I use it?

CheckFree allows you to pay your bills electronically—you don't have to mail your bills; just tell CheckFree which bills to pay and how much and it does it. To use CheckFree, you need a Hayes-compatible modem (see Chapter 2 for setup instructions). Once you subscribe to CheckFree, follow these steps to set up your account:

1. Choose CheckFree from the Activities menu, and then select Set Up Account.
2. Highlight the bank account you want to set up to use with CheckFree.

Chapter 4 *Checks and Reconciliation*

3. Select the Set Up button. The Electronic Payment Account Settings window appears. A completed one might look like this:

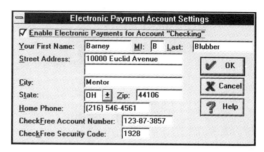

4. Select the Enable Electronic Payments for Account "Checking" check box. "Checking" will be replaced by the name of your account.

5. Fill in your personal and CheckFree information in the text boxes.

6. Select OK to finish and select Close to put the Set Up Account dialog box away. The Set Up Account dialog box now shows a lightning rod next to the setup account. The lightning rod also appears next to the account name in the Account List window.

Now you are ready to set up the payees that you want CheckFree to pay.

Tech Tip: Intuit, the company that markets Quicken, does not provide the CheckFree service. If you have a problem with CheckFree, you need to contact CheckFree Corporation.

How do I make payments with CheckFree?

A CheckFree payment involves two steps: setting up the payee and then paying the bill. Setting up a payee is done once. Paying the bill can be done two ways.

To set up a payee:

1. Choose Chec_k_Free from the Acti_v_ities menu, and then Electronic Payee _L_ist.

2. Select _N_ew.

3. Select _N_ormal Payee or _F_ixed, Recurring Payee, then select OK. Normal Payee is for when the payment amount and date vary. Fixed, Recurring Payee is for when the date and the amount are constant.

4. Enter the payee information in the text boxes. For the phone number, enter the number that you call when you have a billing question. For the Account number field, double-check to be sure that you entered it correctly so that your account is correctly charged. If you are creating a fixed payee, such as a health club membership, you have additional options for the amount, frequency, date, categories, and length of time that Quicken should make these automatic payments. Figure 4-5 shows the Edit Electronic Payee dialog box with entries for a fixed payment. Normal payees do not have the Bank Account, Payment Description, and Duration of Payments sections or the Catego_r_ies button.

5. Select OK to complete the dialog box, then select Close to put the Electronic Payee List window away.

If you are setting up a fixed, recurring payee, then the fixed payments start once you connect your computer to CheckFree.

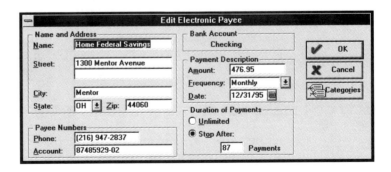

FIGURE 4-5   Payee setup for electronic payments

Chapter 4 *Checks and Reconciliation*

Other payments only are sent to CheckFree as you pay the individual bills.

Now that the payees are established, you can pay bills with CheckFree. You can do this from either the Write Checks window or the Register window.

To pay a bill with CheckFree using the Write Checks window:

1. Switch to the Write Checks window.
2. Select the Electronic Payment check box. If you don't see the check box, you need to set up the account for CheckFree.
3. Write the check as you normally would. You won't enter an address. Lightening rods appear in place of the Address field so you know that CheckFree gets this information from the payee setup information. Also, the date is at least five business days ahead of today's date because CheckFree requires five days advance notice.
4. Select Record.

The CheckFree transaction is recorded. If you look at the transaction in the Register window, you will see XMIT in the Num field marking that this is an electronic payment. After transmission, EPMT replaces XMIT.

To pay a bill with CheckFree using the Register window:

1. Switch to the Register window and the account set up for electronic payments.
2. Select XMIT in the Num field. If the date in the Date field is less that five business days away, Quicken increases the date.
3. Enter the remaining fields as you normally would.
4. Select Record to record the transaction.

After you record the check or transaction, Quicken needs to contact CheckFree to give it this information. To do this, choose CheckFree from the Activities menu, and then Transmit. This is how Quicken contacts CheckFree to give send the payment information. With a fixed, recurring payment, you only need to do this the first time since CheckFree remembers to make the recurring payments for you.

How do I pay a loan with CheckFree?

Loan payments are handled differently for CheckFree because they are fixed and recurring but the amount that goes to interest and principal changes. You can still set this payment up but the steps are more involved. The entire process follows these steps:

1. Choose Check<u>F</u>ree from the Acti<u>v</u>ities menu, and then Electronic Payee <u>L</u>ist.

2. Select <u>N</u>ew.

3. Select <u>F</u>ixed, Recurring Payee, and OK.

4. Enter the payee information in the text boxes. Figure 4-5 shows an example.

5. Select OK to complete the dialog box, and Close to put the Electronic Payee List window away.

6. Choose L<u>o</u>ans from the Acti<u>v</u>ities menu and <u>N</u>ew.

7. Select <u>B</u>orrow Money, select <u>N</u>ew Account, and type an account name for the new liability account in the <u>N</u>ew Account text box. Quicken creates a liability account for you that tracks how much principal is owed on the loan. Select OK.

8. Enter the loan information in the Set Up Loan dialog box and select OK. A completed dialog box might look like this:

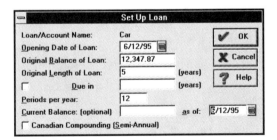

9. Enter additional loan information in the Set Up Loan Payment dialog box that Quicken displays when you finish with the Set Up Loan dialog box. The information you will need includes the interest rate, the amount paid, payment date, and payee.

Chapter 4 *Checks and Reconciliation*

10. Select the Method of Payment button.
11. Select the CheckFree Fixed Payment option button, select the payee from the Fixed Payee drop-down list box, and select OK.
12. Make any changes to the Memo, Next Payment Date, or Category for Interest entries.
13. Select OK.

How do I list my CheckFree transactions?

You can create a Register Report that sorts the payments made by the Num field. This report will have the CheckFree transactions organized together. To create this report:

1. Move to an empty transaction in the register. (If you are at another transaction, you will create a Payee Report instead.)
2. Click the Report button in the Register window's button bar.
3. Select Customize.
4. Select Acct/Chk# from the Sort By drop-down list box to organize the Num field.
5. Select the Transactions option button and then select Payments from the Transaction Types drop-down list box so the report leaves out the deposits you have made.
6. Select OK. The Register Report lists all payments in the register sorted by the Num field. You can scroll through this report until you find the transactions with EPMT, XMIT, and FIXED in this field. These are your CheckFree transactions.

The CheckFree abbreviations that you see in the Num field include

Num Field Abbreviation	Meaning
EPMT	Electronic payment sent to CheckFree
XMIT	Electronic payment to send to CheckFree
FIXED	Fixed electronic payment made automatically by CheckFree

How do I contact CheckFree?

Depending on the information you need, you have three ways to contact CheckFree:

- *You need information about a specific CheckFree payment.* You can see the scheduled payment date, the payee's account number, whether CheckFree received the payment information, and the confirmation number if CheckFree has received it. Highlight the transaction for the payment in the register and choose CheckFree from the Activities menu, and then Inquiry. At this point, you can send a message to CheckFree about this payment. If you select OK, you can enter up to three lines of text to CheckFree. Select Transmit to send this message to CheckFree.

- *You need information from CheckFree that is not specific to a payment.* To send a more general electronic message, choose CheckFree from the Activities menu, and then E-Mail. Select Create, type the message, and then select Transmit. When Quicken is finished, select Done.

- *You need to talk to a person.* The phone number is currently (614)825-3500.

When you send CheckFree a message electronically, you can see the message by choosing CheckFree from the Activities menu, and then E-Mail and Retrieve. Currently, CheckFree does not charge for this support, although calling the (614)825-3500 number will incur any long distance charges.

What's the difference between an electronic payment and an electronic funds transfer?

An electronic payment is a payment made using CheckFree and looks like any other check payment to your bank. An electronic funds transfer is a withdrawal that your bank makes under your direction. An electronic funds transfer can be used to pay bills.

Chapter 4 *Checks and Reconciliation*

Can I stop an electronic payment once I've sent it to CheckFree?

Yes, you can, provided there are at least five business days between when you tell CheckFree to halt the payment and when the payment would be made. To stop a payment before it is made, follow these steps:

1. Highlight the payment transaction in the register.
2. Choose CheckFree from the Acti_v_ities menu and then choose Stop _P_ayment.
3. If the transaction is stopped in time, select OK. Quicken places VOID in the register and remembers the confirmation number.

If you haven't stopped the payment in time for these steps to cancel payment, you can call CheckFree Corporation Technical Support at (614)825-3500. CheckFree doesn't charge when you stop a payment using the steps above but it does have a charge (currently $15) when you stop a payment by calling them.

Tech Terror: Don't void transactions for CheckFree payments to cancel the payment. Instead choose CheckFree from the Acti_v_ities menu and select Stop _P_ayment. Then, CheckFree can get the confirmation number that the transaction is canceled.

How do I stop a series of fixed electronic payments?

Choosing a method to stop fixed electronic payments depends on whether you want to keep the information about the payee. It is useful to keep this information if you may later resume electronic payments.

To keep the payee information while halting future electronic payments:

1. Open the check register that pays the electronic payment.
2. Highlight the last completed transaction for that fixed payment.
3. Choose CheckFree from the Activities menu and then choose Stop Payment.
4. Select OK.
5. Choose CheckFree from the Activities menu and then select Transmit to send your changes to CheckFree.

After these steps, the payee type for this payment changes from FIXED to INACTIVE. The payee remains on the Electronic Payee list.

To remove the payee and halt future electronic payments:

1. Choose CheckFree from the Activities menu and then choose Electronic Payee List.
2. Highlight the payee.
3. Select Delete.
4. Choose CheckFree from the Activities menu and then select Transmit to send your changes to CheckFree.

Now, you no longer have the payee set up. Any confirmation number history is gone.

Which payment you stop depends on the time frame between when the payment is made and the current date. CheckFree can halt payments that are at least five business days from today.

Tech Tip: For scheduled transactions that represent electronic fund transfers that the bank makes from your account, you need to contact your bank to stop the payment. You can then delete the scheduled transaction or alter it so you decide when it is paid rather than having it automatically registered.

Chapter 4 *Checks and Reconciliation*

How do I confirm that a CheckFree payment has been made?

When a payment is made, Quicken gets a confirmation number from CheckFree. You can display this confirmation number as well as other information about the electronic payment. Highlight the payment. Then choose CheckFree from the Activities menu and then choose Electronic Payment Info.

Why can't I transmit to CheckFree when I use OS/2?

You are using an older OS/2 COM driver. Get the newer one and you can transmit to CheckFree. You can get updated COM drivers from CompuServe, the OS/2 bulletin board, or a local bulletin board.

Taxes

As the April 15th tax deadline approaches, most people become a bit frazzled as they rush to pull together all the information they need to file their return. Although Quicken can't file a return for you, it can make the process as painless as possible. Quicken's Tax Planner provides the basics for starting your tax planning. Besides the Tax Planner, Quicken also can organize all of your entries according to their line on the tax schedule. If you prefer you can transfer data from Quicken directly to TurboTax.

Keep in mind, though, that taxes are your responsibility. Quicken can suggest tax form entries but it is not a tax advisor or a complete tax preparation package.

Frustration Busters!

Here are some general hints on how you can improve your tax return.

- Double-check all the math on your tax return.

- Make sure you include your income from all sources including part-time jobs, dividends, and interest.

- Double-check that your entries correctly match the supporting documents such as your W-2s and that you entered them on the correct line.

- Keep a copy of the tax return. You will need it if you are audited, for help preparing next year's tax returns, or if you file an amended return.

- If you itemize deductions, make sure to keep the paperwork that backs up the amount you deducted.

- Make sure to complete all the information carefully. For instance, when you include dependents in your number of exemptions, make sure to include their social security numbers. You also want to make sure that your own social security number is correct.

- Double-check that you entered the correct amount of income tax from the tax table if you used one.

You can also get help with your tax return from the IRS. The IRS provides several helpful sources for completing tax forms. You can call or write the IRS. The IRS's Publication 910, *Guide to Free Tax Services,* has more information. The IRS also has walk-in assistance and volunteer programs to help you. You must call your local IRS office to find out what help is available in your area.

Chapter 5 *Taxes*

Tax Planning

Can Quicken show me how much tax I owe?

Quicken can approximate the taxes that you will owe with the Tax Planner. The window in Figure 5-1 shows how the Tax Planner has calculated your taxable income, deductions, and how much you owe or will have refunded. The Tax Planner's estimates are only as accurate as the information you provide. You'll want to review the entries to make sure that the Tax Planner uses the correct numbers. For instance, if, when entering your Quicken data, you entered your paychecks by their gross amounts instead of breaking them out into gross pay and all the deductions, your income and withholdings, as calculated by Quicken, are incorrect.

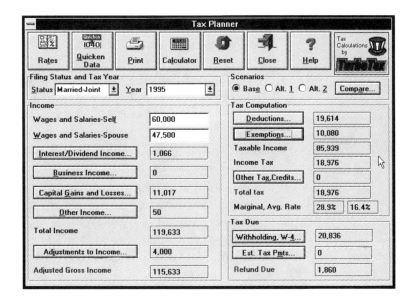

FIGURE 5-1   Tax Planner window

Quicken 4 for Windows Answers: *Certified Tech Support*

Tech Tip: Make sure that you pay enough taxes during the year. If you do not have enough withheld, the IRS can impose underpayment penalties. For example, if you owe over $500, you should check whether you are subject to an automatic underpayment penalty. This penalty applies if the withheld tax is less than 90% of this year's taxes or 100% of last year's (110% if you are filing married filing jointly). Estimating your taxes can warn you that you need to make estimated tax payments to avoid these penalties.

Can Quicken tell me how much I need withheld?

The bottom-right corner of the Tax Planner shows how much tax you owe for the whole year and any refund you may be due or how much you can expect to pay. If the refund or payment is not within an acceptable range, consider changing the amount your employer withholds. To calculate how much you want your withholding to change:

1. Select the Withholding, W-4 button. The Withholding and W-4 Allowances dialog box shows what is already withheld and how much will be withheld. You can also see the projected tax due and how much refund or how much you will owe with these projections.

2. Update the Withholding to Date, Next Pay Date, and Pay Period boxes for yourself and any spouse. At this point, you have an updated estimate for what you still owe or will be refunded.

3. Select the Recalculate Withholding Allowances for Future Withholding check box.

4. Update the Taxable Pay Per Period and Allowances Claimed text boxes for yourself and any spouse.

5. Adjust the amounts in the Allowances Claimed and Additional Withholding per Pay Period boxes to see how changing the number of allowances claimed or amount withheld changes the total taxes withheld. You can even select Recommend when you want Quicken to suggest

Chapter 5 Taxes

the appropriate number of allowances. You can continue making adjustments until the amount after Refund Due or Remaining Tax Due is within the range you want. The final result is what you will want to tell your employer to withhold.

6. Select OK to update the taxes withheld.

What advantage does TurboTax have over the Tax Planner?

TurboTax is a complete tax preparation program. Although the Tax Planner is like TurboTax in that it can take information from Quicken, TurboTax provides guidelines for more detailed tax preparation. It can create tax returns ready to send to the IRS. Quicken's Tax Planner should be used when you want to determine a rough estimate of taxes.

Tax Form Assignments

How does Quicken know which tax lines to enter numbers into?

The tax form assignment for a category tells Quicken where in the tax forms a particular number belongs. You can add other assignments and change the existing ones. Quicken has tax form entries for the following tax forms:

- W-2
- Forms 1040, 2106, 2119, 2441, 3903, 4137, 4684, 4952, 6252, 8815, and 1099R
- Schedules A, B, C, D, E, F, and K-1

Tech Tip: Making tax form assignments is a lot easier when you have a copy of the tax form in front of you.

Can I add categories to tax form lines to use in the Tax Planner?

You can add and alter the tax form lines that categories are assigned to. For example, when you use Quicken for a small business, you frequently have categories set up that you include in your Schedule C; however, if the same items were for personal use, they would not be taxable. To add a tax form to any category:

1. Choose Category & Transfer from the Lists menu.
2. Highlight the category that you want to change and select Edit from the button bar.
3. Select the Tax-related check box.
4. Move to the Form drop-down list box and select the tax form line where entries from this category are included.
5. Select OK and the category is now assigned to a tax form entry.

Can I prevent categories from being included in the Tax Planner's tax forms?

You can change and remove the tax form assignment for a category. For example, suppose you assigned the Gifts Received category to Form 1040:Prizes, awards, gambling, and you want to remove this tax form assignment. To do this:

1. Choose Category from the Lists menu.
2. Highlight Gifts Received as the category that you want to change and select Edit from the button bar.
3. Move to the Form drop-down list box and press HOME or select the top entry from the list so the drop-down list box is empty.
4. Select OK and the category is no longer assigned to a tax form entry.

Chapter 5 *Taxes*

Tech Tip: If you want a category removed from Tax Summary reports (described later in this chapter), edit the category and clear the <u>T</u>ax-related check box. You will also want to remove the entry in the <u>F</u>orm drop-down list box so transactions assigned to the category do not appear in the Tax Schedule report and the Tax Planner.

Why are some categories marked as tax-related without a specific tax form entry?

With some of Quicken's categories, the connection between the category and the tax form entry is clear. For example, state taxes go on Schedule A in the line for state and local income taxes. But what about interest expense? If it is for credit card purchases, car loans, or installment purchases, then it is not deductible. If it is for buying a home, it is deductible on one line on Schedule A. If the interest is for borrowing money for an investment, then it becomes investment interest which is reported on a different line on Schedule A. Marking these categories as tax-related makes them show up in Tax Summary reports without including them in specific lines in the Tax Planner. If you use a category for transactions that belong to a specific tax form entry, you can edit the category to add the tax form. Then the Tax Planner will pick up the amount.

How do I include expenses and income from my categories in the Tax Planner?

If the income and expenses in a category belong on your tax form, you can assign a tax form entry to the category. The Tax Planner will include the expenses and income when you import your Quicken data, as described in the answer to the next question.

Tech Tip: If only some of the income and expenses of a category belong on the tax form, create subcategories for the category and reassign the category for the tax-related transactions to the subcategory instead.

Importing Quicken Data into the Tax Planner

Can I see what my taxes will be like using my Quicken data?

You can put your Quicken data into the Tax Planner and the Tax Planner will display it in the appropriate places. When you are in the middle of a year, you can even annualize the numbers to estimate what taxes you owe if your finances continue in the same way. To bring Quicken data into the Tax Planner:

1. Select the Quicken Data icon from the top of the Tax Planner. Quicken creates a Tax Schedule report in the background. When the Tax Planner gathers the data, you see a window like the one in Figure 5-2. You can see how Quicken takes your income and deductions made so far to estimate what these amounts will be for the entire year.

2. Any tax item can be switched between using the annualized amount or the year to date amount by

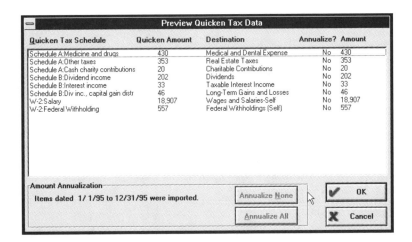

FIGURE 5-2   Quicken data brought into the Tax Planner

double-clicking it. You can only annualize the results when the Tax Planner imports less than the entire year's worth of data.

3. Select OK to put these numbers into the Tax Planner and estimate how much tax you owe.

4. Make any adjustments to the numbers in the Tax Planner. For example, if your Quicken transactions do not include an IRA contribution that you will make, you can select the Adjustments to Income button, enter the IRA deduction after Allowable IRA Deduction, and select OK.

Tech Acct: Make your estimated tax closer to what it will actually be by printing the Tax Summary and Tax Schedule reports. Looking over these reports can alert you to numbers in the Tax Planner that you may change due to transactions that the Tax Planner does not include or incorrectly includes.

Why is the Tax Planner missing some of my latest transactions?

When the Tax Planner imports Quicken data, it imports entire months. This means that the transactions from the current month do not appear in the Tax Planner.

How do I select which year of data is imported into the Tax Planner?

The Tax Planner will import Quicken's data for the year displayed in the Year drop-down list box. Use this list box to select which year of data to import. This Quicken data is not imported until you select Quicken Data again.

Tax Reports

How do I get a report that gives me the numbers that I need to fill out my tax forms?

Quicken has two reports that are useful for calculating taxes. The first one is the Tax Summary report. This report prints the transactions from tax-related categories. This report will point out potential tax-related transactions assigned to categories that do not have a tax form assignment. Figure 5-3 shows the beginning of a Tax Summary report. Create this report by choosing Home from the Reports menu, choosing Tax Summary, and selecting OK.

The other type of report is a Tax Schedule report. This report groups transactions according to the tax form assignments, which can combine entries from several categories. This is the same entry that you see when you edit the category and look at the Form drop-down list box. Figure 5-4 shows the beginning of a Tax Summary report. Create this report by choosing Home from the Reports menu, choosing Tax Schedule, and selecting OK.

Tech Tip: If you just want to see the totals for a report, without listing the individual transactions, select Customize, then select the Totals Only check box. Now a report like the Tax Schedule report will only show the tax form lines and the totals.

What is the difference between a Tax Summary and a Tax Schedule report?

Both reports show transactions that affect your taxes but they differ by how they organize their information. A Tax Summary report groups transactions for tax-related categories according to their category. A Tax Schedule report groups transactions by the entries made for a category's Form drop-down list box. For example, in a Tax Summary report, the amounts assigned to the Bonus and Salary categories are listed separately. In a Tax Schedule report, they are combined. The previous question tells you how you can create both types of reports.

```
                              Tax Summary Report
                              1/1/95 Through 12/13/95
12/6/95                                                                      Page 1
ROBIN-Checking

   Date      Num       Description       Memo           Category    Clr    Amount

             INCOME/EXPENSE
              INCOME
               Int Inc

   1/13/95            Interest Earned                   Int Inc                2.57
   2/13/95            Interest Earned                   Int Inc                3.23
   3/13/95            Interest Earned                   Int Inc                3.54
   4/13/95            Interest Earned                   Int Inc                3.84
   5/13/95            Interest Earned                   Int Inc                2.14
   6/13/95            Interest Earned                   Int Inc                2.72
   7/13/95            Interest Earned                   Int Inc                1.87
   8/13/95            Interest Earned                   Int Inc                2.52
   9/13/95            Interest Earned                   Int Inc                1.98
  10/13/95            Interest Earned                   Int Inc                1.87
  11/13/95            Interest Earned                   Int Inc                2.51
  12/13/95            Interest Earned                   Int Inc                3.48

               Total Int Inc                                                  32.27

              Salary

   1/1/95             Payday                            Salary               800.00
   1/16/95            Payday                            Salary               800.00
   2/1/95             Payday                            Salary               800.00
   2/16/95            Payday                            Salary               800.00
   3/1/95             Payday                            Salary               800.00
   3/16/95            Payday                            Salary               800.00
   4/1/95             Payday                            Salary               800.00
   4/16/95            Payday                            Salary               800.00
   5/1/95             Payday                            Salary               800.00
   5/16/95            Payday                            Salary               800.00
   6/1/95             Payday                            Salary               800.00
   6/16/95            Payday                            Salary               800.00
   7/1/95             Payday                            Salary               800.00
   7/16/95            Payday                            Salary               800.00
   8/1/95             Payday                            Salary               800.00
   8/16/95            Payday                            Salary               800.00
   9/1/95             Payday                            Salary               800.00
   9/16/95            Payday                            Salary               800.00
  10/1/95             Payday                            Salary               800.00
  10/16/95            Payday                            Salary               800.00
  11/1/95             Payday                            Salary               800.00
  11/16/95            Payday                            Salary               800.00
  12/1/95             Payday                            Salary               800.00

              Total Salary                                                18,400.00

              TOTAL INCOME                                                18,432.27

              EXPENSES
               Charity:

                Cash Contrib.

   1/5/95             F.E.O.P.C.      Monthly contribution   Charity:Cash Contrib.   -15.00
   3/5/95             F.E.O.P.C.      Monthly contribution   Charity:Cash Contrib.   -15.00
```

FIGURE 5-3   Tax Summary report

How can I find out where the Tax Planner got its numbers from?

You can see the detail of the numbers that appear in the Tax Planner by looking at the Tax Summary and Tax Schedule reports. They may be different from what you see in the Tax Planner if the Tax Planner annualizes the amounts.

```
                          Tax Schedule Report
                          1/1/95 Through 12/6/95
12/6/95                                                                              Page 1
ROBIN-Checking

      Date      Num       Description          Memo              Category    Clr   Amount

                Form 1040

                   IRA contribution-self

     3/31/95           Prowley Investment Fund                   IRA                -500.00
     6/30/95           Prowley Investment Fund                   IRA                -500.00
     9/30/95           Prowley Investment Fund                   IRA                -500.00

                   Total IRA contribution-self                                    -1,500.00

                Schedule A

                   Cash charity contributions

     1/5/95            F.E.O.P.C.             Monthly contribution  Charity:Cash Contrib.   -15.00
     3/5/95            F.E.O.P.C.             Monthly contribution  Charity:Cash Contrib.   -15.00
     4/5/95            F.E.O.P.C.             Monthly contribution  Charity:Cash Contrib.   -15.00
     4/12/95           Boston University                            Charity:Cash Contrib.  -500.00
     5/5/95            F.E.O.P.C.             Monthly contribution  Charity:Cash Contrib.   -15.00
     6/5/95            F.E.O.P.C.             Monthly contribution  Charity:Cash Contrib.   -15.00
     7/5/95            F.E.O.P.C.             Monthly contribution  Charity:Cash Contrib.   -15.00
     8/5/95            F.E.O.P.C.             Monthly contribution  Charity:Cash Contrib.   -15.00
     9/5/95            F.E.O.P.C.             Monthly contribution  Charity:Cash Contrib.   -15.00
     10/5/95           F.E.O.P.C.             Monthly contribution  Charity:Cash Contrib.   -15.00
     11/5/95           F.E.O.P.C.             Monthly contribution  Charity:Cash Contrib.   -15.00
     12/5/95           F.E.O.P.C.             Monthly contribution  Charity:Cash Contrib.   -15.00

                   Total Cash charity contributions                                -665.00

                Schedule B

                   Interest income

     1/13/95           Interest Earned                            Int Inc            2.57
     2/13/95           Interest Earned                            Int Inc            3.23
     3/13/95           Interest Earned                            Int Inc            3.54
     4/13/95           Interest Earned                            Int Inc            3.84
     5/13/95           Interest Earned                            Int Inc            2.14
     6/13/95           Interest Earned                            Int Inc            2.72
     7/13/95           Interest Earned                            Int Inc            1.87
     8/13/95           Interest Earned                            Int Inc            2.52
     9/13/95           Interest Earned                            Int Inc            1.98
     10/13/95          Interest Earned                            Int Inc            1.87
     11/13/95          Interest Earned                            Int Inc            2.51

                   Total Interest income                                            28.79

                W-2

                   Salary

     1/1/95            Payday                                     Salary           800.00
     1/16/95           Payday                                     Salary           800.00
     2/1/95            Payday                                     Salary           800.00
```

FIGURE 5-4   Tax Schedule report

How do I print my Tax Planner results?

The Tax Planner can print a report of the Tax Planner tax projections. Select the <u>P</u>rint button at the top of the Tax Planner and select OK to create this report. Figure 5-5 shows this report.

Chapter 5 *Taxes*

[Figure: Printed tax planner report showing Tax Summary, Sch A–F deductions and income categories, Other Income or Losses, Other Taxes/Credits, Federal and State/Local Tax Payments, Adjustments to Income, and Alternative Minimum Tax Computation sections]

FIGURE 5-5   Printed report created by the Tax Planner

Tech Tip: If you want a picture of the Tax Planner window, you can press the PRINT SCREEN key, then switch to a graphics program like Paintbrush or a program that accepts bitmaps, like most word processors. After you paste the Clipboard picture into that application, you can use that application to print the picture.

Entering Income into the Tax Planner

How do the numbers in my W-2 match up with the numbers in the Tax Planner?

The best way to see how your paycheck information appears in the Tax Planner is to look at a W-2 and see where the data shows up in the Tax Planner. Figure 5-6 shows a W-2. You can see how the numbers appear in the Tax Planner like the one shown in Figure 5-7. The numbers that you see in the W-2 appear in the following spots in the Tax Planner:

- Box 2 (Federal income tax withheld)   The 2112 in this box appears after the Withholding, W-<u>4</u> button.

- Box 1 (Wages, tips, other compensation)   The 19200 in this box appears in the Wages and Salaries-Sel<u>f</u> text box.

FIGURE 5-6   Sample W-2

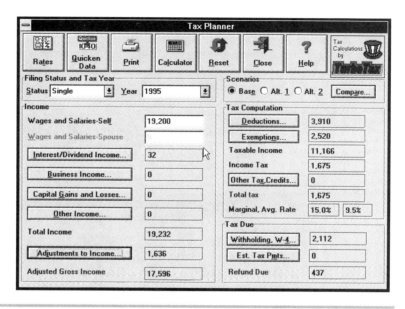

FIGURE 5-7   Tax Planner window showing the numbers from a W-2

- Box 4 (Social security tax withheld)   The 1190.40 in this box does not have any effect if you do not have other business income. However, when you have self-employment income, the Tax Planner uses the number to correctly calculate the social security taxes that you owe on the self-employment income.

- Box 6 (Medicare tax withheld)   The 278.40 in this box does not appear in the Tax Planner because you do not include Medicare taxes on wage income in a Form 1040. If you have self-employment income, you owe Medicare taxes on this income. The Tax Planner will calculate the additional Medicare taxes owed as part of the self-employment taxes that show in the main Tax Planner window after the Other Tax, Credits button.

- Box 18 (State income tax)   The 968.88 in this box appears in the Itemized (Schedule A) and Standard Deductions dialog box as part of the number after State & Local Income Taxes. This number only appears in the main Tax Planner window to affect taxable income if you have enough deductions to itemize.

- Boxes 3, 5, and 17 (Social security wages, Medicare wages and tips, and State wages, tips, etc.) The 19200 in these boxes are the wages upon which the social security, Medicare, and state taxes are calculated. You do not see this number in the Tax Planner because the Tax Planner shows the amount from box 1.

Remember that the tax forms and the Tax Planner combine W-2s when you have more than one.

I changed jobs. Is Quicken's estimate of my annual income still correct?

Assuming you earn more, Quicken's estimate is too low. When Quicken annualizes numbers, Quicken assumes that the average from the beginning of the year will continue for the rest of the year. If you change jobs or change withholding amounts or your deductible expenses do not evenly spread out during the year, the annualized amounts may be wrong. For instance, if you change from a job paying $500 gross weekly to a job paying $1,000 gross weekly on July 1, when you look at your Quicken data with the Tax Planner the income will be wrong. At the end of July, you will see an annualized salary like $29,143 instead of $39,000. The $29,143 is 12 times the seven month average of $2,429 that includes six months of income of $500 and one month of $1,000. The correct amount is $39,000. You can enter new replacement numbers by typing the correct amounts in the appropriate text boxes. For this income example, you need to enter a new amount after Wages and Salaries-Sel_f_. Since a change in earnings also changes your withholdings, you will also need to readjust these numbers.

I previously entered my paycheck as its net amount. How do I calculate my taxes with the Tax Planner?

If you entered paychecks as their net amounts, your income and withholdings are too low. You will need to enter new amounts for the wages and tax withheld. If you have enough itemized deductions, you will also need to add the state and local taxes withheld. If you receive the same amount each paycheck, you can easily enter the new numbers. As an example, suppose that you want to update the Tax Planner to have the correct numbers. For some numbers that are easy to work with, assume that the gross semimonthly pay is $1,000 with $100 deducted for federal taxes, $50 deducted for social security, and $50 deducted for state taxes. To update the Tax Planner for these new numbers, follow these steps:

1. Select Calculator from the Tax Planner to show the calculator.

2. Type **24*1000** to calculate the year's gross wages. Press ENTER or click the = button to perform this calculation.

3. Press ESC or double-click the Calculator's Control menu box to put the calculator away.

4. Type **24000** in the Wages and Salaries-Self text box to enter the year's gross salary.

5. Select the Deductions, then the State & Local Income Taxes buttons to show the State and Local Tax Payments dialog box.

6. Type **0** in the Withholdings to Date text box, type **1/15/95** in the Next Pay Date text box as the first pay date, select Twice/month in the Pay Period text box, and type **50** in the Withholding per Pay Period text box. Quicken calculates the state taxes withheld for the whole year.

7. Select OK twice to return to the main Tax Planner window.

8. Select the Withholding, W-4 button to show the Withholding and W-4 Allowances dialog box.

9. Type **0** in the Withholdings to Date text box, type **1/15/95** in the Next Pay Date text box, select Twice/month in the Pay Period text box, and type **100** in the Withholding Per Pay Period text box. Quicken calculates the federal taxes withheld for the whole year.

10. Select OK to return to the main Tax Planner window. You have updated the income, state taxes, and federal taxes. You don't have to enter social security taxes paid because Tax Planner knows how much is withheld based on your wages. When you perform this for yourself, you will substitute your numbers in place of the ones you used here.

When you earn a different amount each week, you will have to add each paycheck separately.

How do I keep tax-deferred income from showing up in the tax forms?

When you set a tax-deferred account, Quicken recognizes that the income from the account is tax-deferred. This means that you can go ahead and record the income from the tax-deferred account and the income will not appear in the Tax Summary report or in the Tax Planner. In fact, when you create these reports, the default accounts are the nontax-deferred ones. You set up an account as a tax-deferred account by selecting the Tax-Deferred Account check box or by selecting the Yes option button when Quicken prompts for whether the account is tax-deferred.

IRA Deduction in the Tax Planner

Will Quicken calculate my IRA deduction?

If you create expense categories for the IRA contributions, the Tax Planner will show these numbers. You can add these items to categories assigned to the Form 1040:IRA contribution-self, the Form 1040:IRA contrib. working spouse, and the Form 1040:IRA contrib. non-work spouse form entries. The amount you contribute may not be the amount you deduct. You can modify how much is deductible by selecting Adjustments to Income, typing the correct IRA deduction in the Allowable IRA Deduction text box, and selecting OK.

Tech Acct: The IRS has many rules about how much you can contribute and how much you can deduct. The Tax Planner includes all that you have assigned to the IRA category, even if it exceeds what the IRS allows you to deduct. Make sure that you check that the amount entered as deductible in the Tax Planner is actually deductible according to the IRS.

Chapter 5 *Taxes*

How do I enter my IRA contribution when I make it after the end of the year?

If you contribute to last year's IRA, you can actually make the contribution up until when you send in your tax return. However, when you bring your Quicken data into the Tax Planner, the Tax Planner will not include the contribution because it was made after the end of the year. You need to choose Adjustments to Income, enter the IRA deduction in the Allowable IRA Deduction text box, and select OK.

Itemizing

Can Quicken tell me if I am better off itemizing?

The Itemized (Schedule A) and Standard Deductions dialog box shown in Figure 5-8 can calculate what your total itemized deductions are as well as your standard deduction. Quicken uses the higher of the two numbers as the amount of deduction. When the number is higher than the standard deduction, you are better off itemizing. You can get the detailed information that you need to complete Schedule A from this dialog box or from the Tax Summary or Tax Schedule report.

Tech Acct: The IRS now requires written confirmation for charitable contributions over $250. Previously, your canceled check counted as proof but now you need something like a receipt from the receiving charity. Also, with memberships to non-profit organizations, only the amount in excess of what you receive from them is deductible. The charity can tell you this amount. You may want to assign the non-deductible amount to the Dues category so the Tax Planner does not include it as a charitable contribution.

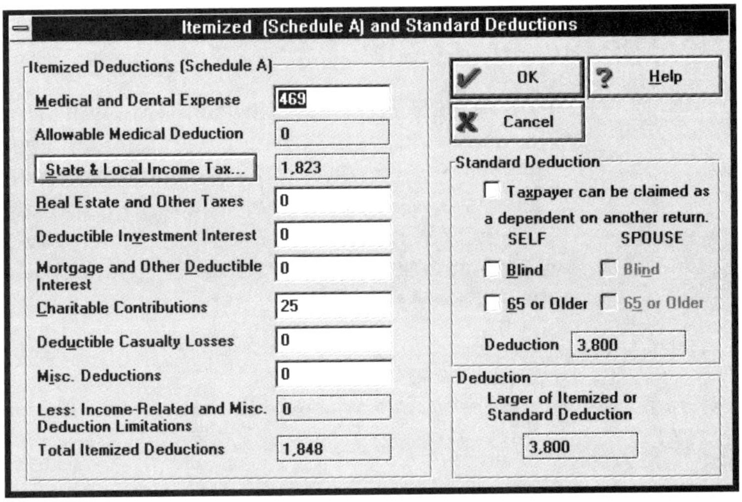

Quicken 4 for Windows Answers: Certified Tech Support

![Itemized (Schedule A) and Standard Deductions dialog box screenshot]

FIGURE 5-8   Itemized (Schedule A) and Standard Deductions dialog box

How do I get my medical and dental bills into the Tax Planner for itemizing deductions?

Quicken's initial home category includes a Medical category for tracking medical expenses. Assign your medical expenses to either this category or one of its subcategories. This category and its subcategories are assigned to specific tax form entries so they will appear in the Tax Planner. When you select Deductions from the Tax Planner, Quicken displays the Itemized (Schedule A) and Standard Deductions dialog box like the one in Figure 5-7. This dialog box includes the total spent and assigned to the Medical category. Since you can only deduct medical expenses that are more that 7.5 percent of adjusted gross income, the box below calculates what part of these deductions is allowed. Therefore, the Allowable Medical Deduction remains 0 unless the Medical and Dental Expense amount is more than 7.5 percent of adjusted gross income.

Tech Tip: If you have to travel to get medical care, create another subcategory to track these expenses. They can also be deducted, but make sure that you review the IRS's rules that limit what you can deduct.

Chapter 5 *Taxes*

How do I set up local income taxes so they appear in the Tax Planner?

Quicken doesn't set up local tax categories for you but the process is similar to how the State subcategory is set up. You want to create a category for recording the local taxes withheld. When you create the category that stores your local taxes, select W-2:Local withholding from the Form drop-down list box—not Schedule A:State and local taxes. If you select Schedule A:State and local taxes, the Tax Planner assumes that the amounts assigned to this category are for past taxes, and does not initially annualize the amount.

How do refund checks affect the taxes that I owe?

If you itemized deductions last year, the state and local tax refunds that you receive this year for last year's taxes are included as income in this year. If you used the standard deduction last year, the refund that you receive for last year's taxes is not included in the tax return. When you deposit your refund state or local refund check, decide whether it will be taxable income. If it is, you can assign it to the Other Inc category so that it will show up on Tax Summary reports as a reminder. This category does not have a specific tax form entry assignment. If the refund is taxable, create a category and assign it to Form 1040:State and local refunds. Federal tax refunds do not affect your taxes, so do not use the Tax:Fed subcategory when you record depositing the refund.

Will the Tax Planner include points on my home mortgage?

You can have the Tax Planner include the deductible amount of points paid on a home mortgage if you enter the transaction in a certain way. How you enter the transaction depends on when the points are deductible. Points for refinancing are spread out over the life of the loan. Previously, points for the initial purchase of a home were deducted the year you bought the home. Now they, too, are deducted over the course of the loan. If the points were deductible the year that you acquired the mortgage, you would assign the cost of points to the Mort Int category. Quicken has assigned this category to Schedule A:Home mortgage interest so the Tax Planner includes the points in the deductions. If you have enough itemized deductions, your deductions will increase.

For points that are not deductible all at once, create an asset account for the points with a zero balance. When you pay the points, select the asset account for the Category field. Then, each year, go to that asset account and add a transaction that decreases the asset account by the deductible portion of the points. Assign the Mort Int category for this transaction. Then the Tax Planner will include only the deductible portion of the points in the deductions that you can claim on Schedule A. The transaction that sets up the points in the account and deducts the proper amount for the year looks like this:

Tech Tip: Since the transaction to record how much of the points are deductible occurs only once a year, you can create a reminder for yourself by making it a scheduled transaction.

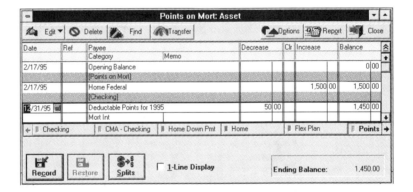

How do I record improvements in the house so that Quicken includes those costs in the home's value when I sell it?

You want an asset account that records your basis in your house. The basis measures what you have invested in property such as your house that determines how much gain or loss you recognize when you sell it. This basis starts off with what you pay for the house, less any deferred gains from sales of previous homes. You get to add onto this basis any improvements that you make to the house. When you spend money on improvements, enter the house's asset account in place of the Home Rpair category. Then the asset account increases by what you spend on the improvement.

Tech Acct: The IRS distinguishes between improvements that enhance the value of a house versus repairs that maintain the house at the same value. Improvements increase the basis; repairs do not.

Schedules B, C, and D

How can I get a list of payers for my Schedule B?

Schedule B requires that you list payers names when you receive more than $400 of interest or dividends (Schedule 1 on Form 1040A). You can create reports that total the payers. For interest, you probably have each payer set up as a separate account. You can create a Transaction report that subtotals the interest you have earned for each account. To create this report:

1. Choose Other from the Reports menu, then select Transaction.
2. Enter the dates in the From and To boxes.
3. Select Customize to modify this report.
4. Select Account in the Subtotal By drop-down list box. While you might be tempted to select Payee, you may notice that when you reconcile bank accounts, Quicken enters Interest Earned for the Payee field regardless of who pays the interest.
5. Select the Totals Only check box to show totals for each account without showing the detail.
6. Select the Accounts option button, then select all accounts where you record receiving interest.
7. Select the Categories/Classes option button to set the categories for the report.

8. Select Clear All to remove all check marks, then select Int Inc and _IntInc to show the interest income in the report. These two categories record interest income. Quicken uses categories with _ starting their name to track investment amounts so you will only have the _IntInc category if you have investment accounts.

9. Select OK to show the report. A sample one might look like this:

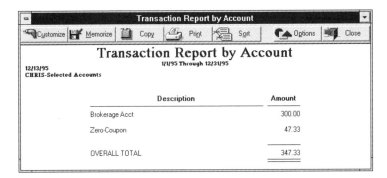

For dividends, how you get the payer list depends on how you record receiving the dividends. If you deposit dividend checks and record them in a checking or savings account, follow the steps above except select Payee in step 4 and select the Div Income category in step 7. For dividends that you enter in an investment account, you will want to follow these steps:

1. Choose Investment from the Reports menu, then select Investment Income.

2. Enter the dates in the From and To boxes.

3. Select Customize to modify this report.

4. Select Security in the Subtotal By drop-down list box.

5. Select the Accounts option button, then select all accounts where you record receiving dividends. You may want to select the Investment button to record the all investment accounts.

6. Select OK to show the report.

I have a separate business on the side. How do I enter it into the Tax Planner?

The Tax Planner displays your business income after the <u>B</u>usiness Income button. You can type in your business income by selecting this button and then entering the appropriate amounts in the <u>R</u>evenue, Cost of <u>G</u>oods Sold, <u>M</u>eals and Entertainment Expense, and <u>O</u>ther Allowable Expenses boxes. A better long term solution if you are recording your business transactions is to assign the business categories to the specific lines in Schedule C. Then, when you import your Quicken data into the Tax Planner, Quicken already shows the appropriate numbers in these text boxes.

Tech Tip: The IRS has hobby loss rules that limit what you can deduct from a business that is run more like a hobby than a business. If your business shows a loss, make sure to check to see whether you are affected by these rules.

How do I get Schedule C information?

You can quickly create a Tax Schedule report that lists the transactions that appear in Schedule C if you assign Schedule C lines to your business categories. Not only that, but the Tax Planner will summarize the Schedule C information as your business income. The Tax Planner will also calculate any self-employment taxes that you owe.

Tech Tip: The Tax Schedule report will include transactions and totals for Schedule C items.

How do I get the numbers from my Investment account for the stock I sold so that I can prepare Schedule D?

The tax information that you need to prepare Schedule D is more detailed than what you see in the Tax Planner. The best way to get the information for Schedule D is to create a Capital Gains report. Create this report by choosing Investment from the Reports menu, then choosing Capital Gains. Select OK to create this report. Many of these columns match the ones you need to complete on your Schedule D.

Self Employment Taxes and Tax Credits

Can Quicken calculate other taxes, such as self-employment taxes?

The Tax Planner can calculate self-employment taxes to include them with the rest of the taxes that you owe, just like Form 1040 does. When you select Other Tax, Credits from the Tax Planner, the Schedule C/F boxes already have the entries that are entered as business and farm income. You can adjust this income using the Other Income text boxes. The Tax Planner takes this income into account as well as salary and wage income to calculate self-employment taxes, as you can see here:

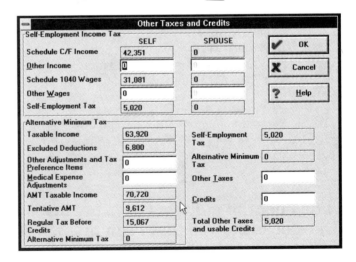

The Tax Planner will also estimate the alternative minimum tax if it applies. However, the Tax Planner will not calculate some credits such as the credit for child and dependent care expenses.

My spouse's business income appears as mine when we calculate self-employment taxes. Will this be a problem?

Since Business Income in the main Tax Planner window doesn't separate which self-employment income belongs to you or your spouse, the Tax Planner shows it entirely in the Self column of the Other Taxes and Credits dialog box. To make sure that the Tax Planner correctly calculates the self-employment taxes, enter the spouse's business income as a negative number in the first Other Income text box and as a positive number in the second. This transfers it out of your column and into your spouse's.

How do I calculate credits in the Tax Planner?

The tax law provides for credits that can decrease your tax liability or increase your refund. These can include the credit for child and dependent care expenses and the Earned Income Credit (EIC). The only way to include these additional credits in the Tax Planner is to calculate them separately and add the credit. To add any tax credit, such as the EIC to the Tax Planner:

1. Select the Other Tax, Credits button.
2. Type the amount of the credit in the Credits text box.
3. Select OK.

Tech Tip: If you are taking advantage of the credit for child and dependent care expenses, assign the Childcare category to the Form 2441:Child care - day care or Form 2441:Child care - household tax form. The amounts that you assign to this category will not appear in the Tax Planner, but they will appear in the Tax Schedule report that will help you complete Form 2441 in order to claim this credit.

Withheld, Estimating, and Estimated Taxes

How do I remove what I paid for last year's taxes from this year's withholding?

If you assign what you paid for last year's taxes to the same category as other federal taxes withheld, your federal withholding is too high. You will need to reduce the amount withheld by the amount of what you paid for last year's taxes. You can reduce the amount of federal taxes withheld in the Tax Planner by selecting Withholding, W-4 and typing the correct amount in the Withholdings to Date text box. Select OK and Quicken recalculates your refund or taxes due based on the new withholding.

Tech Acct: This is only an issue with state and other taxes if you assigned the payment or refund check to the same category as state and local withholdings. The question, "How do refund checks affect the taxes that I owe?" described how to handle refunds for taxes that you deducted in prior years. If you make payments for the prior year's taxes, you may need to create a separate category and assign it to Schedule A:State and local taxes.

Can I estimate the taxes that I will owe for the whole year based on what I have already earned?

When the Tax Planner cannot import an entire year of transactions, the Tax Planner suggests annualizing many of the items that appear in the Tax Planner. When you select Quicken Data, you see a window like the one in Figure 5-2. The Quicken Amount column shows the current total amount. The Amount column shows the annualized version. You can annualize individual categories by double-clicking them in this window.

How do I enter the estimated taxes that I have paid?

You can enter the estimated federal tax payments and have them included in the Tax Planner, but you will want to follow these steps for creating the category:

1. Choose Category & Transfer from the Lists menu.
2. Select New to create a new subcategory.
3. Make the following entries:

   - Name   Type **Estimated Pmt** in this text box for the category name.
   - Description   Type **Estimated Payments** in this text box for the category description.
   - Type   Select the Subcategory of option button, then select Tax from the adjoining drop-down list box.
   - Tax-related   Select this check box.
   - Form   Select Form 1040:Fed. estimated tax from this drop-down list box.

4. Select OK to create this category, then select Close to put the window away.

Now you have a category created just for estimated tax payments. When you record the transaction for the estimated tax payment, enter Tax:Estimated Pmt for the category. When you import Quicken data into the Tax Planner, these estimated tax payments are included and appear after the Est. Tax Pmts button in the main Tax Planner window.

For estimated state and local payments, you also want to create a subcategory just for the estimated tax payments. This subcategory, however, should be assigned to Schedule A:State and local taxes.

Updating the Tax Planner

How do I find out what my taxes will be if the rates change?

You can modify the tax rates the Tax Planner uses when you select Rates from the top of the Tax Planner. You can enter the new rates and tax bracket amounts. Select OK and the Tax Planner uses the new rates.

How does Quicken update itself for tax changes?

Quicken has the tentative IRS tax information for the next two years. However, since the product is finished before the tax laws are, Quicken lets you adjust the tax rate, tax bracket amounts, exemption amounts, and deduction amounts. You can enter these numbers after you select the Rates button from the top of the Tax Planner window. From the Tax Rates for Filing Status dialog box, enter the new information and select OK.

Tech Tip: Intuit has a phone number that you can call to get updated information about how tax law changes affect the way you use the Tax Planner. Currently, this number is 415-858-6081.

Planning

Can I plan for more than the current year?

Quicken includes tentative IRS tax information for the next two years. You can plan taxes for either year by choosing that year from the Year drop-down list box. Selecting the year chooses the amounts for tax brackets, exemption amounts, and standard deductions for that year.

Can I test out Tax Planner changes without destroying the entries I have already made?

The Tax Planner can store a base scenario and two alternatives. When you start working in the Tax Planner, you start using the base scenario. You can copy the base scenario to one of the alternatives, then make changes to the alternatives to show how possible changes will affect your tax return. To start using one of the alternate scenarios, select the Alt. <u>1</u> or Alt. <u>2</u> option button at the top of the Tax Planner. You will see the prompt for whether you want to copy the current scenario.

Select <u>Y</u>es if you want to start out with the same entries as the last scenario you used, or <u>N</u>o to start with 0 for all entries. Now you can alter the entries you have and make new ones knowing that the other scenarios will not change. When you want to print the scenario results, just select the <u>P</u>rint button since this prints the displayed scenario. The real value in having different scenarios comes from comparing the results. Select the Comp<u>a</u>re button and Quicken shows comparisons like the ones in Figure 5-9.

FIGURE 5-9 Tax Scenario Comparisons dialog box to compare different tax possibilities

Investments

When you invest, you put aside today's immediate desires for larger ones down the road. Investment possibilities come in all shapes and sizes. They vary in the potential risk entailed and the return that they offer. They provide a hedge against inflation that does not exist if you stuff your money in a mattress. Some investment opportunities you may see are described in the following Frustration Busters! box.

Quicken can help track investments of all types, providing support for the diversity you need in a good investment portfolio. It cannot provide complete guidance for how to treat your investment transactions at tax time. The IRS has so many rules about investments that you will probably need to contact your accountant for the best tax treatments. Your accountant will know the latest changes that affect your return.

FRUSTRATION BUSTERS!

If investments are new to you, you might be surprised by the vast array of investment instruments. These are some of the most commonly held investments:

- Bonds   Debt that is bought and sold between investors rather than held by banks.

- Individual Retirement Account (IRA)   A tax-deferred investment that invests in other types of investments. Its tax-deferred status makes it easier to accumulate assets for when you retire.

- Limited Partnership   A partnership that allows investors to supply part of the capital required for a business and to share in its proceeds. The limited partners are protected from losing more than their initial investment.

- Mutual fund   A professionally managed investment fund. The idea behind a mutual fund is that its professional management and larger scale investing will give a better return than investors can earn by themselves.

- Option   An option lets you purchase stock at a specific price. This becomes valuable when that price is less than the stock's current price.

- Real Estate Investment Trust (REIT)   A limited partnership that invests in real estate.

- Rights   Rights allow you to buy stock that is about to be issued.

- Stock   Stock represents ownership in a company. It provides income to its stockholders through dividends and increases in its share price. Stocks can also be split. A *stock split* increases the number of shares without changing the percentages of ownership so a 2 for 1 stock split means that instead of 50 shares, you now own 100 but you still have the same percentage of company stock that you held before.

- Unit Trust   Mutual fund that invests solely in bonds. Investors frequently receive both interest income and a return of capital as the bonds that the trust invests in mature.

Setting Up Investment Accounts

Should I use investment accounts for all my investments?

While an investment account is appropriate for many types of investments, some investments are better handled differently. Table 6-1 suggests what types of accounts to use for tracking different kinds of investments.

Account Type	For this Type of Investment
Regular investment account	■ Stocks, bonds, and mutual funds for which you want to track a cash balance ■ Real estate investment trusts (REITs) or partnerships ■ Unit trusts ■ IRA or Keogh accounts ■ Variable annuities
Investment account telling Quicken that the account monitors a single mutual fund	A single mutual fund account that has no cash balance
Checking, Savings, or Money Market account for the checking portion of the account, and an investment account for everything else	Cash management accounts (CMAs)
Money Market if you write checks or, if you don't, an investment account telling Quicken that the account monitors a single mutual fund	Money Market funds
Investment or asset account	■ Employer retirement plans (401(k)) depending on the information that your plan provides ■ CDs or treasury bills ■ Fixed annuities ■ Collectibles and precious metals
Asset account	■ Real estate ■ Stocks that have a constant share price

TABLE 6-1 The appropriate account types for your investments

How do I decide when to add a new investment account?

You should set up an investment account for each group of securities that you think of as a unit. Whether you set up one or several accounts is entirely up to you. You might want to follow these two suggestions:

- Use different accounts for each broker.
- Use different accounts for each mutual fund.

What do the different investment actions mean?

In Quicken's investment accounts, you record actions. Actions represent some investment action. Buying, selling, receiving, and earning income are just some examples of the actions that you record in the investment account. The following table lists the available investment actions and when you might use them:

Action	Purpose of this Action
Buy	Records buying a security with cash from an investment account
BuyX	Records buying a security with cash from another account
CGLong	Records cash received from a long-term capital gains distribution
CGLongX	Records long-term capital gains distribution and transfers the cash received to another account
CGShort	Records cash received from a short-term capital gains distribution
CGShortX	Records short-term capital gains distribution and transfers the cash received to another account
Div	Records cash dividends earned from stock in an investment account
DivX	Records transferring cash dividends to another account
IntInc	Records interest income earned from holdings in an investment account
MargInt	Records paying a margin loan
MiscExp	Records paying miscellaneous expenses
MiscInc	Records miscellaneous income
ReinvDiv	Records reinvesting dividends in additional shares
ReinvInt	Records reinvesting interest in additional shares
ReinvLg	Records reinvesting long-term capital gains distribution
ReinvSh	Records reinvesting short-term capital gains distribution

Chapter 6 *Investments*

Action	Purpose of this Action
Reminder	Used with the Billminder feature to notify you of a pending event
RtrnCap	Recognizing cash from the return of capital
Sell	Records selling a security and leaving the proceeds in an investment account
SellX	Records selling a security and transferring the proceeds of a sale to another account
ShrsIn	Records transferring shares into an investment account when no account supplies the fund for purchasing them
ShrsOut	Records transferring shares out of an account
StkSplit	Records changing the number of shares resulting from a stock split
XIn	Records transferring cash into an investment account
XOut	Records transferring cash out of an investment account

Stock Symbols and Names

How do I find out the symbol for a stock?

If you never use any external stock price information services, having the correct symbol doesn't matter. However, if you plan to update stock prices using Portfolio Price Update or retrieve historical prices using CompuServe, you need the correct ticker symbols to retrieve the correct security information.

You can find out the symbol for a security through various sources including:

- Your brokerage statement
- Your broker
- Newspapers such as the *Wall Street Journal*

When you enter ticker symbols for major exchanges, keep these rules in mind:

- NASDAQ symbols end with a capital letter. This last letter describes the type of security issued by a company, such as the class of common stock, preferred stock, or bonds.

- All AMEX and NYSE symbols start with a colon.
- Don't put a space after the colon for AMEX and NYSE symbols.
- AMEX and NYSE symbols end with specific letters that describe the type of security issued by a company.
- AMEX and NYSE symbols must have the correct capitalization.

How do I tell Quicken that one of the companies that I invested in changed its name?

You need to change the name and symbol that you use for the security. Quicken will keep all the old price information and transaction information although they use the new name. To rename a security:

1. Choose Security from the Lists menu. Quicken shows the Security List window listing all the stocks you have set up.
2. Highlight the stock for the company that changed its name and select Edit.
3. Make new entries in the Name and Symbol text boxes.
4. Select OK, then select Close to put the Security List window away.

Investment Goals

Why do I want to use investment goals?

Investment goals divide your investments into groups so you can match similar types of investments—even ones in different accounts—and see if they meet your expectations. For example, financial analysts often recommend diversifying among different types of securities. Some will be riskier but offer more growth. You can create investment goals for each type of security. Investment goals are set for each security with these steps:

Chapter 6 *Investments*

1. Choose Security from the Lists menu.
2. Highlight the security whose goal you want to change and select Edit.
3. Select the investment goal from the Goal drop-down list box.
4. Select OK, then select Close to put the Security List window away.

Besides the investment goals that Quicken provides, you can create new ones:

1. Choose Security Type from the Lists menu and select New.
2. Enter the investment goal name in the Type text box.
3. Select whether you want prices for this security type shown like 6.625 or like 6 5/8 by selecting the Decimal or Fraction option button.
4. Select OK, then select Close to put the Security Type List window away.

Tech Tip: You can have limit reports only show specific security types. When you show a report and you want to choose which security types are in the report, select Customize, then select the Select to Include and Security Types option buttons. From the list, you can choose which security types appear in the report.

How do I see what I own?

You can see a list of all your holdings with the Portfolio View window or a modified Portfolio Investment report. To create a report that shows all of your holdings:

1. Choose Investment from the Reports menu, then choose Portfolio Value.
2. Select Customize since you want to include all your investment accounts.
3. Select the Accounts option button to see the list of the accounts the report will show.

4. Select the Investment button to include all investment accounts.

5. Select OK to create the report in a window.

6. Select Print in the button bar and then the Print button in the dialog box to print this report like the one shown in Figure 6-1.

The Portfolio Value window also lists securities and shows what you own and their current price. To see this window, choose Portfolio View from the Activities menu. The window initially features only one investment account. This is the account listed in the Accounts drop-down list box at the top of the window. You can select All Accounts from this drop-down list box to see all of your holdings. Figure 6-2 shows an example of this window.

Tech Tip: You can print a report of the contents of your Portfolio View window. From this window, choose Print Summary from the File menu. Selecting the Print button prints a report showing all the columns of information.

```
                              Portfolio Value Report
                                   As of 12/6/95
12/6/95
CHRIS-Selected Investment Acct                                                    Page 1
                                 * Estimated Prices

          Security              Shares      Curr Price    Cost Basis   Gain/Loss    Balance

     ABC Company                 250.00       27 1/2       3,940.00    2,935.00    6,875.00
     American Express             30.00       75.000         822.50    1,427.50    2,250.00
     Brody Bonds                  50.00      101.243       4,973.82       88.33    5,062.15
     Endura Products              60.00       15.000         630.00      270.00      900.00
     FabricART                    25.00       78.000         500.00    1,450.00    1,950.00
     Fun-it Parks                200.00        3.000       1,060.00     -460.00      600.00
     Home Free Inc.               75.00       55.000       3,825.00      300.00    4,125.00
     Mouse Computers           3,000.00       43.000       3,050.00  125,950.00  129,000.00
     Mutual Fund                 497.79       16.970 *    8,317.32      130.26    8,447.58
     Nill & Growth                10.00       75.000 *      750.00        0.00      750.00
     POSE Company                 50.00       25.000       1,250.00        0.00    1,250.00
     Series EE Bonds              10.00       87.330 *      873.30        0.00      873.30
     Smith Corporation           185.00       34.000 *    5,688.75      601.25    6,290.00
     TransGlobe                  150.00       32.000       4,500.00      300.00    4,800.00
     WoolART                     300.00       42.000          10.00   12,590.00   12,600.00
     -Cash-                    2,206.75        1.000       2,206.75        0.00    2,206.75

     Total Investments                                    42,397.44  145,582.34  187,979.78
```

FIGURE 6-1   Portfolio Value report showing all of your investments

Chapter 6 *Investments*

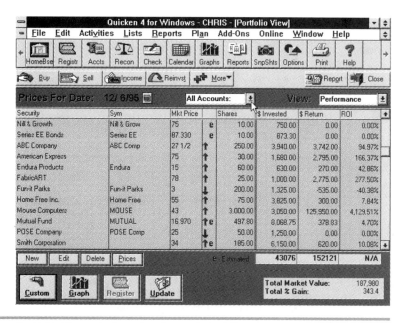

FIGURE 6-2   Portfolio View window showing your holdings

How do I see what I earned on my investments?

Quicken's Investment Income report shows the income earned from investments. To create this report:

1. Choose Investment from the Reports menu, then choose Investment Income.
2. Select Customize since you want to make sure that the report includes all your investment accounts.
3. Select the Accounts option button to see the list of the accounts that the report will show.
4. Select the Investment button to include all investment accounts.
5. Select OK to create the report in a window.
6. Select Print in the button bar and then the Print button in the dialog box to print this report like the one shown in Figure 6-3.

```
                        Investment Income Report
                          1/1/95 Through 12/6/95
12/6/95                                                                    Page 1
CHRIS-Selected Investment Acct
                                                      1/1/95-
                            Category Description      12/6/95

                            INCOME/EXPENSE
                              INCOME
                                _DivInc              410.84
                                _IntInc              300.00
                                _IntIncTaxFree     1,087.21
                                _LT CapGnDst          46.31
                                _RlzdGain         10,969.80
                                _ST CapGnDst           8.42

                              TOTAL INCOME        12,822.58

                              EXPENSES
                                Expenses - Other      0.00

                              TOTAL EXPENSES          0.00


                            TOTAL INCOME/EXPENSE 12,822.58

                            TRANSFERS
                              TO Cash Mgmt Acct: Check  -400.00
                              TO Checking          -12,525.00
                              FROM Checking          8,605.00

                            TOTAL TRANSFERS        -4,320.00

                            Balance Forward
                              Employee Stock Option    0.00
                              Mutual Fund          1,394.88

                            Total Balance Forward  1,394.88


                            OVERALL TOTAL          9,897.46
```

FIGURE 6-3   Investment Income report

Stock Options and Stock Rights

How do I record buying and selling options?

Options are a security that gives you the privilege of buying another security at a specific price, called the *option price*. For example, you may have options so you can buy a fixed number of shares of ABC Company stock at $20 a share. When shares of ABC Company sell for more than $20, this option is worth

Chapter 6 *Investments*

something. An option can also have value when investors think that the stock will be worth more than the option price before the options expire. (Options have expiration dates.)

To Quicken, an option is a type of security. In Quicken, you have four types of transactions you perform for options. One is buying the options, a second is buying the security that the option belongs to, a third is selling the options, and a fourth is writing off the option when it expires while you still have it. To enter buying options:

1. Switch to the Portfolio View window or the investment's Register window that will hold the investment in the options.
2. Select Buy from the button bar.
3. Enter the following information:
   - Date   Enter the date that you buy the options.
   - Security   Enter a name for the options. Ideally, you want to describe the security the option belongs to, the fact that it is an option, when it expires, and the price of the security bought with the option. As an example, for options that let you buy stock in ABC Company at $20 a share before August, a name might be ABC Opt 20 by Aug. In the Set Up Security dialog box, you can enter other information about the security for the option and then select OK.
   - Number of Shares   Enter the number of options you bought.
   - Commission/Fee   Enter any commission that you paid.
4. Enter the account that the money to buy the options comes from in the Transfer Acct drop-down list box.
5. Select OK to finish the transaction of buying options.

When you receive options without buying them, record them with the ShrsIn action, which records acquiring shares without using the Buy or BuyX action.

The second type of transaction that you record for options is exercising the options. You enter this in Quicken by selling the options and buying the underlying security. To record this transaction:

1. Switch to the Portfolio View window or the investment's Register window that holds the investment in the options.
2. Select <u>S</u>ell from the button bar.
3. Enter the following information:
   - <u>D</u>ate   Enter the date that you use the options to buy the security.
   - Security   Enter the name for the options.
   - <u>N</u>umber of Shares   Enter the number of options you exercised.
   - <u>P</u>rice   Enter the price per share that you paid for the options.
4. Select OK to finish selling the options.
5. Select <u>B</u>uy from the button bar.
6. Enter the following information:
   - <u>D</u>ate   Enter the date that you buy the underlying security.
   - Security   Enter a name of the security bought with the options. If you have not bought this security before, you will see the Set Up Security dialog box. You can enter other information about the security and select OK.
   - <u>N</u>umber of Shares   Enter the number of shares of the security that you bought.
   - <u>P</u>rice   Enter the option's price per share that you paid for the security.
   - <u>C</u>ommission/Fee   Enter the total amount that you initially paid for the options. In the ABC Company example, if you paid $2 for 100 options, you would enter $200. Putting the amount paid for the options here means that Quicken correctly records what you invested in the security. You have invested the option price plus the options you purchased to buy it at its option price.
   - Transfer Acct   Enter the account that supplies the money to buy the security.

Chapter 6 *Investments*

- **Amount to transfer** Enter the additional amount that you paid for the stock.

7. Select OK to finish the transaction of buying options. The three transactions in an investment Register window might look like this:

Date	Action	Security	Price	Shares	Amount	Clr	Cash Bal
	Memo		Xfer Acct	Xfer Amt	Comm Fee		
1/9/96	BuyX	Mauseo Opt by Mar	2	500	1,015 00		197 00
	Purchased options for Mauseo		[Checking]	1,015.00	15 00		
2/18/96	Sell	Mauseo Opt by Mar	2	500	1,000 00		1,197 00
	Used Mauseo options to buy						
2/18/96	BuyX	Mauseo Corp	15	500	8,500 00		197 00
	Bought Mauseo stock w/option		[Checking]	7,500.00	1,000 00		

Besides exercising stock options, you can also sell them. When you sell them, you sell the security you set up for the options just as you sell any other security.

The fourth transaction you may need for options is when they expire before you have used them. After the options expire, they are worthless so they have the same treatment as worthless securities. To write off the options or any worthless security, follow these steps:

1. Switch to the Portfolio View window or the investment's Register window that holds the investment in the options.

2. Select Sell from the button bar.

3. Enter the following information:

- Date Enter the date that the options expire.
- Security Enter the name for the options.
- Number of Shares Enter the number of options you bought.
- Price Enter **0**.

4. Select OK to sell the options.

Tech Tip: Selling the options doesn't remove them from your Register window but it does tell Quicken that you no longer own shares; this way you don't see it in your investment reports when you tell Quicken to only include what you own.

I have options that expire soon. How do I remind myself to check whether I want to use them?

You can add investment reminders to investment accounts. You can do this by choosing <u>M</u>ore in the button bar and then <u>R</u>eminder. Then enter a date, investment account if this drop-down list box is available, description, and memo in the appropriate boxes. When you select OK, Quicken adds a transaction like the one here:

Date	Action	Security	Price	Shares	Amount	Clr	Cash Bal	
	Memo							
3/31/96	Reminder	Mauseo options exp					197	00
	Options expire today							

One result from this transaction is that once the date occurs, the Quicken Reminders dialog box shows that you have an investment reminder due.

Another method for reminding yourself about anything, including investment options, is adding a note to the Financial Calendar. The Financial Calendar also lets you add notes to specific dates. These notes also appear in the Quicken Reminders dialog box, and they appear on the Financial Calendar as a square of color.

I just received stock rights. Do I count them as stock?

Stock rights give you the chance to buy stock that is about to be issued. For publicly held corporations, these stock rights can be bought and sold. You can record receiving them, using them to buy the stock, and selling them. The transactions are identical to the ones that you enter for stock options, which were described earlier in this section.

Tech Acct: Stock rights can be a taxable dividend. If yours fall into this category, record receiving the value of the stock rights as dividend income, then enter the Buy transaction that buys the stock rights with the dividend's proceeds. When the stock rights are a non-taxable dividend, record receiving them with the ShrsIn action.

Employee Stock Options

How do I record stock purchases made with my qualified employee stock options?

When you receive *qualified stock options* from your employer, you don't have to recognize income from them until you sell the stocks; therefore, you don't owe tax on the stocks until you sell them.

When you buy stock with stock options, you are exercising these options. Since the transactions you will enter have many steps, follow along with this example. This example assumes that on 1/1/95, you received stock options that allow you to buy 50 shares at $25 apiece. On 2/7/95, you exercised these options. On 6/3/96, you sold these shares for $50 apiece. Later, when you enter your own stock options, change the numbers below to your own. Here are the steps to perform:

1. Choose Security Type from the Lists menu, then select New in the button bar to create a new security type.

2. Type **Exercise Price** for the type name, select the Decimal or Fraction option button for whether you want prices for this security type shown like 6.625 (decimal) or like 6 5/8, and select OK. Now you have a security type to record the exercise price of your options.

3. Select Close to put this window away.

4. Choose Security from the Lists menu, then New in the button bar to create a new security.

5. Type **POSE Company Opt** as the name for the stock options, choose Exercise Price from the Type drop-down list box, and then select OK. This creates a security representing the stock options. If you have already set up the stock that you have the options for, you don't perform the next two steps.

6. Select New again to create another stock.

7. Type **POSE Company** as a name for the stock, choose Stock from the Type drop-down list box, and then select OK.

8. Select Close to put the Security List window away.

9. Switch to the Portfolio View window or the investment account's Register window. If you are in the Portfolio View window, choose the investment account from the top drop-down list box.

10. Select More from the button bar and then ShrsIn to record a ShrsIn action. Enter the following information for the transaction:
    - Date **1/1/95** as the date that the options are available
    - Security **POSE Company Opt** for the stock option's name, not the name of the stock
    - Number of Shares **50** for the number of shares of options
    - Price per Share **25** for the per share price of the stock you can buy with the options

11. Select OK to record this transaction. Now you have a record of the options that you have available and what the option price is.

12. Select Buy from the investment account's Register window. You want to record buying the stock with the options. Enter the following information for the transaction:
    - Date **2/7/95** as the date that you exercise the options
    - Security **POSE Company** for the stock's name
    - Number of Shares **50** for the number of shares of options
    - Price **25** for the per share price of the stock bought with the options
    - Transfer Acct **Checking** as the account that supplied the money to exercise the options

13. Select OK to record this transaction.

14. Select More from the investment account's Register window's button bar and then ShrsOut for the ShrsOut action that records removing the stock options from your investments. You need to record the options that you no longer have because you used them to buy the stock. Enter the following information for the transaction:
    - Date **2/7/95** as the date that you exercise the options

Chapter 6 *Investments*

- Security **POSE Company Opt** for the stock option's name
- Number of Shares **50** for the number of options that you no longer have

15. Select OK to record this transaction.

When you sell the stock later, you enter a standard Sell transaction for the POSE Company stock. Quicken correctly reports the gain or loss from the sale. When you look at your investment holdings, they include the security you set up for the stock options, although once you exercise the options, your holdings become 0. The transactions for acquiring the options, exercising them, and selling the stock might look like this:

Date	Action	Security	Price	Shares	Amount	Clr	Cash Bal
	Memo						
1/1/95	ShrsIn	POSE Company Opt	25	50	1,250.00		0.00
	Granting stock options						
2/7/95	BuyX	POSE Company	25	50	1,250.00		0.00
	Shares bought w/options		[Checking]	1,250.00			
2/7/95	ShrsOut	POSE Company Opt		50			0.00
	Using options to buy stock						
6/3/96	SellX	POSE Company	50	50	2,500.00		0.00
	Stock bought with options		[Checking]	2,500.00			

Tech Acct: What makes a stock option plan qualified or nonqualified is how it is set up, not anything to do with your finances. Your employer can tell you whether the stock option plan is qualified or unqualified.

How do I record my nonqualified employee stock options?

With nonqualified stock option plans, you can recognize taxable income twice. The first time is when you exercise the options (buy the stock). This taxable income is treated just like other wage income. The income you recognize now is the difference between the share price paid to exercise the options and its market value. Later, when you sell the stock, you can recognize additional taxable income between the difference of the selling price and the market value when you exercised the options. How you record these transactions depends on whether you keep the stock purchased with these options.

If you hold onto the stock after exercising the options, perform the following steps. This example assumes that on 5/16/95 you exercise options to buy 500 shares of Twiddle Inc stock at $10 a share while the market value of the stock is $20.

1. Choose Security from the Lists menu, then select New in the button bar to create new securities.
2. Type **Twiddle Opt** as the name for the stock options, choose Stock from the Type drop-down list box, and then select OK. This creates a security representing the stock options.
3. Select New again, type **Twiddle Inc** as the name for the stock, choose Stock from the Type drop-down list box, and then select OK. You only have to do this if it is the first time you are buying that stock.
4. Select Close to put the Security List window away.
5. Switch to the Portfolio View window or the investment account's Register window. If you are in the Portfolio View window, choose the investment account from the top drop-down list box.
6. Select Buy from the button bar. Enter the following information for the transaction:
   - Date **5/16/95** as the date that you exercise the options
   - Security **Twiddle Opt** for the stock option's name, not the name of the stock
   - Number of Shares **500** as the number of shares of options
   - Price **10** for the per share price of the stock bought with the options
   - Transfer Acct **Checking** as the account that provided the money to buy the stocks
7. Select OK to record this transaction.
8. Select Sell from the button bar. Enter the following information for the transaction:
   - Date **5/16/95** as the date that you exercise the options
   - Security **Twiddle Opt** for the stock option's name

- **Number of Shares 500** as the number of shares of options
- **Price 20** for the per share price

9. Select OK to record this transaction. You have bought and sold these options to correctly recognize the gain from exercising them.

10. Select <u>B</u>uy again, then enter this information:

- **Date 5/16/95** as the date that you exercise the options
- **Security Twiddle Inc** for the stock's name, not the stock option's name
- **<u>N</u>umber of Shares 500** as the number of shares of stock
- **Price 20** as the per share market price of the stock

11. Select OK to record this transaction.

The investment account now shows the stock valued at its market price when you exercised the options. Later, when you sell the stock, Quicken correctly reports the gain or loss as the difference between the sales price then and the market value when you exercised the options. It does not include the gain of the difference between the option price and the market price on the day of exercise. You already recognized this gain when you exercised the stock. When you look at the Register window, the options and the stock might look like this:

Date	Action Memo	Security	Price	Shares	Amount	Clr	Cash Bal
5/16/95	BuyX	Twiddle Opt	10 [Checking]	500 5,000.00	5,000 00		0 00
5/16/95	Buy	Twiddle Inc	20	500	10,000 00		-10,000 00
5/16/95	Sell	Twiddle Opt	20	500	10,000 00		0 00

If you sell the shares at the same time that you exercise them, you will need the broker's statement to record this transaction in the account where you deposit the proceeds, *not* in an investment account. This statement will include the proceeds from the sale, what the options cost, what is taxable to you, what the taxes are, and the final amount that you receive. To the IRS, the proceeds are taxable just like a salary. You will want to enter the net result the same way you enter your salary.

Tech Tip: When you use the Tax Planner, remember to include the gain from exercising the options in Wages and Salaries.

Individual Retirement Accounts

How do I keep track of my IRA?

You can create an investment account for your IRA indicating that it is a tax-deferred account. Then, Quicken will not record the income and expenses from the IRA in the tax summary information. As you make contributions, they are recorded as transfers to this account. You can record IRA earnings in the investment account. Figure 6-4 shows an investment account for an IRA. This IRA invests in a mutual fund.

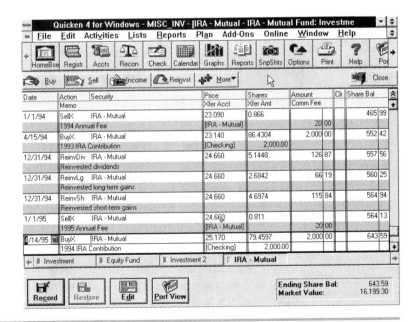

FIGURE 6-4   Investment in an IRA's mutual fund

Chapter 6 *Investments*

How do I enter my IRA's or mutual fund's annual fee?

IRAs and some mutual funds have their annual fee paid out of what is in the account. The way the fund manager handles this is to sell some of the mutual fund or IRA's assets equal to the amount of the fee. You can record this transaction following these steps:

1. Enter the date for this transaction in the Date field.
2. Select SellX from the Action field.
3. Enter the share price and the number of shares sold in those fields.
4. Select the same investment account for the Xfer account field as the one holding this transaction. If you do select a different account, it doesn't really matter, since the final transaction amount is zero. However, if you select a different account, you will have blank transactions filling up your register in that other account.
5. Type the amount of the fee in the Commission field. It will always be the same amount as the Price multiplied by the Shares field so the commission equals the sales price of the portion of the mutual fund sold to cover the annual fee.
6. Select Re<u>c</u>ord, then select <u>N</u>o so you do not specifically identify which lots are sold. The top transaction in Figure 6-4 shows the transaction paying 1994's annual fee; the next to last one shows the annual fee for 1995.

401(k) Plans

How do I enter my 401(k) into Quicken?

This depends on the type of information that you receive. If you receive a statement that states each purchase, including the number of shares and the share price, create an investment account. You can even create separate investment accounts for each fund that your 401(k) invests in. When each fund has a separate investment account, they may be set up as an investment account for mutual funds as in Figure 6-4. The next question tells you how to enter payroll deductions to the 401(k) plan.

If your statement only tells you the current value, create an asset account and update the account's new value with each statement you receive.

How do I enter my paycheck's 401(k) contributions into Quicken?

When you enter your paycheck, you can include the 401(k) contribution. Ideally, your paycheck transaction should include all the deductions. Then you can take advantage of Quicken's Tax Planner to estimate your taxes.

Follow these steps:

1. Go to a blank transaction in the account's register where you will enter your paycheck deposit.
2. Make the appropriate entries in the Date, Num, and Payee fields.
3. Enter the amount of your paycheck as the transaction's amount.
4. Make any entry in the Memo field.
5. Select Splits to open the Splits window.
6. Enter the category, memo, and amount of the gross pay.
7. For each deduction, enter the category, memo, and amount. The amount will be entered as a negative number. The 401(k) contribution is recorded like any other deduction. The category for the 401(k) contribution is the account name created for tracking your 401(k) contribution. You know that you are done when the amount after Remainder is 0 and there are no lines that contain amounts but not categories. A Splits window that shows the different deductions and the categories they belong to appears in Figure 6-5.
8. Select OK to complete the Splits window.
9. Select Record to complete the transaction.

Chapter 6 *Investments*

FIGURE 6-5 Splits window showing the complete payroll deductions

Quicken records the paycheck deposit. When you show the investment account's register, you will see a transaction like this:

Date	Action	Security	Price	Shares	Amount	Clr	Share Bal
		Memo					
11/17/95	BuyX	401(k) plan	12.759	15.675	200 00		15 67
		Est. price as of 11/17/95	[Checking]		200.00		

Quicken uses the latest share price to estimate what the number of shares and price are for the amount contributed. You will need to update the shares and price when you find out exactly what they are for the date that the 401(k) contribution is made. The amount will not change.

If the 401(k) is set up as an asset account, you can still perform the same split payroll transaction. However, after completing the transaction, you may still need to adjust the amount.

Tech Tip: Make sure that your payroll transaction is memorized. That makes entering it subsequent times much easier.

My company contributes to my 401(k). Do I put that in my investment account?

You can if you want Quicken to track what it is worth. To record the contribution:

1. Display the Portfolio View window or the investment account's Register window where you want the 401(k) contributions recorded. If you are in the Portfolio View window, choose that investment account from the top drop-down list box.

2. Select Income from the Register window's button bar for the investment account. Enter the following information for the transaction:

   - Date   The date of the contribution
   - Miscellaneous   The amount of the contribution
   - Category for Misc.   A category name, such as Employer 401(k), created for tracking this amount

   You can leave the Security drop-down list box empty.

3. Select OK to record this transaction.

4. Select Buy from the investment account's Register window. Enter the following information for the transaction:

   - Date   The date of the contribution
   - Security   The name of the security that the 401(k) plan buys
   - Number of Shares   The number of shares of stock bought
   - Price   Per share price of the stock bought with the employer contribution

5. Select OK to record this transaction.

The miscellaneous income represents the employer's contribution used to buy the securities. You will still need to add the transaction for your own contribution. You can do it as part of your regular paycheck deposit. This is described in the previous question.

Chapter 6 *Investments*

Tech Tip: If you record your 401(k) as a mutual fund investment, add your employer's share with the SharesIn action.

Check Writing from an Investment Account

How do I write a check from my investment account?

Cash management accounts can combine the use of a broker and check writing features into one account. In Quicken, however, you have two separate accounts. One account is an investment account that handles all of your investment transactions. The other account is a checking account that handles the check writing feature of the cash management account.

Each time you write a check from the cash management account, add the transaction for the check in the Quicken checking account specifically created for this cash management account. You also want to transfer money from the investment account to this checking account. For example, if you sell stock to cover a check, you enter a SellX action to sell the stock and transfer the proceeds to the Quicken checking account. When the check is less than the proceeds of the transaction, enter the amount to transfer so that the difference remains in the investment account as a cash balance. After both transactions, the checking account for this cash management account remains at zero. Figure 6-6 shows the register entries in the cash management account's Quicken checking account and the one from the investment account transferring funds into this one. The checking account is named CMA - Checking and the investment account is named CMA - Invest.

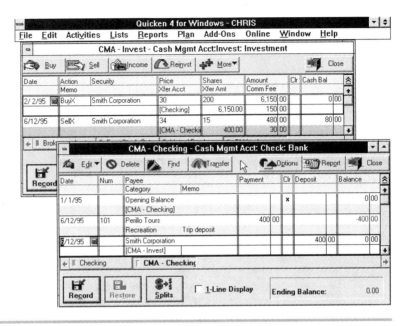

FIGURE 6-6   Register entries for writing a check from an investment account

Buyouts, Spin-offs, and Return of Capital

A company I invested in was just bought out by another company. How do I convert my stocks from the old company into the new?

When you replace one set of shares with another in a buyout, you can rename the security, then adjust the shares. To do this:

1. Choose Security from the Lists menu.
2. Highlight the old stock in the list and select Edit in the button bar.
3. Replace the old stock information with the new and select OK.
4. Select Close to put the Security List window away.

Chapter 6 *Investments*

5. Switch to the investment's Register window.
6. Select <u>M</u>ore in the button bar, then <u>S</u>tkSplit for the action you want.
7. Select the security from the Security drop-down list box. It will have the new stock's name.
8. Enter either the total number of new and old shares or a ratio in the <u>N</u>ew Shares and <u>O</u>ld Shares text boxes. As an example, if you own 1000 shares in ABC company and it converts to 2000 in the XYZ company, you can enter either **2000** and **1000** or **2** and **1**.
9. Enter the newer share price if you know it. Split stocks decrease share price because each share owns proportionally less. For example after a 2 for 1 stock split, each share is worth half of what one used to. It now takes two shares to have the same ownership percentage.
10. Select OK to make the change.

The result is that the investment account now shows the new stock name. The basis in these shares remains the same even if the number of shares is different.

I just received some shares in a spin-off. How do I enter these new shares?

A *spin-off* is when a company divides. It's the business world equivalent of a single cell splitting into two and the two resulting cells going in separate directions. In this cell-splitting analogy, part of the cell's original material remains with one cell and part goes off with the new one. With a business spin-off, you need to record how much of the original amount invested in the security belongs to the original company and how much belongs to the spin-off. The original company is returning part of what you invested in the form of stock from the newly formed company. So you must record the capital returned from the original company and the purchase of the new stock. These are the steps:

1. Switch to the investment account's Register window or the Portfolio View window.

2. Select More in the button bar and then RtrnCap to show the Return of Capital dialog box that records a RtrnCap action.

3. Enter the following information:
   - Date   Enter the date of the spin-off.
   - Security   Select the original company.
   - Amount   Type the portion of the original investment allocated to the newly formed company.

   The amount you enter is a fraction of what you had invested in the original company. This fraction is the proportion of the new stock's value to the total value. You look at the market value after the spin-off to decide how much of your original investment remains in the original company and how much belongs to the spin-off. Suppose you have 100 shares of the original company and they are worth $6,000 on the date of the spin-off. You originally invested $6,000 in this company. The spin-off gives you 50 shares in the new company that is worth $24 a share on the date of the spin-off for a total of $1,200. The stock in the spin-off is worth one-sixth of the total ($1,200/$7,200) so the amount of capital returned from the original stock that represents your value in the spin-off is $1,000 or $6,000 ÷ 6. Your completed dialog box might look like this:

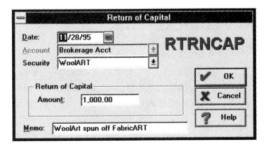

4. Select OK to finish the transaction.
5. Select Buy in the button bar.
6. Enter the following information:
   - Date   Enter the date of the spin-off. It is the same date that you entered in step 3.

Chapter 6 *Investments*

- Security   Enter the name of the subsidiary company. You will also need to add the information about this new security such as symbol, type, and goal.
- Number of Shares   Enter the number of shares you received in the new company.
- Total of Sale   Enter your investment in the new company. It is the same number that you entered for Amount in step 3.

Your completed dialog box might look like this:

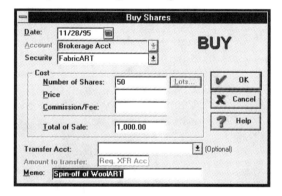

7. Select OK to finish the transaction. The two entries in the investment register might look like this:

Date	Action	Security	Price	Shares	Amount	Clr	Cash Bal
	Memo						
11/28/95	RtrnCap	WoolART			1,000 00		1,197 00
	WoolArt spun off FabricART						
11/28/95	Buy	FabricART	20	50	1,000 00		197 00
	Spin-off of WoolART						

At this point, the cash invested in the investment account remains the same, assuming that you recorded the new company in the same investment account as the original company. You may want to add the price history for this new stock. To do so:

1. Switch to the Portfolio View window.

2. Select Price Update from the View drop-down list.

3. Highlight the new company in the Portfolio View list.
4. Select Prices.
5. Add any day's price by selecting New, entering a date and price, and then selecting OK. Repeat this for each day's prices that you want to record.
6. Select Close to put the Price History window away.

I just received a return of capital from my investment. How do I add this to my investment account?

A return of capital returns part of what you originally put into an investment. This is different from dividends and capital gains distributions, which represent what your investment has earned. When you receive a return of capital, you are changing your basis in that security. Your basis is what you use to calculate gains or losses from sales. To record a return of capital:

1. Switch to the investment account's Register window or the Portfolio View window.
2. Select More in the button bar and then RtrnCap to show the Return of Capital dialog box that records a RtrnCap action.
3. Enter the following information:
   - Date   Enter the date of the transaction.
   - Security   Select the company.
   - Amount   Type the amount returned.
4. Select OK to finish the transaction.

At this point, the cash invested in that security has decreased and the amount of the return of capital appears in the Ending Cash Balance. If you received a check for this return of capital, you will subsequently record a XOut action that records receiving the proceeds and depositing them into a bank account.

Tech Terror: Your transaction may seem as though it didn't work correctly when you look at the market value. After performing a return of capital transaction, you may need to readjust the market value.

Stock Dividend

How do I record my stock dividend?

Stock dividends change the number of shares you own without changing your basis, or your investment in the security. Both stock dividends and stock splits increase the number of shares you own without changing your ownership percentage. Stock splits and stock dividends are recorded with the same StkSplit action. To enter a stock dividend:

1. Switch to the investment's Register window containing the transactions for the stock that received the stock dividend.
2. Select More in the button bar, then StkSplit to open a dialog box that records the StkSplit action.
3. Select the security that provided the stock dividend from the Security drop-down list box.
4. Enter either the total number of new and old shares or a ratio in the New Shares and Old Shares text boxes. As an example, if you own 1000 shares in ABC company and receive a 5% stock dividend, you can enter either **1050** and **1000** or **1.05** and **1**.
5. Enter the new share price in the Price After Split text box if you know the new share value.
6. Select OK to add the stock dividend.

Tech Acct: Usually the difference between a stock dividend and a stock split is the extent of the conversion. For example, a stock dividend might increase the number of shares by five percent while a stock split might double them.

How do I record stock dividends when I receive fractional shares?

As described previously, stock dividends increase the number of shares you own without changing how much you have invested in the security. The previous question explained how you enter stock dividends. If you receive fractional shares, when you enter the number of new shares and old shares the numbers you enter simply have numbers after the decimal point.

Tech Tip: If you don't remember how many shares of a stock you currently have before the stock dividend, go to the Portfolio View window and make sure that it shows the accounts where you have that stock to display the old number of shares.

Tax-deferred Transactions, Gifts, and Inheritances

How do I enter tax-deferred information into Quicken?

When you set up an account as a tax-deferred account, Quicken recognizes that the income from the account is also tax-deferred. This means that you can go ahead and record investment dividends and gains in the account and Quicken automatically acknowledges that the income is tax-deferred.

Tech Acct: When you sell tax-deferred mutual funds, you don't have to tell Quicken that you are redeeming some of your earlier tax-deferred income. When you received the tax-deferred income, it was used to buy more shares. By selling the shares bought with the income, you recognize that income.

How do I record gifts of stock?

Gifts of stock are different in two ways from stock that you buy. First, you add the shares using the ShrsIn action. You do not use Buy or BuyX since that would make Quicken expect that you are spending money, either in the investment account or in another. Second, the amount you invested is not the amount the security is worth on the day you received the gift. It is the amount the person who gave you the gift invested in it. For example, if your Aunt Clara gives you 50 shares of GM that she bought at $25 per share, your investment is $1,250, even if it is now worth $5,000. It is important that you know what she had invested in it when you sell it since the difference between what she bought it for and what you sell it for is gain that you recognize.

Chapter 6 *Investments*

1. Switch to the investment's Register window where you want to record receiving the stock.
2. Select More in the button bar, then ShrsIn to open a dialog box that records the ShrsIn action.
3. Select the security that you received from the Security drop-down list box.
4. Enter the number of shares in the Number of Shares text boxes.
5. Enter the donee's share price in the Price per Share text box.
6. Select OK to record receiving the stock.

How do I record inherited investments?

Inherited stock is added just like gifts of stock—with one advantage. You add inherited investments to your Quicken investment account using the ShrsIn action. However, your amount invested in this stock is not the same amount as the person you inherited from paid for it. Instead, the amount invested in the stock is the fair market value on the date of that person's death. This means that if your Aunt Clara died and you received 50 shares of GM from her estate, you record the $5,000 it was worth on the date of her death rather than the $25 per share that she originally paid for it. The steps you would perform are the same ones in the previous question.

Bonds and Treasury Bills

I just bought a bond that includes accrued interest. How do I enter this in my investment register?

To record buying this bond, you must record two transactions. The first one records buying the bond and the second records the accrued interest. Accrued interest is interest paid to the previous owner, which they earned while holding the bond. You are reimbursed for the accrued interest when you receive the next interest payment. The steps to record the bond are:

1. Select Buy on the button bar of an investment's Register window or the Portfolio View window.

2. Enter the following information in the Buy dialog box:
   - Date   Enter the date that you buy the bond.
   - Account   Enter the investment account that stores the records for the bonds, if this drop-down list box is available.
   - Security   Enter a name for the bond.
   - Number of Shares   Enter the face value of the bond divided by 100. When you buy a $1,000 bond, enter **10**.
   - Commission   Enter any commission paid.
   - Total of Sale   Enter the actual cost of the bond. Make sure to omit any accrued interest.
   - Transfer Acct   Enter the name of the account that provides the money to buy the bond.

3. Select OK. Quicken calculates a bond price that is approximately $100. When newly issued bonds have a higher interest rate than the bond you bought, your bond is worth less than $100 and when newly issued bonds have a lower interest rate than yours, your bond is worth more. However, you need to report the accrued interest so when you receive the next interest payment, you do not incorrectly record all the interest as earned while you held the bond.

4. Select More from the button bar and then select MiscExp to show the dialog box that records a MiscExp action.

5. Enter the following information in the Miscellaneous Expense dialog box:
   - Date   Enter the date you buy the bond.
   - Account   Enter the investment account that stores the records for the bonds if this drop-down list box is available.
   - Security   Enter the bond's security name.

Chapter 6 *Investments*

- **Amount** Enter the accrued interest that you paid on the bond.
- **Category** Select _Accrued Int from this drop-down list box.

6. Select OK.

When you receive the next interest payment, enter it as interest income. Quicken realizes that you only earned the difference between the interest payment and accrued interest.

Do I enter redeeming a bond the same way I enter selling it?

Redeeming bonds is a different transaction than selling the bond. When you sell the bond, enter a sell transaction just like selling stock. When you redeem the bond, you are returning it to its issuer and they return the bond's face value. Enter this transaction as a return of capital.

When I enter my interest income from my bonds, Quicken tells me, "Interest is excluded from transfer." How do I record receiving and depositing my interest checks?

Quicken does not let you directly transfer the interest income from the investment's Register window to your checking account. There are two ways you can record the interest from your investments. The first way is to go ahead and record the interest income in the investment account, then transfer the interest to the checking account. These transactions might look like this:

Date	Action / Memo	Security (Opt.)		Amount	Clr	Cash Bal
6/30/95	IntInc	Brody Bonds		300 00		497 00
6/30/95	XOut / Received Brody Bonds Interest		[Checking]	300 00		197 00

The second way is to enter depositing the interest check in your checking account's register. Quicken already has categories for interest income. However, since the interest payments are not added in the investment account's register, the Investment Income report does not show this interest.

Do I handle redeeming treasury bills the same way I handle selling stock?

No, redeeming treasury bills is different because part of what you receive is interest income. When you receive the proceeds, you will be told how much of that yield is interest. Record this as interest income. Then, record a Sale transaction for the difference between what you received and the interest. The transactions for buying and redeeming treasury bills might look like this:

Date	Action	Security	Price	Shares	Amount	Clr	Cash Bal
	Memo		Xfer Acct	Xfer Amt	Comm Fee		
4/6/92	BuyX	Treasury Bills	865.424	10	8,704 24		0 00
	Bought treasury bills		[Checking]	8,704.24	50 00		
10/10/95	IntInc	Treasury Bills			1,087 21		1,087 21
	Interest from treasury bill						
10/10/95	Sell	Treasury Bills	891.279	10	8,912 79		10,000 00
	Sold treasury bills						
10/10/95	XOut				10,000 00		0 00
	Cashed in T-Bills		[Checking]				

I just got a 1099-OID on zero-coupon bonds. What do I do with it?

The 1099-OID for zero-coupon bonds that you received represents the interest earned. Zero-coupon bonds are sold at a discount and redeemed at their full value. The difference between how much it is bought for and how much it is redeemed for is the interest earned. For example, you might buy a $1,000 zero-coupon bond due in 5 years for $750. Over 5 years, you earn $250 in interest. Even though the interest isn't paid out until you redeem the bond, you receive the 1099-OID that tells you the amount of income to recognize. The amount of this interest increases the value of the bond. To enter this in

Chapter 6 *Investments*

Quicken, you enter an Income transaction for the amount of the interest reported on the 1099-OID. At this point, you have a negative cash balance and you need to increase the value of the bond. Select More from the button bar and select RtrnCap to enter a RtrnCap action that returns the capital. Select the security for the zero-coupon bonds from the Security drop-down list box. For the amount, enter a negative amount of the interest. For example, if your 1099-OID reports $47.33 in interest, you type **-47.33** as the return of capital. When you select OK to complete this transaction, the value of the bond has risen by the amount of interest, and the cash balance returned to the amount is was before you entered the interest. These transactions might look like this:

Date	Action	Security	Price	Shares	Amount	Clr	Cash Bal
	Memo		Xfer Acct	Xfer Amt	Comm Fee		
2/2/95	BuyX	Nill & Growth	75	10	750 00		0 00
	Bought $1000 face value		[Checking]	750.00			
12/31/95	IntInc	Nill & Growth			47 33		47 33
	1995 interest earned						
12/31/95	RtrnCap	Nill & Growth			-47 33		0 00
	Increase value of N&G bonds						

How do I enter my Series EE bond?

Series EE bonds are bonds that are bought at less than their face value. Once their redemption date passes, you can redeem them at their face value plus the interest earned after the redemption date. You don't owe taxes until you redeem the bonds. When you buy the bond, record the purchase by buying the bond, and setting up a security for the bond if necessary. When you redeem the bond, enter a Sell transaction that sells the bond for the amount for which you bought it. Then enter an Income transaction for the difference between what you paid and what you received. These transactions might look like this:

Date	Action	Security	Price	Shares	Amount	Clr	Cash Bal
	Memo				Comm Fee		
8/19/93	BuyX	Series EE Bonds	87.330	10	873 30		0 00
	Bought Series EE Bonds		[Checking]	873.30			
5/2/96	Sell	Series EE Bonds	87.330	10	873 30		873 30
	Sold Series EE Bonds						
5/2/96	IntInc	Series EE Bonds			126 70		1,000 00

Limited Partnerships

How do I record what I receive from my limited partnership?

At the end of a year, a limited partnership issues a Schedule K-1 (Form 1065). This form identifies the information that you need to include in your tax return. This is information that you cannot enter correctly until you receive the Schedule K-1. Schedule K-1 (Form 1065) breaks out what you must record as ordinary income, capital gains and losses, and dividends. After you have this form, you can enter the items in the form into the investment account where you record your limited partnership transactions.

Tech Acct: Limited partnerships have several special rules. For example, when your limited partnership incurs a loss, you may not be able to deduct all of it. This is an area in which you will need tax guidance to correctly prepare your tax returns.

Capital Gains and Investment Values

I am preparing schedule D. How do I list my capital gains?

Quicken's Capital Gains report shows the short-term and long-term capital gains that you earned by buying and selling stock. To list your capital gains:

1. Choose Investment from the Reports menu, then choose Capital Gains.

2. Select Customize since you want to make sure that you include all investment accounts.

3. Select the Accounts option button to see the list of the accounts that the report will show.

4. Select the Investment button to include all investment accounts.

5. Select OK to create the report in a window.

6. Select Print in the button bar and then the Print button in this dialog box to print this report like the one shown in Figure 6-7. Many of these columns match the ones you need to complete on your Schedule D.

Tech Tip: Remember to look carefully over these transactions before completing your tax return. For example, wash sales (when you sell stock at a loss, then buy the same stock within 30 days) and sales to related parties require different tax treatment but Quicken does not necessarily identify these transactions for you. Also, when a sale includes some securities held short-term and some long-term, Quicken includes all of them in the long-term section.

How do I find out what my investments are currently worth?

The Portfolio View window shows what investments are worth when you supply the current market price. You can show this

```
                              Capital Gains Report
                              1/1/95 Through 12/6/95
12/6/95                                                                                Page 1
CHRIS-Selected Investment Acct

         Acct                Security        Shares   Bought    Sold    Sales Price  Cost Basis  Gain/Loss

                          SHORT TERM

   Brokerage Account       Fun-it Parks        50    5/9/95   9/13/95      190.00      265.00      -75.00
   Brokerage Account       FabricART           25   11/28/95  11/30/95   1,825.00      500.00    1,325.00
   Cash Mgmt Acct:Invest   Smith Corporation   15    2/2/95   6/12/95      480.00      461.25       18.75
   Employee Stock Option   POSE Company Opt    50    1/1/95   2/7/95    1,250.00    1,250.00        0.00

                          TOTAL SHORT TERM                               3,745.00    2,476.25    1,268.75

                          LONG TERM

   Brokerage Account       Low Grow Foods      75   5/20/91   3/6/95    9,275.00    1,150.00    8,125.00
   Brokerage Account       American Express    35   1/24/94   5/25/95   2,225.00      857.50    1,367.50

                          TOTAL LONG TERM                               11,500.00    2,007.50    9,492.50

                          OVERALL TOTAL                                 15,245.00    4,483.75   10,761.25
```

FIGURE 6-7 Capital Gains report

window by choosing Portfolio View from the Activities menu. You can move to the investments and enter the prices in the Market Price column as has been done in Figure 6-8. As you enter prices in the Market Price column, you are adding a price history to each security for the date at the top of the window. As you enter new prices, the "e" in the column between Market Price and Shares disappears so you know that the price is not an estimate. Quicken supplies the entries in the other columns.

It is also possible to update stock prices with Portfolio Price Update, which uses your modem to connect to an outside service to return the current security prices.

Brokerage Accounts

How do I indicate that I've transferred shares from one broker to another?

If you completely transfer your shares from one broker to the next, you can edit the account information to change the old broker information to the new. Then, continue using the same account with the updated information.

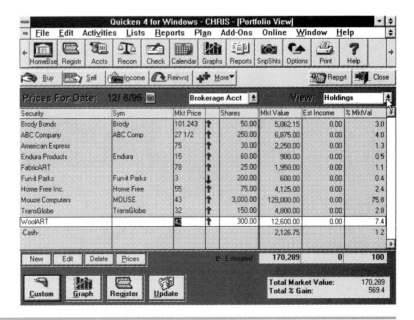

FIGURE 6-8 Portfolio View window showing new prices for your holdings

Chapter 6 *Investments*

Another way to handle this is to create a new investment account, then transfer the transactions from one account into another. If you transfer all the investments handled by the old broker to the new one, you can export the transactions from the old investment account to the new one. Chapter 2 has the steps for transferring transactions between accounts. If only a few transactions apply to the investments that you transferred to the new broker, you may be better off entering them yourself in the new account and then removing them in the old one.

I just added more money to my investment account at my brokerage. How do I add this amount to my Quicken investment account?

One of Quicken's actions is designed just for this purpose. You can select More from the button bar in an investment account's Register window or the Portfolio View window and then select XIn to record this action. In the Transfer Cash In dialog box, enter the amount and the account providing these funds. When you select More from the Portfolio View window, you can also select the investment account into which these funds go. The following dialog box shows some entries already completed. When you select OK, Quicken adds a transaction to the investment account for receiving the funds and one to the bank account for providing them.

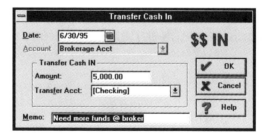

How do I record what I add and take out of my brokerage account?

Taking money out of a brokerage account and putting money in are recorded as transfers. Investments have a XIn and XOut action for recording these transfers. You can select More in the button bar, then XIn or XOut. From the next dialog box, you can enter the date, investment account, amount, which account the money comes from, and a memo. Selecting OK completes the transfer.

My brokerage statement lists interest that my money earned after I sold stocks. How do I record this interest?

After you sell securities, you can leave the money with your broker if you plan to buy other securities. Leaving the money with the broker makes buying subsequent securities easier since the money is readily available for your next purchase. Brokers often pay interest on this money. This interest is just like interest that you earn from the investments in that brokerage account. In the Register window for the account that you set up for that brokerage account, select Income from the button bar. You can enter the income, then select OK to add this interest. You didn't assign a particular security so the interest is not included in any of the security's returns.

Different Security Prices

Does Quicken track when I buy securities at different prices?

When you buy stock more than once, you will want to keep track of how much you paid for each group of shares. Each purchase of shares is called a *lot*. Keeping the lots separate lets you control how much gain you recognize when you sell some of your shares because you can choose which shares you sell. For example, suppose on three separate occasions, you buy 50 shares of the same type of stock at $25, $50, and $75 dollars a share respectively. When you sell 50 shares at $100 per share, you can have a $75 per share gain if you sell the first batch, $50 per share gain if you sell the second batch, or $25 per share gain if you sell the third batch.

Chapter 6 *Investments*

In prior versions of Quicken, you kept each lot separate by changing the security name for each purchase. The separate names allowed Quicken to keep track of the different purchases, yet updating them was inconvenient. With the latest version of Quicken, you can use the same name for the separate purchases. When you sell part of your holdings in the stock, you have the opportunity to select which shares you will sell. To see this feature in action, follow these steps:

1. Select Sell from the Portfolio View window or investment account's Register window to open the Sell Shares dialog box.
2. Enter the sales date, investment account, and stock name.
3. Enter the total number of shares you are selling.
4. Select the Lots button. Now you see a dialog box like the one shown here. You can see how the lots are separated to show their purchase date, purchase price, and number of shares. You can select which lots the shares that you are selling come from.

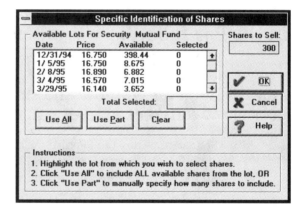

5. Move to each lot that you want to include in the ones you are selling and select Use All or Use Part. If you select Use Part, you will need to type how many shares to sell from that lot and then select OK. When you want to use as much of a lot as necessary to select the remaining shares, select Use All and Quicken figures out the part of the lot that you are selling.
6. Select OK when you finish selecting the shares you are selling.

7. Continue with other entries in the Sell Shares dialog box.
8. Select OK to complete the transaction for selling shares.

If you don't select specific lots, Quicken makes an FIFO assumption. FIFO (first in, first out) assumes that the oldest stock is what you are selling.

Tech Tip: You can see a report of the lots you have for a security. In the Portfolio View window, double-click any stock listed. Quicken creates a Security report that lists the transactions made with the selected securities. From this report, you can see the lots that you have bought and sold.

Tech Acct: The IRS has rules about recognizing long-term and short-term capital gains. The cut-off point for long-term versus short-term in most instances is one year. By selling specific lots, you can choose whether your gain or loss is long-term or short, based on how long you have held the stock you choose to sell.

Working in the Portfolio View Window

Why do the Register window and the Portfolio View window show different market values?

The market value in the Register window and Portfolio View window can differ for two reasons. One has to do with the day that the Portfolio View window shows. The Portfolio View window shows the security values as of a specific date. If you change the date to one before the current date, Quicken may be showing market values using older prices.

Another possibility is that you have price information for a date after today's date for one of your securities. The Register window shows the calculated market value in the Register window using the latest price information. Go through your securities in the Portfolio View window and select Prices. When you see those with a date after today's date, highlight them on the list and select Delete.

Chapter 6 *Investments*

Can I only show one investment account in the Portfolio View window?

The Portfolio View window can show your holdings in specific investment accounts. All you have to do is select the investment account from the Account drop-down list box that is to the right of the Date box. If you want to show more than one account, choose Selected Accounts from this drop-down list box. Quicken shows the Portfolio View Settings dialog box. Here you can select which accounts appear in the Portfolio View window. Select OK and the window only shows the selected accounts. For example, the Portfolio View window in Figure 6-8 shows only the Brokerage Acct investment account holdings.

Tech Tip: When you limit which investment accounts appear in the Portfolio View window, you may also want to hide securities that are not included in that investment account. If you do not, Quicken shows all the securities you have set up, including ones that you use in other accounts and ones that you no longer own. Only the securities that have shares in the selected account have entries in the Shares column and in the last three columns.

Can I combine different views in the Portfolio View window to show what I have invested, how much it's worth, and its percentage of my holdings?

The last three columns of the Portfolio View window can show any three calculations including your investment, its market value, and its percentage of your holdings. You can customize two views that Quicken initially calls Custom 1 and Custom 2 to set what these three columns contain. To customize these views:

1. Choose <u>C</u>ustom at the bottom of the Portfolio View window.
2. Choose the Custom Views tab.
3. Under Set Up Custom 1 View, choose what you want to appear in the three columns and enter a name for this view in the <u>V</u>iew Name text box.
4. Under Set Up Custom 2 View, choose what you want to appear in the three columns and enter a name for this

view in the View Name text box. You only need to do this if you want to change the Custom 2 view as well as the Custom 1 view.

5. Select OK.

Figure 6-9 shows a My Investments view as one of the custom views. It shows $ Invested in the first column, Mkt Value in the second, and % MktVal in the third.

Why does the Portfolio View window still show stock I don't own?

The Portfolio View window initially shows all securities shown in the Security List window. You can change this window to only show stock that you currently own. Then, as you sell your

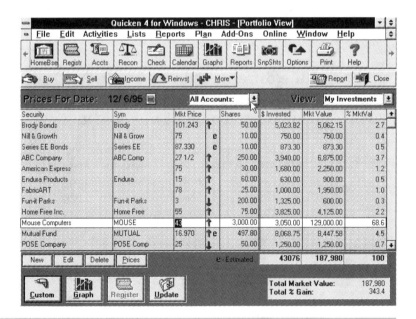

FIGURE 6-9 Portfolio View window customized to show a different final 3 columns

holdings in a security, it no longer appears in the Portfolio View window. To make this change:

1. Show the Portfolio View window.
2. Select Custom and then the Securities tab.
3. Select the Hide Securities You Do Not Own check box.
4. Check that the securities that you want to see only when you own them have Default listed under Status. You can change any security to this by highlighting it and selecting the Default button.
5. Select OK.

Investment Graphs

Why does my investment graph show a different IRR than my Performance report?

IRR represents Internal Rate of Return, which calculates the average annual return. Its rate is the same rate that you would have to earn on a bank account to make the same return as the investment has.

The different IRRs are caused by the different dates in the graph versus the report. Graphs, like the one in Figure 6-10, operate with entire months such as 1/95 to 12/95.

This graph uses the data from the first day of the first month to the last day of the second. Reports can operate on days so you can have a similar period, such as 1/1/95 to 12/5/95, which is close but not the same. The difference in the IRRs is caused by the date range not being identical. When you adjust the dates in the report, the results are the same.

My investment graph is missing one of my securities. How do I get the security to show?

When you click the Graphs iconbar button, select the Investment Graph option button, and select Create, Quicken

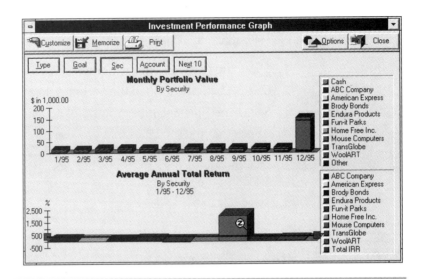

FIGURE 6-10   Investment graph showing IRR for several securities

creates an Investment graph that displays the portfolio value and return on your investments. You can add a missing security to this graph. To make this change:

1. Choose Customize from the button bar.
2. Select Securities from the Customize Graph dialog box.
3. Click the security you want added to the graph so that it has a check mark.
4. Select OK twice to re-create the graph.

If this doesn't fix it, it is because one of your investment accounts does not appear in the graph. Add the account by following these same steps, except that you should select Accounts in step 2 and the account to add in step 3.

Tech Tip: Remember that you can change how the graph presents its information. Clicking the Type, Goal, Sec, or Account button changes to show the security information divided by security type, investment goal, security, or account.

Scheduled Investment Transactions

 Can I create a scheduled transaction for my investments?

You cannot create scheduled transactions for investments. However, you can memorize investment transactions then create a scheduled transaction group that includes these transactions. This works even when the scheduled transaction group only has one transaction. These steps are:

1. Memorize the investment transactions to add to the scheduled group. You memorize investment transactions just like other transactions—by moving to the transaction and choosing Memorize Transaction from the Edit menu.

2. Choose Scheduled Transaction from the Lists menu to show the Scheduled Transaction List window.

3. Select New in the button bar, then Group since you are creating a scheduled transaction group.

4. Select the Investment option button as the type of transaction and the investment account from the Account drop-down list box.

5. Make the normal entries in Next, Group Name, Frequency, Number of Payments, Register entry, and Days in advance boxes just as you would for other scheduled transaction groups.

6. Select OK.

7. Mark transactions to include in the Assign Invest Transactions to Group window.

8. Select Done when you are finished.

At this point, your transaction is scheduled. You will not see it listed in the Financial Calendar. However, when the day for the scheduled investment transaction arises, the Scheduled Transactions Due dialog box, which prompts for the scheduled transactions to record, shows these scheduled transactions.

Storing Prices and Portfolio Price Update

 I'd like the historical prices of some stocks that I'm interested in. Can I put these into Quicken?

You can add stock prices yourself or use an external service to provide these numbers. To enter any price yourself:

1. Switch to the Portfolio View window for your investments. You can choose Portfolio View from the Activities menu, press CTRL+U, or click the Port View button on the iconbar or in an investment's Register window.

2. Highlight the security to which you want to add more price information and select Prices.

3. Select New, enter a date and price, then select OK. Repeat this step for the different days and prices.

4. Select Close to put the Price History window away for the selected security.

 **Tech Tip:** If you have access to CompuServe, you can use it to get historical price information. The advantage of downloading price information from CompuServe is that you can get a lot of prices and dates without entering them yourself. However, downloading the data does not put it into a format that Quicken can use. You can take the downloaded information and create a CSV format file with Excel that Quicken can import. Then you can bring the file into Quicken by choosing Import Prices on the File menu. The Quicken Deluxe edition can retrieve stock prices from CompuServe through the Quicken Quotes program that comes with Quicken Deluxe.

 When can I use the Portfolio Price Update?

Once you sign up for the Portfolio Price Update, you can retrieve stock prices any time of the day, any day of the week.

Chapter 6 *Investments*

How much do I have to pay to use Portfolio Price Update?

Portfolio Price Update charges a monthly fee plus additional fees depending on usage. Since the fees can change, contact Intuit Online Services at (800) 245-2164 for the most recent rates.

How up-to-date are prices in the Price Portfolio Update?

It depends on which type of securities you have. Stocks are delayed by at least 15 minutes. The delay occurs because it takes some time to transfer the information to the Price Portfolio Update. When you update stock prices after the market closes, you get the closing price for that security. Mutual funds, however, are updated only once a day at 5:30 p.m. EST. Updating prices before this time gives you the previous day's closing price.

Can the Price Portfolio Update provide stock indexes such as the Dow Jones?

Price Portfolio Update can provide industrial averages if you include the ticker symbols for them in your portfolio. The following list shows some industrial averages and their ticker symbols.

Stock Index	Ticker Symbol
Dow Jones Industrial Average	^DJI
Dow Jones Transportation Average	^DJT
Dow Jones Utilities Average	^DJU
S&P 500 Composite Index	^SPC

Business

Quicken is built more for personal finances than business records, but if your business doesn't have complex accounting needs, Quicken might be all you need. Quicken has many of the necessary categories already set up to record your business's income and expenses. In this chapter, you will find questions and answers concerning business topics that you are unlikely to encounter when you use Quicken only for personal finances. You'll find that, with a business, you will have a great need for the reports that Quicken can create. For example, Quicken's Payroll reports can help prepare the paperwork for a business with employees. Besides using reports more, business owners often make accounting decisions that an individual doing only personal finances seldom considers. The Frustration Busters box describes one accounting decision that primarily applies to businesses—when to record your income and expenses.

FRUSTRATION BUSTERS!

Cash and accrual basis accounting use different systems of timing when you record financial transactions. As a quick example, suppose you buy office supplies on December 27, 1995 and pay the bill for them on January 10, 1996. Are the supplies an expense of 1995 or 1996? When you use the *accrual system*, you recognize the expense in 1995—when you incurred the expense or earned the income. When you use the *cash basis system*, you recognize the expense in 1996—when you pay the expense or receive the income. Both methods record the same information, but at different times. A third method for reporting business revenues and expenses is the *modified-cash-basis approach*. This method primarily follows the cash basis system, but modifies it to report depreciation.

Most small businesses use the cash basis system because it corresponds to their tax-reporting needs, it is easier, and because the financial reports prepared match the cash-related activities of the business.

The decision can be yours or the IRS's. If your business is organized as a corporation, you must use the accrual method. If inventories are part of your business, you must use the accrual method for revenues and purchases. Your creditors may also have a say in how you set up your accounting system.

One special note: If you use a cash basis system and you make business purchases with your credit card, the IRS expects you to recognize the expense on the date you charged the goods, not the date you paid your credit card bill.

Setting Up Quicken for Business

 Do I need to change Quicken's categories in order to use Quicken for my business?

Quicken will already have many of the categories that you will need for your business if you included the business categories when you created the data file. If the standard business categories are missing from your file, follow these steps to incorporate them:

1. Choose Import from the File menu.
2. Type **Business** in the QIF File to Import text box.
3. Select the Category List check box. It doesn't matter if the other check boxes are selected or cleared.
4. Select OK to import the standard business categories into your file.

Since Quicken cannot provide every category for every business, you may still need to add categories that are unique to your business or remove ones that you will never use. If you already have a chart of accounts, you can modify Quicken to make the category names match it exactly.

Tech Tip: If you will use the Tax Planner or a Tax Schedule report, make sure that the categories that your business will use are selected as tax-related and have the appropriate tax form entry selected.

How do I create a business budget that is separate from my personal budget?

Quicken only stores one budget at a time. So you cannot have one budget for business finances and a second for personal use. The only way to get around this limitation is by using Quicken's forecasting features to create more than one budget, as described in Chapter 8. The only other solution is to create Personal and Business supercategories. Then, you can separate your budget categories into the Personal and Business supercategories. Once you set up and save your budget like this, you can modify the Budget report to specifically include only the Business supercategory with these steps:

1. Select C̲ustomize from the Budget report window.
2. Select the C̲ategories/Classes option button.
3. Select the Su̲percategories option button.
4. Click the supercategories, such as Personal, that you do not want in the budget report, in order to remove the check marks next to these supercategories.
5. Select OK so that the budget only shows the selected supercategories.

Using Quicken for Business Versus Personal Finances

Can I use the same Quicken file for both business and personal use?

Yes, you can use the same Quicken data file to record both personal and business finances. Whether you have one file or two, make sure that you have separate checking accounts. You want a personal checking account for personal expenses and a business one for business expenses. Quicken does not have any qualms about you intermixing your finances, but the IRS does.

Also, set up different categories for your income and expense items. For instance, make sure to record business utilities in a separate category or subcategory than the one for your personal utility use. Then, you can assign tax form entries on Schedule C to the business utility categories. Quicken will include them in Tax Summary and Tax Schedule reports and, also, display them in the Business Income section of the Tax Planner. If you do not have categories set up specifically for business, another option is to use classes to separate business and personal transactions such as adding /B after the business transactions. Classes provide a different way to organize transactions so you can use them to separate your business transactions from your personal ones. The disadvantage of using classes is that pulling the numbers into the Tax Planner and separating them in the Tax Summary and Tax Schedule reports is not as easy. When you use classes, you have to manually calculate what does or does not belong in the Tax Planner, and then enter the adjusted numbers.

Tech Tip: If the business is a corporation and you are not the sole shareholder, create separate files for your personal finances and those of the business. The finances of a corporation and a shareholder should be kept separate, and it is easier to do so when they are in different files.

How do I record expenses that are part personal and part business?

If you record your personal and business transactions in the same Quicken data file, you will record the expenses as usual. You should have separate business categories or at least a class that you use to indicate which transactions are business ones. Use these business categories or classes to separate the parts of the transaction that are for personal use and for business use. The following Splits window shows a transaction where part is for business and part is personal.

Quicken 4 for Windows Answers: *Certified Tech Support*

Tech Acct: If you intermingle your business and personal funds, substantiating all of your business expenses is more difficult if you are audited.

Payroll

What kind of categories and accounts do I need for my payroll?

When you record payroll in Quicken, you want to create specific categories and accounts. The categories record what you pay for wages and for payroll taxes. You want an overall Payroll category with several subcategories for the separate payroll items. You can take advantage of assigning tax forms to categories to help assemble your tax reports. You will want to create the following categories, using the suggested tax form entries.

Category	Tax Form	What It Represents
Comp FICA	Schedule C:Taxes and licenses	What your business pays for FICA taxes (Social Security)
Comp FUTA	Schedule C:Taxes and licenses	What your business pays for federal unemployment taxes
Comp MCARE	Schedule C:Taxes and licenses	What your business pays for Medicare taxes
Comp SUI	Schedule C:Taxes and licenses	What your business pays for state unemployment taxes
Payroll	Schedule C:Wages paid	The salaries and wages paid to employees
Payroll:Gross	Schedule C:Wages paid	The gross amount paid to employees

You also want liability accounts that track what you owe for the various withholdings and taxes.

You will want the following liability accounts:

Account	Description
Payroll-FICA	FICA taxes paid by both the employee and the employer
Payroll-FUTA	Federal unemployment taxes paid by the employer
Payroll-FWH	Federal income taxes withheld from employees' earnings
Payroll-MCARE	Medicare taxes paid by both the employee and the employer
Payroll-SUI	State unemployment taxes paid by employer
Payroll-SWH	State income taxes withheld from employees' earnings

You can potentially combine some of your liabilities in the same account, such as creating a Payroll Taxes liability account for all payroll liabilities. However, creating separate liability accounts for the different payroll liabilities makes keeping track of the different payroll withholdings and taxes easier. In the payroll questions that follow, the answers use these account names and categories.

How do I record employee wages in Quicken?

The best way to record paying employees is to create the categories and accounts suggested by the answer to the previous question. Once you have these accounts and categories, you can follow the steps described in the answer to the next question to enter payroll transactions.

How do I record employee withholdings?

As an employer, you need to do more than write a paycheck to keep your payroll records up-to-date. You have to calculate taxes that you withhold from your employee's wages and calculate employer taxes. You can enter many of the taxes and withholdings in the transaction that records each paycheck. You can see the steps that you perform for your employees by following an example. This example uses the payroll categories and accounts suggested earlier. This example also assumes the following information:

- Your employee, Robin Meyers, is paid a salary of $800 twice a month.
- You withhold $88.00 for federal taxes and $40.37 for state taxes from each paycheck. These numbers come from the tables that the IRS and state tax department provide. (While this example skips local taxes or other types of withholdings, they would follow the same pattern. They have their own categories and accounts in addition to the ones you use for federal and state taxes.)
- FICA of $49.60 is withheld from each paycheck. FICA was 6.2% of wages up to $61,200 for 1994. Additionally, you withhold $11.60 from each paycheck for Medicare taxes, which are 1.45% of wages. Besides withholding these amounts from the employee's wages, you, as the employer, are also responsible for matching FICA taxes of $49.60 and Medicare taxes of $11.60.

With this information, you are ready to enter the payroll. Here are the steps you perform to record payroll for January 15, 1996:

1. Move to the next blank transaction in the account register where you write the payroll check.
2. Type **1/15/96** in the Date field.
3. Select Next Chk# for the Num field.
4. Type **Robin Meyers** in the Payee field since you are entering Robin Meyer's paycheck.
5. Type **000-00-0001** in the Memo field for Robin's social security number. Entering it in this field can help you organize Payroll reports by employee.
6. Select Splits to open the Splits window. In this window you will enter the total pay, withholdings, and payroll taxes.

7. Enter the following information:

Category	Memo	Amount
Payroll:Gross	Gross Earnings	800.00
[Payroll-FWH]	Federal Withholding	-88.00
[Payroll-SWH]	State Withholding	-40.37
[Payroll-FICA]	FICA Withholding	-49.60
[Payroll-MCARE]	Medicare Withholding	-11.60
Payroll:Comp FICA	Payroll Taxes-FICA	49.60
Payroll:Comp MCARE	Payroll Taxes-MCARE	11.60
[Payroll-FICA]	FICA Matching Withheld	-49.60
[Payroll-MCARE]	Medicare Matching Withheld	-11.60

The complete entries match the ones in Figure 7-1. The first five lines record the gross earnings and the amounts withheld. The last four lines record matching employer payroll expenses. QuickFill will make entering the categories easier but since some of the entries in the Category column are similar, make sure that you select the correct account or category.

For some of the categories, you are entering liability accounts since the balances represent money you owe. These are amounts that you withhold from the employee or are taxes that you owe. Enter the amounts for the liability accounts as negative numbers. The gross pay and the taxes that you record paying are positive numbers.

8. Select OK to set the transaction's total and close the window.

9. Select Payment since the $610.43 is a payment and select OK.

10. Select Record to record the transaction. The transaction looks like this:

Date	Num	Payee			Payment	Clr	Deposit	Balance
		Category	Memo					
1/15/96	1487	Robin Meyers			610 43			1,275 51
		--Splits--	✓✗ 000-00-0001					

Quicken 4 for Windows Answers: Certified Tech Support

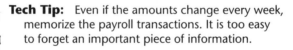

FIGURE 7-1 The Splits window, showing the complete payroll breakdown

You can see how all the payroll deductions are entered in the Splits window. The Splits window can handle up to 30 items. Besides recording the pay and all of its withholdings, you as an employer must record payroll taxes, such as federal and state unemployment taxes. The next question describes the steps to perform.

Tech Tip: Even if the amounts change every week, memorize the payroll transactions. It is too easy to forget an important piece of information.

How do I enter the separate amounts for payroll taxes?

Besides FICA and Medicare, employers pay other taxes, including unemployment taxes and workman's compensation. Paying FICA and Medicare taxes are most easily done when you enter paychecks, as described in the previous question. You will want to record other employment taxes separately. For example, unemployment taxes apply to a different cap (maximum salary amount) than FICA.

Quicken's Payroll reports can monitor the income earned by your employees so that it knows when an employee has earned enough that you no longer need pay these taxes for the rest of the year.

Also, these taxes are often calculated and paid less frequently since you might calculate them every quarter instead of every pay period. As an example, suppose that on April 5, 1996, you calculate the unemployment taxes on Robin Meyer's wages for the first quarter of 1996. During this period Robin earned $4,800, which is less than the cap for unemployment taxes. For this employee, your business owes $38.40 of federal and $259.20 of state unemployment taxes. These numbers come from the .8% federal unemployment and the 5.4% state unemployment tax rates. To enter this transaction:

1. Type **4/5/96** in the Date field.
2. Enter the check number in the Num field entry.
3. Type **State Unemployment Bureau** in the Payee field.
4. Type **259.20** in the Payment field.
5. Select Payroll:Comp SUI in the Category field.
6. Type **State Unemployment Taxes** in the Memo field.
7. Select Record.
8. Enter the next check number in the Num field entry.
9. Type **Internal Revenue Service** in the Payee field since they collect federal unemployment taxes.
10. Type **38.40** in the Payment field.
11. Select Payroll:Comp FUTA in the Category field.
12. Type **Federal Unemployment Taxes** in the Memo field.
13. Select Record. The two transactions look like this:

Date	Num	Payee		Payment	Clr	Deposit	Balance
		Category	Memo				
4/5/96	1603	State Unemployment Bureau		259 20			2,964 16
		Payroll:Comp SUI	State Unemployment Taxes				
4/5/96	1604	Internal Revenue Service		38 40			2,925 76
		Payroll:Comp FUTA	Federal Unemployment Tax				

When you calculate your unemployment taxes, you will need to learn the rules for your state. States have different rules about how the taxes are paid, including the rates and the income caps.

States also have their individual rules about workman's compensation and any other taxes that they levy.

How do I generate the numbers that I need for my employees' W-2s?

Create a Payroll report to provide these entries. You create this report by choosing Business from the Reports menu, then choosing Payroll. When you select OK, Quicken creates a report that separates the payroll entries by payee. Figure 7-2 shows a Payroll report that includes the information for Robin Meyers. You can see how these same numbers appear on the W-2 since this payroll information created the W-2 shown in Figure 5-6 of the Taxes chapter.

Tech Terror: The Payroll report expects that your payroll categories start with the word "Payroll." If you name your categories something else, you need to customize the report to select the payroll categories that Quicken does not include.

```
                                    Payroll Report
                               1/1/96 Through 12/31/96
12/31/96                                                                              Page 1
BUSINESS-All Accounts
                                                                           OVERALL
         Category Description    Internal Revenue Ser...   Robin Meyers   State Unemployment ...   TOTAL

         INCOME/EXPENSE
           EXPENSES
             Payroll:
               Comp FICA              0.00           1,190.40        0.00       1,190.40
               Comp FUTA             56.00               0.00        0.00          56.00
               Comp MCARE             0.00             278.40        0.00         278.40
               Comp SUI               0.00               0.00      486.00         486.00
               Gross                  0.00          19,200.00        0.00      19,200.00

             Total Payroll           56.00          20,668.80      486.00      21,210.80

           TOTAL EXPENSES            56.00          20,668.80      486.00      21,210.80

         TOTAL INCOME/EXPENSE       -56.00         -20,668.80     -486.00     -21,210.80

         TRANSFERS
           FROM Federal tax withheld  0.00           2,112.00        0.00       2,112.00
           FROM FICA taxes collected  0.00           2,380.80        0.00       2,380.80
           FROM Medicare taxes        0.00             556.80        0.00         556.80
           FROM State taxes withheld  0.00             968.88        0.00         968.88

         TOTAL TRANSFERS              0.00           6,018.48        0.00       6,018.48

         OVERALL TOTAL              -56.00         -14,650.32     -486.00     -15,192.32
```

FIGURE 7-2 Payroll report

How do I get the numbers from Quicken for payroll taxes I have withheld?

The Payroll report in Figure 7-2 shows the payroll taxes withheld from your employees. The FROM Payroll-FICA entry is the social security tax paid and withheld by you and your employees. The FROM Payroll-MCARE works the same way for Medicare taxes. The FROM Payroll-FWH is the federal tax withheld. The FROM Payroll-SWH is the state tax withheld.

Can Quicken provide the numbers that I need to complete Form 940 and Form 941?

Form 940 reports the liabilities owed and deposits made for federal unemployment tax. Form 941 calculates the payroll taxes paid by your company and withheld from your employees. The Payroll report like the one in Figure 7-2 includes the information you need for Form 940 and Form 941.

How do I get Quicken to remind me when payroll taxes are due?

You can add a reminder to the Financial Calendar and Quicken will show the reminder. To create this reminder:

1. Choose Financial Calendar from the Activities menu or click the Calendar iconbar to show the Financial Calendar window.
2. Move to the date on the Financial Calendar when you want the reminder.
3. Select Note in the button bar.
4. Type the text that you want for the reminder.
5. Select a color from the Color drop-down list box.
6. Select Save. The day now includes a small box to indicate that it has a note.

Each day can have only one note. To see the note, double-click the note's box.

Sales Tax

How do I track the sales tax that I have collected?

When you record a sale, record it less the sales tax you collected, then assign the sales tax collected to the liability account created for sales tax. For example, when you deposit the day's sales, the transaction and its Splits window might look like this:

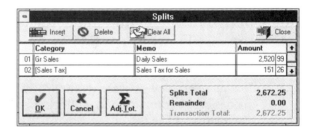

Sales Tax is a liability account that records all the sales tax you have collected. Each day you make your deposit, you increase what you owe for sales tax. You can create reports from this liability account recording what you have collected and paid. When you write a check to pay the sales tax bill, select the Sales Tax liability account and any sales tax you still owe will be decreased by the amount of the check.

Tech Tip: Add a scheduled transaction for paying the sales tax so Quicken will remind you when it is due. You can enter **0** as the amount of the transaction since you don't know how much sales tax you will owe. When you pay the bill, you can adjust the payment amount.

Job Costing

Can I do job order costing in Quicken?

Quicken's class feature lets you divide the transactions that you assign to categories in different ways. You can use this feature to assign different classes to different projects. Create separate classes for each job or project that you want tracked. Then, as you enter income and expense transactions, you can assign them to different classes according to the jobs or projects. The following Splits window, in which a supplies bill is paid, shows how the different items are assigned different classes according to the project that the supplies are for.

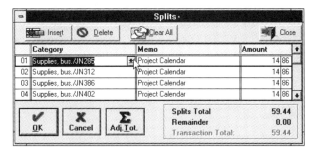

Tech Tip: To create a report that features a project or job, customize the report. Select the Matching option button, then select the class for that project or job from the Class Contains drop-down list box.

How can I divide my expenses by store or department?

The previous question about job order costing describes how you can create classes to track different projects. You can also use classes to divide expenses and income according to store, department, or any other criteria.

How can I divide rental income and expenses by different properties?

The question in this chapter about job order costing describes how you can create classes to track different projects. You can also use classes to divide expenses and income according to properties. For instance, if you have four rental properties, any income or expense item is assigned to one of the four classes that represent each property. Then you can create a Job/Project report by choosing **B**usiness from the **R**eports menu, then Job/Project. Figure 7-3 shows a Job/Project report. You can use this report to complete your Schedule E to report rental income.

Tech Tip: Other reports can have columns for each class. To change a report to divide items according to the class, choose C**u**stomize from the report's button bar and select Class from the Col**u**mn drop-down list box. When you select OK, the report includes separate columns for each class, just like the example in Figure 7-3.

Job/Project Report
1/1/95 Through 12/16/95

12/16/95
RENTING-All Accounts

Category Description	103 N. Kendall	425 Western	4392 Curtis	942 State St.	OVERALL TOTAL
INCOME/EXPENSE					
INCOME					
Rent Income	5,040.00	7,200.00	4,620.00	5,040.00	21,900.00
TOTAL INCOME	5,040.00	7,200.00	4,620.00	5,040.00	21,900.00
EXPENSES					
Business Tax	1,392.84	1,932.83	1,285.28	1,273.41	5,884.36
Insurance	279.85	468.22	372.15	437.28	1,557.50
Int Exp	2,855.00	4,236.83	3,163.88	3,793.97	14,049.68
L&P Fees	106.18	106.18	106.18	106.46	425.00
Lawn Care	220.00	220.00	220.00	220.00	880.00
Repairs	0.00	148.82	738.28	204.85	1,091.95
TOTAL EXPENSES	4,853.87	7,112.88	5,885.77	6,035.97	23,888.49
TOTAL INCOME/EXPENSE	186.13	87.12	-1,265.77	-995.97	-1,988.49
TRANSFERS					
TO 103 N. Kendall	-862.60	0.00	0.00	0.00	-862.60
TO 425 Western	0.00	-1,121.77	0.00	0.00	-1,121.77
TO 4392 Curtis	0.00	0.00	-1,468.24	0.00	-1,468.24
TO 942 State St.	0.00	0.00	0.00	-1,131.67	-1,131.67
FROM Checking	862.60	1,121.77	1,468.24	1,131.67	4,584.28
TOTAL TRANSFERS	0.00	0.00	0.00	0.00	0.00
OVERALL TOTAL	186.13	87.12	-1,265.77	-995.97	-1,988.49

FIGURE 7-3 Job/Project report separating income and expenses by class

Depreciation

 How do I record depreciation in Quicken?

Quicken cannot calculate depreciation but it can record it. After you calculate the depreciation, you can enter it by following these steps:

1. Switch to the register where you have recorded the assets.
2. Enter the date for recording the depreciation.
3. Type a payee name, such as **1995 Depreciation Expense**.
4. Enter the depreciation amount in the Decrease column.
5. Select the category where you want the depreciation expense recorded. You may want to create a new category for this expense. You can assign it to the Schedule C:Other business expense tax form.
6. Select Re**c**ord. The completed transaction might look like this:

Date	Ref	Payee		Decrease	Clr	Increase	Balance
		Category	Memo				
12/16/94		Opening Balance				50,000 00	50,000 00
		[Equipment]					
12/31/95		1995 Depreciation Expense		5,000 00			45,000 00
		Depreciation					

Tech Acct: The IRS has many rules about how much depreciation you can record. For instance, the number of years over which you depreciate an asset is determined by the IRS, not by how long you plan to use it. You will need to review these rules to make sure that you depreciate the correct amount.

How do I record Section 179 deductions?

Section 179 is a special deduction available to businesses. Section 179 lets you deduct up to $17,500 of business equipment purchases in the year of purchase rather than depreciated over the asset's life. IRS Publication 534 has more information on this deduction. Recording this deduction is just like recording depreciation, described in the question, "How do I record depreciation in Quicken?" The only difference is the Payee field entry, which would contain **Section 179 Deduction**.

Owner Withdrawals and Keogh Contributions

How do I record what I take out of my business for my personal use?

Withdrawals that the owners make from a business reduce the owners' investment in their business. As such, it is neither income nor an expense. When the same Quicken file holds your personal and business financial records, the withdrawal is handled as a transfer between your business and personal checking accounts. You can easily enter the transaction following these steps:

1. Go to the account register in which you are writing the check for the withdrawal.
2. Move to the next empty transaction at the end of the account register.
3. Enter date of the withdrawal in the Date field.
4. Type your name in the Payee field.
5. Type the amount of the withdrawal in the Payment field.
6. Type **Transfer - Withdraw** in the Memo field.
7. Select your personal checking account for the Category field.
8. Select Re*c*ord to record the transaction.

9. Choose Go To Transfer in the Edit menu or press CTRL+X to view the transaction in your personal checking account.
10. Modify the Payee and Memo fields if you want.
11. Select Record to update the changes.

When your personal Quicken data is in a separate file, you enter writing a business check in your business Quicken file and depositing it in an account in your personal Quicken file. You will enter a transaction in each file for the owner's withdrawal. Create a category in both files that you will use for the transfer transaction. In the business Quicken file, the category is an expense category. In the personal Quicken file, it is an income category. However, in both files, the category is not tax-related. Do not assign it to any tax form. When you make the owner's withdrawal in the business file, you select the withdrawal expense category for the owner's withdrawal. In the personal file, you select the owner's withdrawal income category for the deposit.

Tech Acct: When the business is a corporation, your withdrawals are either salary or dividends. Thus, you record the withdrawal as payment of wages or payment of dividends. For payment of dividends, you need to create an expense category.

How do I record Keogh contributions?

Keogh contributions are contributions made to a retirement plan for sole proprietors and partnerships that have a different set of rules than IRAs. Keogh contributions appear on the sole proprietor or partner's tax return as an adjustment to income rather than as an expense in the business. You will want to create a category or modify the RRSP (Regular Retirement Savings Plan) category to make it tax-related and add the Form entry of Form 1040:Keogh deduction. Then, when you write the check for the Keogh contribution, assign it to this category. The amount will appear in the Tax Summary report, in the Tax Schedule report, and after Adjustments to Income in the Tax Planner.

Business Deductions

 Can I keep my business mileage in Quicken?

Driving for business purposes is a deductible expense and can be deducted in one of two ways. You can deduct the business portion of your actual automotive expenses or you can deduct using the standard deduction rate based on the number of miles driven for business. With either method you need to keep good records. You can create an investment account that tracks your mileage. When you create this investment account, set it up to track a single mutual investment fund. Then, as you make business trips, enter the mileage as Buy transactions. A sample transaction to record this information might follow these steps:

1. Go to the next empty transaction in the investment Register window.
2. Type **1/19/96** in the Date field for the date of the trip.
3. Select BuyX for the Action field.
4. Type **45** in the Number of Shares text box as the number of miles you drove.
5. Type **Visited potential client** in the Memo field because you need to include the purpose of the trip in your records.
6. Select the same investment account as the one you are working in for the Xfer Account field. Using the same account prevents cluttering up another account with transactions that have no effect on the other account.
7. Select Record to record this transaction. Figure 7-4 shows this type of investment account with several transactions entered. Notice that the price is left empty. It really doesn't matter what price you put. You can leave it as zero or put in any number.

When you are done and you want to see your mileage deduction, switch to the Portfolio View window and update the prices. Updating the share's price to .30 (the standard deduction

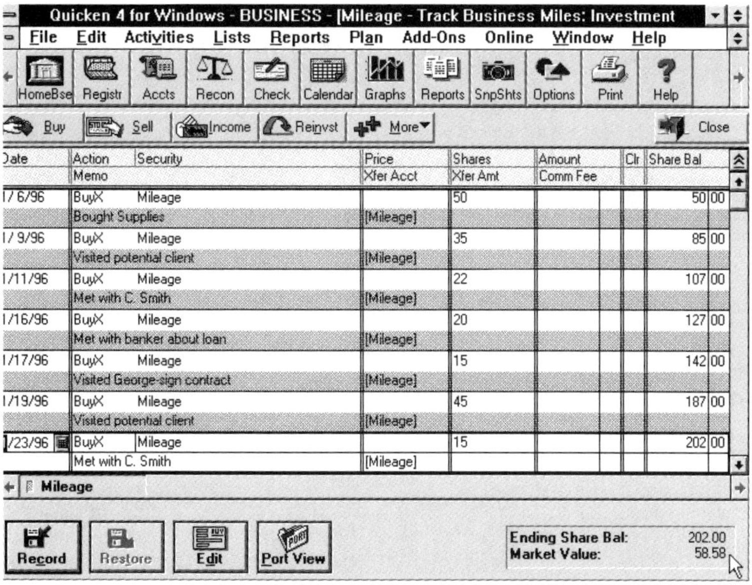

Chapter 7 *Business*

FIGURE 7-4 Investment account set up to track business mileage

rate in 1995) makes the market value of this "investment" equal to the deduction. This deduction is in addition to tolls and parking fees that you have paid while on business trips. When you record these expenses, you can assign them to the Car category that Quicken includes in the standard business categories. This category is already set up as tax-related and assigned to Schedule C: Car and truck expenses. Leave the Auto category for personal automobile use. If you plan to use the standard mileage deduction, create a subcategory under the Car category to record the tolls and parking fees that you can deduct in addition to the standard mileage deduction. The standard mileage deduction will not appear in the Tax Planner when you import Quicken data, although what you assign to the Car category is. You will want to total the standard mileage deduction and toll and parking expenses. In the Tax Planner, select Business Income and increase the amount in the Other Allowable Expenses text box by the amount that the standard mileage deduction, toll, and parking exceeds the total for the Car category.

Tech Acct: You can also use Quicken to track mileage that you drive for charitable purposes. The standard deduction for these miles is 12 cents per mile. If you have enough itemized deductions, these miles can help reduce your taxes. Be aware that the IRS has many rules concerning who is eligible to use the standard rate, and how to calculate the deduction. If you plan to take this deduction for your business or as an itemized deduction, you can get the IRS Publication 917, Business Use of a Car, for more details.

Do I have to adjust the Tax Planner for my business income for the less-than-full deduction that I get for meals and entertainment?

The Tax Planner assumes that only 50% on meals and entertainment expenses are deductible. Assign these expenses to the Meals & Entertn category included in the default Business categories. When you import the Quicken data, the Tax Planner shows the meals and entertainment separately and calculates the allowable deduction.

Accounts Receivable and Accounts Payable

How do I record accounts receivable?

Quicken can record accounts receivable using an asset account even though Quicken is not designed to have full accounts receivable features. Accounts receivable in Quicken need their own asset account. Create the asset account with a zero balance, then mark the Clr field for the transaction so the opening balance transaction does not appear in reports. Once you have the account, you are ready to record your accounts receivable. Suppose you want to record invoice #5001 dated 6/12/95 for ABC Corporation for $510. To record this account receivable, follow these steps:

   1. Go to the next empty transaction in the Register window for the accounts receivable asset account.

Chapter 7 *Business*

2. Type **6/12/95** in the Date field for the invoice's date.

3. Type **5001** in the Num field for the invoice number. With later invoices, you can type **+** if you want Quicken to add the next sequential invoice number for you.

4. Type **ABC Corporation** in the Payee field to record who owes this money.

5. Type **510** as the invoice amount in the Increase column since you are increasing the accounts receivable that you have.

6. Select Gr Sales in the Category field.

7. Type **Invoice Billing** in the Memo field.

    If you wanted to divide the amounts in the invoice into different categories, you would open the Splits window, then enter categories, memos, and amounts there.

8. Select Re<u>c</u>ord to create the account receivable that looks like this:

Date	Ref	Payee		Decrease	Clr	Increase	Balance
		Category	Memo				
6/12/95	5001	ABC Corporation				510 00	510 00
		Gr Sales	Invoice Billing				

When ABC Corporation pays this invoice on 6/17/95, you will perform these steps:

1. Open the Register window for the accounts receivable asset account.

2. Go to the transaction for the invoice that ABC Corporation is paying.

3. Select <u>S</u>plits to open the Splits window, then move to the next empty line.

4. Select the checking or other account where you are depositing the invoice's payment in the Category field.

5. Type **Invoice Paid 6/17/95** in the Memo column.

6. Type **-510** as the invoice amount paid by ABC Corporation.

7. Select Adj. <u>T</u>ot so that the Splits Total is now zero.

8. Select <u>O</u>K to close the Splits window.

Quicken 4 for Windows Answers: *Certified Tech Support*

9. Click the Clr column to mark the transaction as cleared. Clearing invoices that are completely paid makes creating reports on your outstanding balances easier.

10. Select Re$\underline{c}$ord to record paying the invoice. When you select $\underline{S}$plits for this transaction, the transaction and its Splits window might look like this:

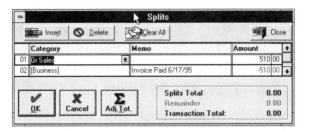

11. Select $\underline{G}$o To Transfer from the $\underline{E}$dit menu or press CTRL+X to switch to this transaction in the checking account where the deposit is made.

12. Make any changes to the transaction, such as DEP in the Num field or the description in the Payee field. You cannot change the date so the date continues to have the date of the invoice rather than when it was paid.

How do I create an accounts receivable report?

When you have an account set up for accounts receivable, you can easily create an accounts receivable report listing what your customers owe. Just follow these steps:

1. Choose $\underline{B}$usiness from the $\underline{R}$eports menu and then choose A/$\underline{R}$ by Customer.

2. Select $\underline{C}$ustomize to make changes, if necessary.

3. Select the $\underline{A}$ccounts option button, then clear the other asset accounts except for the account that you created for accounts receivable.

4. Select OK to create the report. Figure 7-5 shows what this report, when created for three months in 1995, might look like.

Chapter 7 Business

```
                           A/R by Customer by Month
                               4/1/95 Through 6/30/95
7/16/95                                                                          Page 1
BUSINESS-Selected Accounts
                                                                        OVERALL
         Payee                         4/1/95     5/1/95     6/1/95      TOTAL

         Ace Water Control Division      0.00       0.00     693.83      693.83
         Acme Mail Order Inc             0.00   4,678.28   5,372.46   10,050.74
         Beagle Blazons                  0.00     393.68       0.00      393.68
         Carolyn Camping Store           0.00       0.00     573.81      573.81
         Davis Landscaping               0.00       0.00     182.27      182.27
         FEETS                           0.00       0.00      27.88       27.88
         Franklin Mint                   0.00   2,781.28   5,167.97    7,949.25
         Irish Cat Shop                238.38       0.00       0.00      238.38
         Jones Art Supply                0.00       0.00   4,738.27    4,738.27
         Lim & Associates                0.00       0.00   1,047.29    1,047.29
         Mandy Jones                     0.00       0.00      49.27       49.27
         Martin Inc.                     0.00       0.00     937.38      937.38
         Mathers Printers                0.00     383.28       0.00      383.28
         Memorial Towers                 0.00       0.00     592.23      592.23
         Monty Maps                      0.00       0.00      39.58       39.58
         Pennsylvania Supplies           0.00       0.00      87.27       87.27
         Rob & Seal Outfitters           0.00     259.32     392.82      652.14
         Smith & Grant                   0.00     963.38      46.27    1,009.65

         OVERALL TOTAL                 238.38   9,459.22  19,948.60   29,646.20
```

FIGURE 7-5   A/R by Customer report to show outstanding accounts receivable balances

This report sorts your accounts receivable according to the payees. It omits the bills that your customers have already paid because when a customer pays the bill, you clear that transaction. This report omits all cleared transactions from the accounts receivable account.

If you need a report listing the invoices for each payee, create a Register Report for the accounts receivable account. You create this report by moving to an empty transaction and selecting Rep**o**rt in the button bar. Then, you can customize the report to subtotal by payee and omit newly cleared and reconciled transactions. The beginning of this report appears in Figure 7-6.

How can I record the bills that I owe?

When you do your accounting using the cash basis or modified cash basis, you want to enter bills as they are paid. Yet, you also want Quicken to remind you about the bills you owe so that you do not pay late fees and can take advantage of any discounts that

Register Report by Payee by Payee
1/1/95 Through 6/30/95

7/16/95
BUSINESS-Accounts Rec

Page 1

Date	Num	Description	Memo	Category	Clr	Amount
6/16/95	5016	Ace Water Control Division	Invoice Billing	Gr Sales		693.83
		Total Ace Water Control Division				693.83
5/1/95	4000	Acme Mail Order Inc	Invoice Billing	Gr Sales		4,678.28
6/13/95	5002	Acme Mail Order Inc	Invoice Billing	Gr Sales		5,372.46
		Total Acme Mail Order Inc				10,050.74
5/14/95	4011	Beagle Blazons	Invoice Billing	Gr Sales		393.68
		Total Beagle Blazons				393.68
6/15/95	5012	Carolyn Camping Store	Invoice Billing	Gr Sales		573.81
		Total Carolyn Camping Store				573.81
6/15/95	5010	Davis Landscaping	Invoice Billing	Gr Sales		182.27
		Total Davis Landscaping				182.27
6/15/95	5009	FEETS	Invoice Billing	Gr Sales		27.88
		TOTAL FEETS				27.88
5/4/95	4001	Franklin Mint				2,781.28
6/14/95	5006	Franklin Mint	Invoice Billing	Gr Sales		5,167.97
		Total Franklin Mint				7,949.25
4/18/95	3005	Irish Cat Shop	Invoice Billing	Gr Sales		238.38
		Total Irish Cat Shop				238.38
6/14/95	5007	Jones Art Supply	Invoice Billing	Gr Sales		4,738.27
		Total Jones Art Supply				4,738.27
6/14/95	5005	Lim & Associates	Invoice Billing	Gr Sales		1,047.29
		Total Lim & Associates				1,047.29
6/13/95	5004	Mandy Jones	Invoice Billing	Gr Sales		49.27
		Total Mandy Jones				49.27
6/14/95	5008	Martin Inc.	Invoice Billing	Gr Sales		937.38
		Total Martin Inc.				937.38
5/18/95	4020	Mathers Printers	Invoice Billing	Gr Sales		383.28
		Total Mathers Printers				383.28
6/16/95	5015	Memorial Towers	Invoice Billing	Gr Sales		592.23
		Total Memorial Towers				592.23

FIGURE 7-6 Register Report listing accounts receivable by payee

can apply. To do this, enter your bills as checks to print with dates after today's date so they become postdated checks. Quicken will remind you of these bills to pay as checks that you need to print. To create one of these transactions:

1. Move to the next empty transaction in the Register window for the account you will use to pay the bill.
2. Enter the date you want to pay the bill in the Date field.
3. Select Print in the Num field.
4. Make entries in the Payee, Memo, Category, and Payment fields just like paying any other bill in a Register window. You can also select Splits to assign multiple categories to the transaction.
5. Select Record to record this transaction.

Now, the Quicken Reminders window shows that you have checks to print. When you pay the bill, you can enter any updated information such as a different date or a check number if you write the check by hand. The account's Register window shows both today's balance and the balance for when the bills are paid.

Tech Tip: You can also enter the bills as a scheduled transaction. However, the A/P by Vendor report will not create a report of the bills that need to be paid.

How can I list who I need to pay?

You can create an accounts payable report. This report lists all unprinted transactions from your bank accounts. (This assumes that the unpaid bills are entered as unprinted checks. The previous question tells you how to enter your bills as unprinted checks.) To create this report, follow these steps:

1. Choose Business from the Reports menu and then choose A/P by Vendor.
2. Select Customize to make a few changes.

3. Select the Accounts option button, then clear asset accounts that do not have your business's bills, such as your personal checking account.
4. Select OK to create the report.

Like the A/R by Customer report, this report sorts the unpaid bill according to the payee.

Budgeting

Quicken's registers and reports can provide a good picture of your financial history. Quicken's budgeting features let you plan for the future—an essential part of realizing your financial goals.

If budgeting has always seemed like a chore, you need to look at it in a new light. Budgeting allows you to make informed decisions about how you spend your money. With a budget, you can evaluate purchases against your plan to see if they fit into the financial scheme you've set for yourself.

FRUSTRATION BUSTERS!

The first time you plan a budget, the process may seem overwhelming. Follow this strategy to put together your budget entries, remembering that you can always make adjustments after a few months.

First identify your short- and long-term financial goals. You are much more likely to stick to your financial plan if you view it as a means to an end. Perhaps your short-term goal is to save up enough money for a down payment on a car, and your long-term financial goal is to pay off your mortgage in 18 years instead of the 26 years remaining. If you have a long list of financial goals, you will have to prioritize them. Decide which are the most important since it may be difficult to save for all of them at the same time. Normally, you will place short-term goals at the top of your list.

After identifying your goals, you can quantify the amount of money you need to attain them. For example, do you need to save $1,000 for a down payment on a car or are you trying to save the entire purchase price in order to avoid interest on a car loan? The financial planners discussed in Chapter 10, "Financial Planning," can help you quantify goals and ensure that they can be realistically achieved in the time frame that you select.

Next, identify all of your short-term fixed expenses. For example, your current mortgage payment may be $850 a month or you might have $200 a month in car payments. Your Quicken entries can be a good source for the amount of these fixed expenses. Quicken can create a budget from these entries, providing a starting point for what you plan to spend.

Look at your other Quicken categories and decide how many of the remaining expenditures are discretionary and how many are required. For example, food expenditures may be $500 a month but you might feel that the essentials cost you $250. You will need to decide if you want to continue your restaurant dining three nights a week or perhaps cut back to one evening and shift these expenditures toward one of your saving goals. As you complete your budget plan, you will also need to ensure that planned outflows do not exceed inflows and that you have allocated sufficient savings to meet your most important goals.

Chapter 8 *Budgeting*

After a month or two, go over what you spent versus what you had planned to spend. The areas in which you spent a lot more than you had planned should be examined in more detail. You might decide to add subcategories to let you monitor them a little closer.

Budget Reports

How do I compare what I planned to spend with my actual expenditures?

The Budget report compares what you spend to what you planned in your budget. Your account's transactions provide the numbers for what you have spent and your budget provides the numbers for what you planned to spend. To create this report:

1. Choose <u>H</u>ome from the <u>R</u>eports menu, then choose Monthly <u>B</u>udget.
2. Select OK in the Create Report dialog box.

Figure 8-1 shows the beginning of a Budget report. Quicken organizes your account data by category and compares each month's planned and actual spending.

Tech Acct: Try out Quicken's Discretionary and Non-Discretionary supercategories. By breaking out your budget into these supercategories, your budget report focuses on the spending patterns that you are able to change, rather than what you cannot.

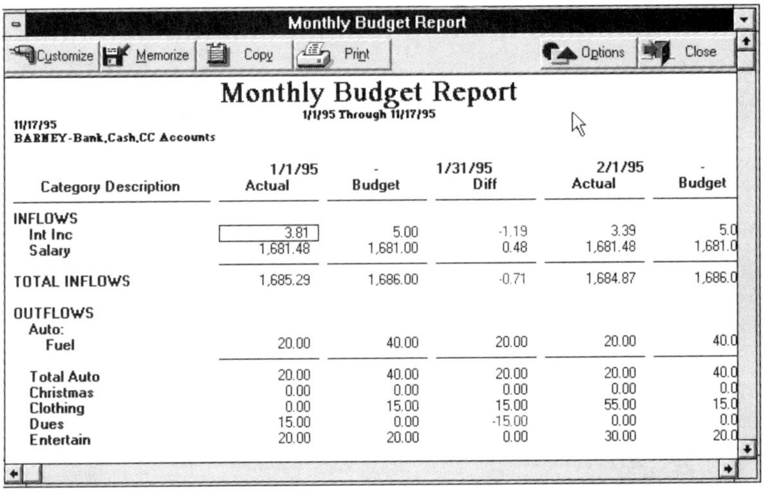

Quicken 4 for Windows Answers: *Certified Tech Support*

[Monthly Budget Report screenshot]

FIGURE 8-1   Budget report to compare planned spending against actual spending

My Budget report doesn't show the most recent budget. What happened?

When you create the Budget report, Quicken uses the last *saved* budget data. All you need to do is go to the Budget window and click the Save button. When you return to the Budget report, it will show the new numbers.

Why is my Budget report title missing the beginning characters?

When you change the Budget report's default title, Quicken adds "by Month" to the end of it. Quicken can't allow your custom title to expand too far or it interferes with the report's date. Instead, Quicken may cut off the beginning of the report title. Shorten the title and you won't have this problem. You can change the report's title by selecting Customize in the button bar. Change the entry in the Title text box and select OK.

Chapter 8 *Budgeting*

How do I print my Budget report sideways so that I can fit it on one page?

If your printer can print sideways, then you can change Quicken's printer settings to print budgets or other Quicken reports sideways. To make this change:

1. Choose Printer Setup from the File menu and then select Report/Graph Printer Setup to bring up the Report Printer Setup dialog box.

2. Select Settings. At this point, you see Window's Control Panel. If your printer has settings for orientation, you will be able to change those settings here. The dialog box that you see varies according to which printer you selected in the Printer drop-down list box in Quicken's Report Printer Setup dialog box.

Tech Tip: The printer settings that you change here affect all of your Windows applications.

3. Make the changes to the printer settings and select OK.

4. Select OK to put away Quicken's Report Printer Setup dialog box.

If the report is too large to fit sideways on a page, you can try changing the report's font size. Directions for changing this setting and many others (in any of your reports) are discussed in Chapter 9, "Reports and Graphs."

Creating Budget Entries

Can I create a budget using existing data?

Yes, you can. In fact, if you have kept good records, it is the best way to get realistic numbers for your budget. Quicken creates a budget for what you plan to spend using your past entries of what you have already spent. To create a budget out of past data:

1. Select the Create button in the Budget window to show the Automatically Create Budget dialog box.

2. Enter the beginning date and ending date in the From and To text boxes. Quicken initially looks at last year's

data but, if you only have a partial year of data or you want to use part of the current year's, you may want to enter new dates.

3. Set whether you want the exact amount or a rounded amount by choosing 1, 10, or 100 from the Round Values to Nearest drop-down list box.

4. Choose how you want the budget amounts divided over the year. Choose Use Monthly Detail when you want amounts to appear in the budget for the months in which your expenditures were actually made. Choose Use Average for Period when you want the total averaged over a span of time. As an example, for auto insurance that is paid once a year, choosing Use Monthly Detail budgets the insurance expense in the same month in which you paid for it, while choosing Use Average for Period spreads it out over the year.

5. Select Categories to bring up the Select Categories to Include dialog box and choose which categories you want Quicken to calculate budgeted amounts for, based on the past data. From the Select Categories to Include dialog box, select the categories that Quicken will include in the budget it creates. Initially all the categories are selected so you only have to change the ones that you do not want in your budget. Categories with check marks get budgeted amounts from past data while the ones without don't. Select OK when you are done.

6. Select OK to create the budget.

Tech Tip: When you don't have a full year's worth of data on which to base your budget, enter the part of the year that you do have data for in the From and To text boxes and make sure to select Use Average for Period. Then Quicken creates a budget for the whole year and not just the section where you have data.

Chapter 8 *Budgeting*

I didn't enter all of last year's data. Can I create a budget from last year's numbers using just the months that I do have?

Certainly. You just tell Quicken the date range for which you want actual transaction entries used to create budget amounts. When you create the budget with the <u>C</u>reate button in the button bar, remember to type the dates in the <u>F</u>rom and T<u>o</u> text boxes. For example, typing **8/94** in the <u>F</u>rom text box and **12/94** in the T<u>o</u> text box creates a budget using just five months of 1994's data. Make sure to select Use <u>A</u>verage for Period so Quicken annualizes the budget amounts. This means that if you have an average of $40 for gas for five months, the budget has $40 for gas for all twelve months.

Tech Terror: If you include the full year to create the budget but you only have entries in a few of the months, your budget will be too low. The months without transactions bring down the average for each category. For example, if you type **1/94** and **12/94** but you only have entries starting in August, Quicken sums the total auto expense and divides it over 12 months rather than the five months of entries actually available.

Can I apply all of my January's numbers to the rest of the year's budget?

Certainly. You can copy the January amounts for all of your budget categories for the rest of the year. All you have to do is:

1. Move to the January column since you want to be in the column containing the numbers that you want applied to the rest of the year.

2. Select the E<u>d</u>it button in the Budget window, then select Fill <u>C</u>olumns.

3. Select OK when Quicken prompts for whether you want to fill all of the year with the entries in the selected column.

Quicken copies all the numbers in the current column to the columns for the rest of the year, overwriting any previous entries in these columns.

How can I repeat one category's budget amount for the rest of the year?

To have Quicken repeat a budget amount for the rest of the year:

1. Move to the budgeted number that you want to repeat for the rest of the year. If you are in the first column, normally January, the budget amount applies to the whole year but if you are at, for instance, July's number, it only applies to August through the end of the year.

2. Select the E_dit button in the Budget window, then select Fill R_ow Right.

3. Select OK when Quicken prompts about filling the rest of the year with the current entry.

Quicken copies the current number for the rest of the year for just the category you selected. For the budget shown in Figure 8-2, most of the numbers are entered in the first column and copied to the others. Then, monthly variations, such as dues due in April, are added.

Tech Tip: Applying budget amounts to later months extends through the last column of the Budget window. When you use a calendar year, this is through December. Quicken has a customization option to allow the use of a fiscal year instead of a calendar year. When you extend budget amounts through the year, they continue to the last column of the budget window, even when the last month is not December.

How do I budget for savings?

When you set aside money for savings, Quicken must take money from one account and put it into another. To enter this into the Budget window, you need to see entries for the

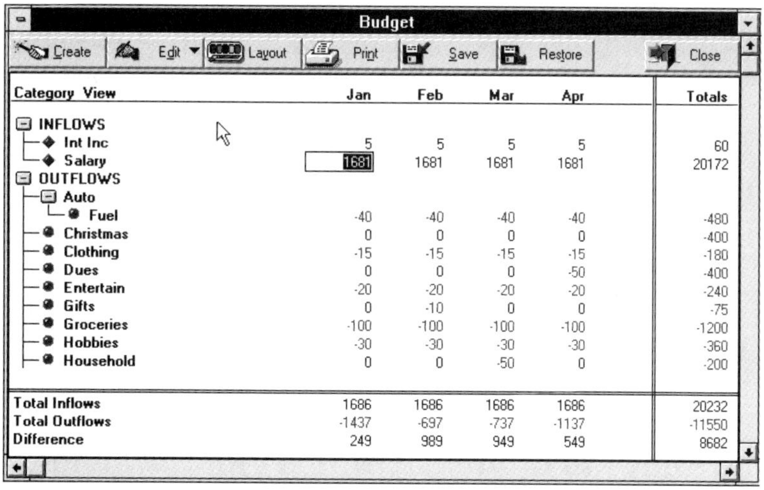

FIGURE 8-2   Budget window

accounts. To add these to the Budget window, select Layout in the Budget window's button bar, then select Show Transfers, and select OK. Now the Budget window includes FROM and the account name in the Inflows section and TO and the account name in the Outflows section. At this point, enter the amount you plan to set aside in the row for FROM and the account where the money comes from (as in FROM Checking), and in the row for TO and the account where the money goes (as in TO Savings).

When you look at your Budget report, you can change which transfers Quicken shows. Just select Customize from the button bar and the Show Rows option button. From the Transfers drop-down list box, select Exclude All, Exclude Internal, or Include All. Exclude All omits showing all transfers, such as when you put aside money into savings. Include All shows all transfers. This choice can include transfers like the one from your checking account to your credit card account when you pay your credit card bill (assuming that you set up your credit cards as separate accounts). Exclude Internal only omits the transfers between the accounts that are combined in the monthly Budget report. Use this when you put aside money in a separate account specifically set up for your savings. You will then also want to select the Accounts option button and remove any check mark next to the account that holds your savings. The report will show transfers to and from this account but will not include this account's transactions in the other categories. When you select OK, the report changes to reflect the changes you have made.

Tech Acct: When you budget savings, make sure they are paid as part of your nondiscretionary bills. Otherwise, it becomes too easy to be a little short at the end of the month as you use what should be savings for impulse purchases.

I am paid every other week rather than twice a month. Do I have to figure out which months include three paychecks?

No, you can let Quicken do it for you. To do this:

1. Move to a budget amount for the category you want to calculate.
2. Select E<u>d</u>it from the Budget window's button bar and select 2-<u>W</u>eek.
3. Enter the amount of the salary in the <u>A</u>mount text box.
4. Select the first date with a paycheck like this in the <u>E</u>very two weeks starting text box.
5. Select OK.

Why does my budget have categories that start with an underscore, as in _DivInc?

These categories are for the income and expenses associated with your investment accounts. You can enter budget amounts for the inflows and outflows that you expect. The following section of a Budget report shows these categories and the actual amounts that have come from the investment account transactions.

Category Description	11/17/95 Diff	1/1/95 Actual	Budget	11/17/95 Diff
_DivInc	0.00	410.84	0.00	410.84
_DivIncTaxFree	0.00	0.00	0.00	0.00
_IntInc	0.00	300.00	0.00	300.00
_IntIncTaxFree	0.00	1,087.21	0.00	1,087.21
_LT CapGnDst	0.00	46.31	0.00	46.31
_RlzdGain	0.00	9,644.80	0.00	9,644.80
_ST CapGnDst	0.00	8.42	0.00	8.42
_UnrlzdGain	0.00	0.00	0.00	0.00
Total Other Income	0.00	11,497.58	0.00	11,497.58

Tech Terror: Budget reports normally do not include investment accounts. Don't be surprised if you see 0's for the actual data. If you want to see the amounts for these categories, you need to include the investment accounts in the Budget report. You choose which accounts a report includes by selecting Customize from the button bar then the Accounts option button. Select the accounts to include, then select OK to re-create the report with the selected accounts.

Hiding Budget Numbers

Can I hide items that are not in my budget?

Yes, the Budget window initially includes all categories but you can change the Budget window to only show the ones with entries. To hide these zero-amount categories:

1. Choose the Layout button in the Budget window's button bar.
2. Select the Hide Budget Zero Categories check box and select OK.

Repeating these steps and clearing the Hide Budget Zero Categories check box will display all categories again.

My Budget report doesn't contain expenditures that I didn't budget for. How do I add these to the Budget report?

A Budget report initially contains only the categories with non-zero budget amounts. You can expand the categories in the report to also include categories in which you've spent money without budgeting. To do this:

1. Switch to the Monthly Budget Report window by selecting it from the Window menu.
2. Select Customize from the button bar.
3. Select the Show Rows option button.
4. Select Non-Zero Actual/Budgeted from the Categories drop-down list box.
5. Select OK to show the report with all categories that have amounts either in the actual column or the budgeted column.

Supercategories

Can I create parent categories for my regular categories?

Supercategories in a budget let you divide categories in different ways. You can use them to change the groups of categories that you see in your budget. Your data file already has some supercategories set up but you can create your own. You can also select which accounts belong to each supercategory.

To create a supercategory:

1. Select the Edit button on the window's button bar and then select Supercategories. The Manage Supercategories dialog box that you see lists the categories and the supercategories.
2. Select New to create a new supercategory.
3. Type a name for this supercategory and select OK.

Chapter 8 *Budgeting*

4. Assign the categories that belong to this supercategory or select OK to put the dialog box away.

While you have the Manage Supercategories dialog box open, you can rearrange the supercategory that each category belongs to. A category can only belong to one supercategory. A supercategory can include both income and expense categories. To create or change supercategory assignments:

1. Select the Edit button on the window's button bar and then select Supercategories.
2. Highlight the category that you want to assign from the list of categories.
3. Highlight the supercategory that you want this category to belong to.
4. Select Assign.
5. Repeat steps 2 through 4 until you are finished, then select OK.

To show the budget organized by supercategories:

1. Select the Layout button on the window's button bar.
2. Select Show Supercategories and select OK.

Figure 8-3 shows supercategories in a budget. Besides the Discretionary and Non-Discretionary ones that Quicken already provides, this budget has Before Home Purchase and After Home Purchase supercategories with some new categories assigned to them.

Tech Tip: You can also change the supercategory that a category is assigned to by dragging the category name from one supercategory heading to the next. This only works when you show the supercategories in a Budget window.

How do I organize my budget reports by supercategories?

If you save your report while you show the budget organized by supercategories, the Budget reports that you create are organized by supercategories.

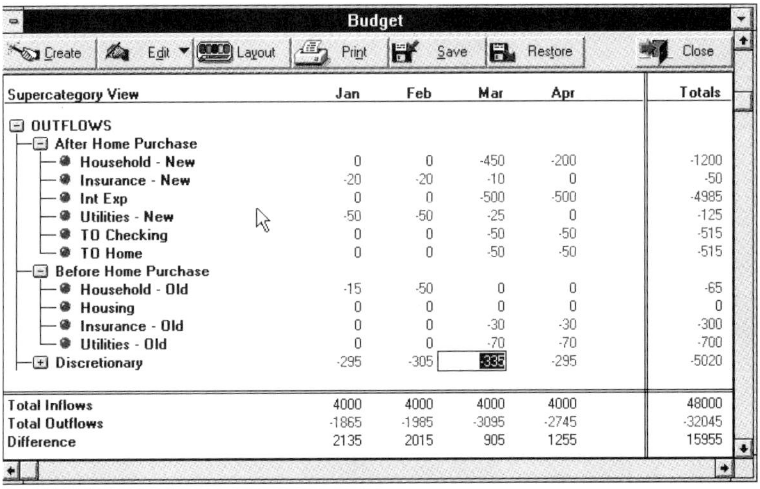

[FIGURE 8-3 image showing a Budget window]

FIGURE 8-3 A Budget window showing a budget arranged by supercategories

How do I make supercategory assignments to categories that appear on my Budget report but not in my budget?

You can assign supercategories to categories that do not appear in the Budget window when you choose the Edit button in the button bar and then Supercategories.

Budget Differences

Why don't the budget numbers in the Budget window match my Budget report?

Usually the numbers match but if they don't it is typically because you are matching one month's worth of budget with more or less than a month for the Budget report. For example, if you combine three months into one for the budget report, you will see the combined total for the three months. You can also have that problem when the budget shows less than a whole month. For instance, creating a budget report on the 15th of the month shows half of the budgeted amounts for each category.

When I use the autocreate feature for a budget, why do the budgeted amounts and actual amounts differ?

It might seem that when you base your budget on your actual data that the difference between what you planned to spend and what you actually spent is less than a dollar. This is the budget that you create with the Create button in the Budget window's button bar as described earlier in the chapter. You will always have slight differences because budget amounts are rounded to the nearest dollar while actual amounts include the pennies. Your budget may be quite different from the actual amounts for the following reasons.

- You have averaged out the budgeted amounts but the actual expenses are not evenly spread out. For instance, suppose that over the course of the year you spend $240 on clothes. The automatic budget has $20 for each month. Your real expenses may be more sporadic because you spend $50 in March, $60 in July, $35 in September, and $95 in November. In this case, over the course of the year, you stayed in budget but individual months may be under or over budget.

- Your basis for the budget is last year but you don't have all of last year's transactions entered. When you created the budget, the amounts that you do have were spread over the entire year rather than just the few months of transactions that you supplied. For example, over five months last year, you spent $1,200 on groceries. When Quicken uses these five months of food expenses for the year's budget, each month is budgeted $100. You will need to revise your budget to have more realistic amounts.

- You are in the middle of the month. The Budget report apportions the budget amount for the current month. This means that if you have $300 budgeted for rent, the Budget report shows $150 on the 15th. However, if you already have paid rent, your budget report shows a negative $150, even if rent is a monthly expense.

Budget Window

Why does the Budget window display an account I have deleted?

A file that is slightly damaged can show an account in the budget that does not appear in the Account List window. If this happens, follow these steps:

1. Switch to the Budget window.
2. Enter an amount for this account.
3. Choose Category & Transfer from the Lists menu. You can go through this list and find the deleted account that is being treated as a real category.
4. Highlight the category that was previously an account.
5. Select Delete from the Category & Transfer List window's button bar and select OK. The category disappears from both the Category & Transfer List window and the Budget window.

Why can't I see my subcategories in the Budget window?

The categories and supercategories in a Budget window can be expanded to show the entries below them or collapsed to hide them. Next to each subcategory or supercategory is a button that contains a - or +. When a category is collapsed to hide its subcategories, it shows the + button like the one here:

Chapter 8 *Budgeting*

Clicking this button shows the subcategories and changes the button to a - one like the one here:

You can also click these buttons in front of Inflows and Outflows or any supercategories to hide or display the categories listed underneath them.

Can I show a budget for time periods other than months?

You can show the budget divided by months, quarters, or a year. To switch which period that the budget reports on, all you have to do is select Layout from the Budget window's button bar. Then select Month, Quarter, or Year from underneath Columns, and then select OK. When you switch from months to quarters or years, the monthly data is totaled for each of the columns. However, your monthly detail is not lost. When you return to showing months, you will find that Quicken remembered each month separately.

Exporting Budget Data

How do I export my budget so I can put it into my word processor or spreadsheet?

You can copy your budget to Windows' Clipboard. Once it is here, you can paste it into other applications such as a word processor or spreadsheet. To do this:

1. Select Edit from the Budget window's button bar and select Copy All to copy the budget to the Clipboard.
2. Open your other application.

3. Choose that application's command that pastes the Clipboard data. For example, for most Microsoft products, choose Paste in the Edit menu.

At this point, you have a useable copy of the budget information in that other application. Figure 8-4 shows a copy of a budget placed into an Excel spreadsheet.

Note that pasting your data into a word processor separates the columns with tabs, rather than creating a table.

Tech Tip: You can also copy Quicken reports, such as your budget reports, to other applications. To copy the data, select Copy from the Budget window's button bar. The copied report information does not include the column headings or report title.

FIGURE 8-4 Budget copied to an Excel spreadsheet

Chapter 8 *Budgeting*

Creating Multiple Budgets

Can I create more than one budget?

Quicken can only store one budget at a time. However, you can use the Forecasting feature to have more than one set of numbers, then apply any forecast you have created to the budget. This is a roundabout way to have more than one budget, since Quicken allows more than one forecast and can copy amounts between the Budget and the Forecasting windows. However, it has one drawback: When you copy a forecast to the Budget window, the year's amount is averaged, so if you had different amounts for different months, you will lose the detail. However, the amount for the entire year remains the same. The steps for this process are:

1. Choose Forecasting from the Plan menu to show the Forecasting window. If this is your first time showing this window, you will need to type in dates for the forecast and select OK.

2. Select the Income button to show the currently forecasted income items.

3. For each income item under Known Items, highlight it and select Delete. You want to remove the known items from the current forecast so Quicken picks up all categories from the budget. Also, when you create a budget out of a forecast, Quicken only creates budget amounts for estimated items in the forecast. The budget ignores any items in the forecast added as known items.

4. Select Expense Items from the top of the dialog box to change the Forecast Income Items dialog box to the Forecast Expense Items dialog box.

5. For each expense item under Known Items, highlight it and select Delete.

6. Select Done to leave the Forecast Expense Items dialog box.

7. Select Create in the window's button bar.

8. Select Advanced to see more budget options.

Tech Tip: Quicken still remembers supercategory assignments and Budget window settings.

9. Select the Estimated Items option button so that Quicken will look at your budget rather than at the scheduled transactions for categories where you have scheduled transactions.

10. Select the From Budget Data option button and then select Done.

11. Select OK to create the forecast out of the budget.

12. Select Scenario from the button bar.

13. Select New, type a name for the scenario such as **First Budget**, and select OK.

14. Select <Base Scenario> from the Scenario Data text box and select Done.

15. Choose Budgeting from the Plan menu to show the Budget window, then enter a new budget. Remember to select Save when you are done.

16. Repeat steps 7 through 14 for each budget you want to create but enter different scenario names in step 13. At this point, Quicken remembers the different budgets as forecast scenarios.

17. Select Scenario from the button bar.

18. Select the scenario you want in the Budget window from the Scenario Data drop-down list box, select the Current Scenario Only option button, and select Done to show the forecast that you want to see in the Budget window.

19. Select Track, select OK, and then select Done to copy the forecast to the Budget window.

You can also create budgets from the Forecasting window by creating the income and expense items. When you are done, you can copy this forecast to the Budget window just like other budgets that you have copied into the Forecasting window.

Reports and Graphs

Reports and graphs are among Quicken's most useful features. You can get a quick overview of your financial status, savings patterns, savings goals, and taxes. Quicken's report customization features allow you to create reports tailored to your specific needs. The Frustration Busters box below provides a synopsis of the customization options so that you can create the reports that are most useful to you.

Frustration Busters!

With the wealth of customization options, you may be confused about where to find the settings you want. Here are the option buttons that you see in the Customize Report dialog box:

- Report Date   You can set the report dates either at the top of the Customize Report dialog box or with this option button. A report can have a beginning and an ending date as well as the date the report is prepared. Comparison reports utilize more than one beginning and ending date.

- Report Layout   With this option, you can set the report's title, select what the report shows in its columns and rows, and choose whether the report shows the cents or just dollar figures, the detail for split transactions, the memo and category field entries, or just totals for the transactions. You can sort the transactions or group them by some basis.

- Account   These options let you choose which accounts with their transactions appear in the report.

- Transactions   These options let you choose the transactions to be included. For example, you can select whether reconciled, newly cleared, or uncleared transactions appear in the report; you can select transactions according to their amount; you can omit tax-deferred transactions; you can show unrealized gains; and you can show specific transaction types such as deposits, payments, and unprinted checks.

- Show Rows   With this option, you can limit the detail presented on the rows in the report. You can choose which transfers appear in a report. You can choose whether categories that have subcategories show the individual subcategory detail or combine their subcategories to present a single row of entries. You can also select categories to appear in Budget reports based on whether any amount was budgeted in the category or spent in the category—or you can include all of them.

- Categories/Classes   With this option, you select the categories, classes, or budget supercategories that appear in the report.

- **Select to Include** You can select the actions, categories, securities, security types, and investment goals that appear in the report.

- **Matching** These options let you select only the transactions that meet specific criteria. The criteria can be an entry in the Payee, Memo, or Category fields as well as any class you have created. For investment reports, you can also select specific securities.

Remember that not all options are appropriate for every report. Quicken only makes appropriate options available.

Types of Reports

How can I see where I am spending my money?

Several types of reports can show your spending patterns. For example, you can create a report that lists all the transactions sorted by amount. To create this report:

1. Select Other from the Reports menu and then Transaction to display the Create Report dialog box.
2. Set the date for transactions that you want listed in the Report Dates section.
3. Select Customize to make some changes to the report.
4. Select Amount from the Sort By drop-down list box.
5. Select the Transactions option button to limit the transactions appearing in the report.
6. Select Payments from the Transaction Types drop-down list box so the report omits deposits.

7. Select OK to create the report.

Now you have a report with the transactions sorted from highest to lowest, as in Figure 9-1. The report shows payments made from the Checking, Pocket Money, and Credit Card accounts. This report omits internal transfers.

Tech Tip: A shortcut for changing the accounts that appear in this report is to double-click the list of the accounts already shown in the report. Quicken then shows the Customize Report dialog box with the Accounts option button selected. Once you select the accounts, just select OK to include the selected accounts in the report.

A second option is to create a report that lists the payees and the amount paid to each one. To create this report:

1. Select Other from the Reports menu and then Summary.

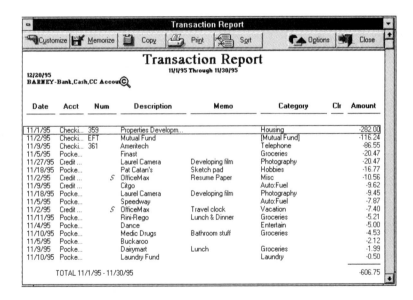

FIGURE 9-1 Report showing transactions

Chapter 9 *Reports and Graphs*

2. Set the date for transactions that you want listed in the Report Dates section.
3. Select Customize.
4. Select Payee in the Row drop-down list box and select OK.

Now the report lists the payee and the amount spent on each one. Figure 9-2 shows a report created with these steps.

Tech Acct: If you are spending too much, make a budget for yourself. Then you can create a Budget report that compares what you spent against what you had planned to spend.

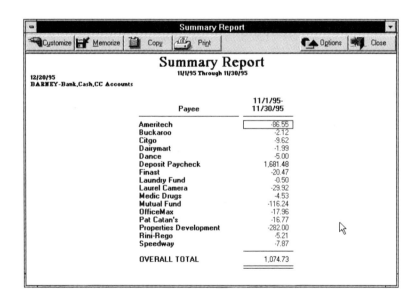

FIGURE 9-2   Report listing what you have paid to each payee

I want to see whether I've spent more this month than last. Can a report show this?

Yes, a Comparison report can compare items such as categories for different time periods. To create a Comparison report that compares the income and expense categories for two different months:

1. Choose <u>H</u>ome from the <u>R</u>eports menu and choose <u>C</u>omparison.

2. Choose Current Month from the top drop-down list box for the first comparison date.

3. Choose Last Month from the drop-down list box for the second comparison date.

4. Choose OK to create the report. This report might look like the one in Figure 9-3.

This report compares what you have spent during the two months. The negative numbers indicate that you have spent more. Use this report to pinpoint areas in which you want to change your spending habits.

I tried to create a Comparison report with last year's data, but last year's data is missing. What happened?

Quicken cannot find last year's data. If you just started using Quicken this year, your data file may not include the older transactions. The other possibility is that you updated your Quicken data file to only include this year's transactions. You can make a year-end copy that consolidates all of last year's transactions. The advantage of having this year-end copy is that your Quicken data file is smaller since it does not include each and every one of last year's transactions. The disadvantage is that you don't have the old data needed to create comparisons between this year's and last year's data.

Chapter 9 Reports and Graphs

```
                          Comparison Report
                         10/1/95 Through 11/30/95
12/2/95                                                                        Page 1
BARNEY-Bank,Cash,CC Accounts
                                        10/1/95-        11/1/95-          $
          Category Description          10/31/95       11/30/95       Difference

          INFLOWS
            Interest Income               3.29           0.00           -3.29
            Salary Income             1,261.11       1,681.48          420.37

          TOTAL INFLOWS               1,264.40       1,681.48          417.08

          OUTFLOWS
            Automobile Expenses:
              Auto Fuel                  20.02          17.49            2.53

            Total Automobile Expenses    20.02          17.49            2.53
            Entertainment                 0.00           5.00           -5.00
            Film Developing              16.77          29.92          -13.15
            Gift Expenses               103.27           0.00          103.27
            Groceries                   129.79          32.20           97.59
            Hobby spending               36.38          16.77           19.61
            Household Misc. Exp         785.33           0.00          785.33
            Housing                     282.00         282.00            0.00
            Insurance                   506.00           0.00          506.00
            Miscellaneous               475.54          10.56          464.98
            Quarters saved for wash       0.00           0.50           -0.50
            Telephone Expense            85.25          86.55           -1.30
            Vacation expenses             0.00           7.40           -7.40
            Water, Gas, Electric:
              Gas and Electricity        36.32           0.00           36.32

            Total Water, Gas, Electric   36.32           0.00           36.32
            Outflows - Other              0.00           2.12           -2.12
            TO Personal Mutual Fund     145.29         116.24           29.05

          TOTAL OUTFLOWS             2,621.96         606.75        2,015.21

          OVERALL TOTAL             -1,357.56       1,074.73        2,432.29
```

FIGURE 9-3 Comparison report comparing spending for two months

Tech Acct: When you create a copy of your data file with the older transactions, you may want to keep the previous year's transactions. For instance, when you create the version of the file that you will use in 1996, tell Quicken to delete the transactions earlier than 1/1/95 because this leaves all of 1995's data to compare with the 1996 data. You may want to delete transactions older than that because if your data file becomes too big (about 800K), Quicken will have problems handling it; you may have to use the rebuild utility that comes with Quicken to rebuild the file if Quicken has difficulty with it.

How do I get my Cash Flow Report to show or hide transfers between accounts?

To choose which transfers appear in a report, follow these steps:

1. Select Customize in the Report window's button bar.
2. Select the Show Rows option button.
3. Select which transfers to show in the report from the Transfers drop-down list box. Your choices are:

   - Exclude All to omit all transfers between accounts. For example, the report will not show the money you transferred from your checking to your savings account.
   - Include All to show all transfers. The report will show all transfers, such as putting money from your checking account into your savings account.
   - Exclude Internal to show only transfers to accounts that are not in the report. If the report only includes the checking account, then the report will show the transfer to the savings account. If the report includes both the checking and the savings accounts, that transfer does not appear.

4. Select OK to update the report to show only the transfers that you want to see.

Targeting Reports

How do I limit reports to business transactions?

Your method for limiting reports depends on how you have marked business transactions: with classes or with separate categories.

If you have marked business transactions with a class, customize the report to include only the transactions with the correct class. For example, if you enter **/b** after the category for all business transactions, you would follow these steps to modify a report to only include business transactions:

1. Select C**u**stomize from the button bar.
2. Select the Matchin**g** option button.
3. Type **b** in the Cla**s**s Contains box to have the class you want the transactions to match appear in the report.
4. Select OK to alter the report to only include the business transactions.

If the business categories use separate categories than your personal transactions, you need to select the categories you wish to appear in the report. To change which categories appear in a report, follow these steps:

1. Select C**u**stomize from the button bar.
2. Select the **C**ategories/Classes option button.
3. Mark the business categories so they have a check mark next to them and clear the personal categories so that they do not.
4. Select OK to alter the report so that it only includes the business transactions.

How do I set the dates for the report?

The Create Report and Customize Report dialog boxes have the settings for dates. For most reports, you can set the date period at the top of the dialog box using the drop-down list box and the From and To date boxes. Many of the reports suggest a default date such as "Year to date." Many of the options you want are in the drop-down list box for the date. The options and the dates they select are:

Date Drop-Down List Box Selection	Description
Include all dates	From the earliest transaction date to the latest transaction date
Current Month	From the first to the last date of this month
Current Quarter	From the first to the last date of this quarter
Current Year	From the first to the last date of this year
Month to date	From the first of the month until today
Quarter to date	From the start of the current quarter until today
Year to date	From January 1 (or the first day of the fiscal year) until today
Earliest to date	From the earliest transaction date until today
Last Month	From the first to the last date of last month
Last Qtr	From the first to the last date of last quarter
Last Year	From the first to the last date of last year
Custom Date	From the date in the From date box to the date in the To date box

You can always set your own dates by entering new ones in the To and From date boxes. If you want to change the default date for your reports, choose the Options button in the button bar of any Report window. Select the date range you want from the drop-down list boxes under Default Report Date Range and select OK.

Tech Tip: You can quickly customize the date in a report. When you double-click with the mouse while pointing at the dates covered in the report, you open the Customize Report dialog box. You will already be at the position for entering new dates for the report.

How do I set my reports to use a fiscal year rather than a calendar year?

A fiscal year uses a different starting point than January 1 for the beginning of the year for financial purposes. If you set Quicken to use a fiscal year instead of a calendar year, Quicken adjusts

Chapter 9 *Reports and Graphs*

the date in reports accordingly. For instance, if you have a report for 1995 and your fiscal calendar starts in July, Quicken knows that the starting date is July 1, 1995, and the ending date is June 30, 1996. To set Quicken to use a fiscal year:

1. Choose Options from the Edit menu.
2. Select the General button.
3. Select the Fiscal Year option button and select the month that starts the fiscal year from the Starting Month drop-down list box.
4. Select Close and then select OK.

How do I change my report to show amounts for each month?

Several reports show beginning and ending amounts or the totals for an entire period for a year. You can change the columns to break out the time covered into smaller periods, such as weeks or months. To set the column heading for a different time period, select Customize from the button bar. With the Report Layout option button selected, select the time period you want for the columns in the Column drop-down list box. Select OK to adjust the report to have the new column headings.

Quicken has many options for column headings. For instance, in the Cash Flow Report in Figure 9-4, the report has columns for each week of the month as well as the final column for the overall total.

Why is my report missing some entries?

Your report may be missing entries for two reasons. First, check that the dates for the report include the dates of the missing transactions. Second, if you just changed a transaction that did not appear in the report but it should now, then you need Quicken to re-create that report. All you do is switch to that report's window and select Customize in the button bar and then select OK.

Cash Flow Report by Week
10/1/95 Through 10/27/95

10/27/95
BARNEY-Bank,Cash,CC Accounts

Category Description	Week of 10/1/95	Week of 10/8/95	Week of 10/15/95	Week of 10/22/95	OVERALL TOTAL
INFLOWS					
Int Inc	0.00	3.29	0.00	0.00	3.29
Salary	420.37	420.37	0.00	420.37	1,261.11
TOTAL INFLOWS	420.37	423.66	0.00	420.37	1,264.40
OUTFLOWS					
Auto:					
Fuel	8.92	0.00	11.10	0.00	20.02
Total Auto	8.92	0.00	11.10	0.00	20.02
Gifts	0.00	59.47	14.94	28.86	103.27
Groceries	0.00	129.79	0.00	0.00	129.79
Hobbies	36.38	0.00	0.00	0.00	36.38
Household	785.33	0.00	0.00	0.00	785.33
Housing	282.00	0.00	0.00	0.00	282.00
Misc	275.54	50.00	150.00	0.00	475.54
Photography	0.00	0.00	16.77	0.00	16.77
Telephone	0.00	85.25	0.00	0.00	85.25
Utilities:					
Gas & Electric	0.00	0.00	36.32	0.00	36.32
Total Utilities	0.00	0.00	36.32	0.00	36.32
TO Personal Mutual Fund	145.29	0.00	0.00	0.00	145.29
TOTAL OUTFLOWS	1,533.46	324.51	229.13	28.86	2,115.96
OVERALL TOTAL	-1,113.09	99.15	-229.13	391.51	-851.56

Page 1

FIGURE 9-4   Cash Flow Report with columns for each week

Layout and Format

Can my reports show the descriptions of categories in place of their names?

Since descriptions are more helpful, you may want categories in reports to show the descriptions rather than the category names. To make the switch for your reports:

1. Choose O**p**tions from the button bar in any Report window.
2. Choose D**e**scription under Category Display and select OK.

Chapter 9 *Reports and Graphs*

Tech Tip: Changing whether Quicken displays names, descriptions, or both for accounts and categories can be done to all of your reports.

Your reports now use the category description in place of the name. Categories that do not have a description continue to show their category name. You can also make the same change for accounts in order to show the account descriptions in reports in place of their names.

Notice that when Quicken alphabetizes the categories, it uses whatever you use to label the categories for the alphabetizing process. Since the category descriptions may start with a different letter than the category names, don't be surprised if the categories are in a different order when you display them by their description.

Why are my report entries shortened?

The report is so wide that Quicken doesn't have enough room to fit all the information. Therefore some of it is cut off. This can include category names, account names, descriptions, and memos. Some solutions to this problem include:

- Removing some of the entries. To remove the category or memo fields from a report that shows them, select C<u>u</u>stomize from the Report window's button bar, then clear the Cat<u>e</u>gory or <u>M</u>emo check box and select OK.

- Limiting what you see for categories and accounts. If showing both the description and name for categories or accounts makes the report too wide, show only one of them. You can set whether the report shows names or descriptions by selecting O<u>p</u>tions in the Report window's button bar.

- Making the report wider. You can do this by changing the orientation from portrait to landscape or by reducing the margins.

- Using a smaller font size to fit more entries across the report.

Tech Tip: Sometimes a report will have abbreviated entries on the screen but will show the entire entry when you print it. If your report only has a few characters missing, preview the report to see whether the printed version has the same problems.

The Customize Report dialog box is missing some options that I've used in other reports. How do I get those other options to appear?

The Customize Report dialog box only shows the options that apply to the current report. You do not see the report options that do not apply.

How do I set the text fonts in reports?

Reports show two fonts—a heading font and a body font. To select the font you use in your reports for these two areas:

1. Choose Printer Setup from the File menu and then Report/Graph Printer Setup.
2. Select Head Font.
3. Select a font, font style, and size for the head text.
4. Select OK to set the heading font.
5. Select Body Font.
6. Select a font, font style, and size for the body text.
7. Select OK to set the body font.
8. Select OK to finish the report and graph setup.

Realize that this setting applies to all Quicken graphs and reports, not just the one you are working on when you make this change.

Tech Terror: The font list will include fonts and font styles that Quicken will not use to print reports. After you change the fonts, print any report to make sure that your choices print.

Can I make the text in a Report window look different?

You can change the fonts Quicken uses to display reports in a Report window. A Report window uses three fonts. The report has a heading, such as Cash Flow Report by Week in Figure 9-4,

Chapter 9 *Reports and Graphs*

heading text, such as Week of 10/1/95 in Figure 9-4, and body text, such as 420.37 in Figure 9-4. To set these fonts, you need to add a few lines to the QUICKEN.INI file. You can modify the file with Windows' Notepad. This file contains several of Quicken's settings. To make this change:

1. Close Quicken.
2. Open the Windows Notepad. Its icon is in the Accessories window in the Program Manager.
3. Choose Open from the File menu.
4. Type **c:\windows\quicken.ini** in the File Name text box and select OK to open this file. You may need to change C:\WINDOWS if this file is in a different location.
5. Move to the beginning of the first blank line after [Quicken] and type:

   ReportTitleFont=*font name*
   ReportHeadingFont=*font name*
   ReportDataFont=*font name*

   For *font name*, enter the font name that you want to use as it appears in list boxes.
6. Choose Save from the File menu.
7. Choose Exit from the File menu.
8. Start Quicken again. The Report windows now use the selected fonts.

How do I change my report's margins?

Report margins are part of the report and graph printer setup. To change your margins in all graphs and reports:

1. Choose Printer Setup from the File menu and then Report/Graph Printer Setup.
2. Type new sizes that you want for the margins in the Left, Right, Top, and Bottom text boxes.
3. Select OK to update the new margins for all graphs and reports.

Printing Reports

How do I fit more columns onto my reports?

You can try two changes to fit more columns on a page. You can print your report sideways (landscape) or change the font size. Printing sideways is a good idea when you want to fit data for a whole year across one page. To rotate a report:

1. Choose Printer Setup from the File menu and then Report/Graph Printer Setup.

2. Select Settings to get to the Control Panel's Setup dialog box for your printer. From here or from one of the dialog boxes available through here, you can change the orientation from portrait to landscape. Printing sideways may take longer, depending on your printer.

3. Select OK until you return to Quicken's Report Printer Setup dialog box, then select OK again to put this dialog box away.

You will probably have to return your printing orientation to portrait for the other items you want to print. Your second option, reducing the size of the font, makes the text smaller so you can fit more on the report. A previous question's answer describes the steps for changing the fonts used in a report. Remember that changing the report's font changes the font size for all reports, not just the one you are working on.

Why does my report look different in a Report window than when I print it?

A Report window shows the contents of the report without the formatting Quicken adds when you print it. The biggest difference between how the report looks on screen and on paper is that long entries such as descriptions and memo fields are truncated on screen.

Chapter 9 *Reports and Graphs*

In order to see how Quicken will print your report, you can preview it. To preview the report before printing it, select the Print button in the button bar and then select Preview. Now you see a preview of how the report looks when printed. Figure 9-5 shows a previewed report. (This is a preview of the printed report that appears in Figure 9-4.) You can look closer at this report by selecting Zoom In. If the report looks the way you want, select Print. If it does not, select Close, then adjust the report to get what you want.

What is the difference between the Print button in the iconbar and in the button bar?

The location—both buttons will print your report when you click them from a Report window.

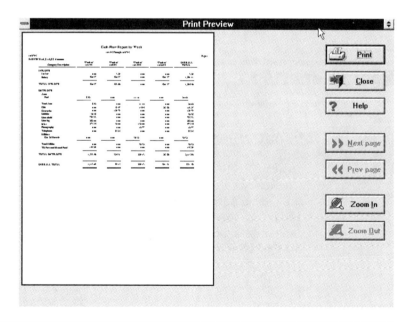

FIGURE 9-5   Preview of a report

How do I print reports on different sized paper?

You can tell Quicken the paper size to print its reports on by telling the Windows Control Panel program the default paper size. Rather than switching programs, you can get to the printer settings in the Windows Control Panel program through Quicken. To do this:

1. Choose Printer Setup from the File menu and then Report/Graph Printer Setup.
2. Select Settings to go to the Control Panel's Setup dialog box for your printer. Each printer causes the Control Panel to show a different dialog box that matches the settings that are appropriate for the selected printer.
3. Select a new paper size and then select OK. The exact way that you select a paper size depends on your printer.
4. Select OK until you return to Quicken's Report Printer Setup dialog box.
5. Select OK to finish your printer setup changes.

QuickZoom Reports

How do I find out where a number in a report came from?

You can create a QuickZoom report that shows where Quicken got the number that you see in the report. To create this QuickZoom report, double-click the number or move to it and press ENTER. When you point to a number for which Quicken can create a QuickZoom report, the mouse pointer changes to the QuickZoom magnifying glass—a magnifying glass with a Z

Chapter 9 *Reports and Graphs*

in it. A QuickZoom report for the 420.37 number in Figure 9-4 might look like this:

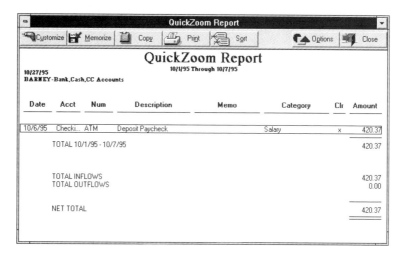

I see a wrong entry in a report. How do I get to that transaction to fix it?

Double-click the number that you think is wrong. Quicken displays a QuickZoom report showing the transactions that generated the number. Double-click the transaction that you think is wrong and Quicken opens that account's Register window and places you at that transaction. When you fix the transaction, the original report and the QuickZoom report update to reflect the correction.

Why does the mouse pointer in a report sometimes display as a C and other times as a Z?

The different character in the mouse pointer's magnifying glass describes what you will see when you double-click what you are pointing to. While the magnifying glass shows a C, such as when you point to the title, double-clicking shows the Customize Report dialog box. You will see this pointer when you point to the report's title, date, or accounts. While the magnifying glass shows a Z, double-clicking shows a QuickZoom report that provides the details regarding the number that you just double-clicked. When you are in a QuickZoom report and double-click a transaction, you switch to that transaction in the account's Register window.

Quicken Reports in Word Processors

How do I put my Quicken report into my word processor?

You can copy your Quicken report to another application using the Clipboard. Copy your Quicken report to the Clipboard by selecting Cop<u>y</u> in the button bar. Then you can switch to your word processor or any other Windows application and paste it there. How the report appears in the other application depends on that application. In Excel, the entries are copied into separate columns and rows. In a word processor, the report's columns are separated by tabs as you can see here:

Tech Tip: You may need to adjust the tab stops in order to have the tabs line up in the word processing document the way they do in Quicken. Also, the copied report does not include the title and column headings.

Another option for putting a Quicken report into a word processor is to print it to a text file, then open the text file into a word processing document. To do this:

1. Select Pri<u>n</u>t from the Report window's button bar.

2. Select the ASCII <u>D</u>isk File or Ta<u>b</u>-delimited Disk File option button to select how you want the document printed. ASCII <u>D</u>isk File will include the report title and heading using spaces to separate the columns. Ta<u>b</u>-delimited Disk

File omits the report title and uses tabs to separate the columns.

3. Select Print to print the report.
4. Type a name for the file and select OK.
5. Switch back to your word processor.
6. Open the file in your word processor. The exact steps to do this depend on the word processor you use.

My columns got messed up when I copied my report to my word processor. How do I get my columns back?

The columns in the report are separated with tabs. The tab stops in your word processor are not in the same positions as the columns in Quicken. Change the tab stops in the word processor and it will restore the report columns, as you can see here:

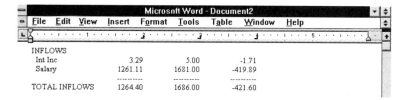

Tech Tip: Most word processors let you right align text at a tab stop. This is the type of tab stop you want to use when you copy your Quicken data. Then the column headings and the numbers line up at the decimal point.

Report Windows

Why do all my reports disappear when I open Quicken again?

Quicken does not re-create the Report windows that you had open the last time you used Quicken. When Quicken remembers which windows are open on a desktop, it skips over all Report windows. You must create the report again. If it is a report that you use often, memorize the report and leave the Memorized Reports window open. Quicken will reopen the Memorized Reports window if it is part of the saved desktop.

How do I keep the report I have just created?

You can memorize a report when you want Quicken to remember all the settings that you used in that report. Then, the next time you want a report, Quicken creates the report with the same settings. To memorize the report:

1. Create a report using the settings that you will want to use repeatedly.
2. Select <u>M</u>emorize from the button bar.
3. Adjust the report's title in the <u>T</u>itle text box so that it has the name that you want for your memorized report.
4. Select how you want the report dates memorized.
5. Select OK.

Later when you want to see that report again, just select the memorized report. To select a memorized report:

1. Choose <u>M</u>emorized Reports from the <u>R</u>eports menu to open the Memorized Reports window.
2. Highlight the memorized report that you want.
3. Double-click the report name or select <u>U</u>se in the button bar.
4. Select OK to create the report. The report's title is the name of the memorized report.

Can I set up my memorized reports so that they always use the same dates?

Quicken can memorize the dates in a memorized report three ways. You can use the Monthly Budget Report in Figure 9-6 as an example of how the three ways work. The memorized report

Chapter 9 *Reports and Graphs*

can repeat the same selections in the date drop-down list boxes, such as remembering Last Month for the Budget report. The memorized report can remember the specific date range as in 10/1/95 through 10/31/95 for the Budget report. Finally, the memorized report can remember the default for the report type which, for a Budget report like the one in Figure 9-6, is "Year to date." To select how the memorized report remembers the dates, select Memorize from the button bar, and then select how you want the dates memorized. The Memorize Report dialog box for memorizing the report in Figure 10-6 looks like this:

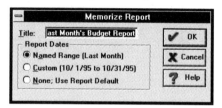

Choose one of the option buttons below Report Dates to select how you want the dates in the report memorized.

Tech Tip: Comparison reports work with two sets of dates. You can set how the first and second comparison date ranges are memorized separately for these reports.

Filtering Reports

Is there any way to ignore transactions with zero amounts so that they do not clutter a report?

You can select transactions according to their amounts. This feature lets you skip items that have a 0 for the Amount field. To remove zero-amount transactions from a report:

1. Select Customize from the Report window's button bar.
2. Select the Transactions option button.

Monthly Budget Report
10/1/95 Through 10/31/95

11/27/95
BARNEY-Bank,Cash,CC Accounts

Category Description	10/1/95 Actual	Budget	10/31/95 Diff
INFLOWS			
Int Inc	3.29	5.00	-1.71
Salary	1,261.11	1,681.00	-419.89
TOTAL INFLOWS	1,264.40	1,686.00	-421.60
OUTFLOWS			
Auto:			
Fuel	20.02	40.00	19.98
Total Auto	20.02	40.00	19.98
Christmas	0.00	0.00	0.00
Clothing	0.00	15.00	15.00
Dues	0.00	0.00	0.00
Entertain	0.00	20.00	20.00
Gifts	103.27	50.00	-53.27
Groceries	129.79	100.00	-29.79
Hobbies	36.38	30.00	-6.38
Household	785.33	0.00	-785.33
Housing	282.00	282.00	0.00
Insurance	506.00	0.00	-506.00
Laundry	0.00	5.00	5.00
Medical	0.00	0.00	0.00
Misc	475.54	100.00	-375.54
Photography	16.77	20.00	3.23
Recreation	0.00	10.00	10.00
Tax:			
Fed	0.00	0.00	0.00
Local	0.00	0.00	0.00
Tax - Other	0.00	0.00	0.00
Total Tax	0.00	0.00	0.00
Telephone	85.25	40.00	-45.25
Utilities:			
Gas & Electric	36.32	30.00	-6.32
Total Utilities	36.32	30.00	-6.32
Vacation	0.00	0.00	0.00
TOTAL OUTFLOWS	2,476.67	742.00	-1,734.67
OVERALL TOTAL	-1,212.27	944.00	-2,156.27

FIGURE 9-6   Monthly Budget Report comparing a month's budget against actual spending

3. Select Greater Than from the A<u>m</u>ount drop-down list box and type **0** in the text box if it is not already there.

4. Select OK to remove the zero-amount transactions from the report.

Chapter 9 *Reports and Graphs*

How can I filter to include more than one item?

The filters for the Payee, Category, Class, and Memo fields only let you enter one matching entry. If you want a report to find two payees or two memo field entries, the filter must be broad enough to find both of them or you must create separate reports. With categories and classes, you can limit the categories and classes that appear in the report by selecting the Categories/Classes option button in the Customize Report dialog box, then selecting the categories and classes you want included.

Tech Tip: Quicken may be running slower because as you make your changes, Quicken has to update your reports. If you are making many changes, put the Report windows away, finish your changes, and then re-create the reports.

Can I create a filter to find transactions that are missing an entry?

You can create filters to find transactions that are missing a Payee, Category, Class, or Memo field entry. When you select Customize and the Matching option button, type ~ in the Payee Contains, Category Contains, Class Contains, or Memo Contains box. For example, typing ~ in the Memo Contains box finds transactions that do not have a Memo field entry.

How do I get rid of uncategorized transactions in my reports?

You can remove uncategorized transactions from reports in two ways. First, you can categorize them. Second, you can tell Quicken to ignore these uncategorized transactions for the reports. Ideally, you want to employ the first method. To find these transactions so that you can assign them to categories:

1. Highlight the number representing the uncategorized transaction. The label for this item varies according to the report. Some examples that you might see include Income-Other or Expense-Other, Inflows-Other, and Outflows-Other.

2. Double-click the number to create a QuickZoom report showing transactions that do not have a Category field entry.

At this point, you can double-click the transaction you want to change in the QuickZoom report in order to switch to that transaction's register entry. Fixing that transaction updates the original report and the QuickZoom report. After you assign categories for all of the uncategorized transactions, you will see the prompt: "No matching transactions found. Change report settings?" If you still have some uncategorized transactions that you do not want appearing in a report, you can customize the report, choose the Categories/Classes option button, and remove the check mark from Not Categorized in the Category list box.

Other Report Settings

What is the difference between cash flow and income & expense organization in reports?

When the Report Layout option button is selected in the Customize Report dialog box, some reports show an Organization drop-down list box. This drop-down list box frequently offers the choices of Cash flow basis and Income & expense. If you select Cash flow basis, the report displays cash inflows from transfers in the income category and cash outflows in the expense categories. In a report organized by Income & expense, the transfers are separate from the income and expense categories.

Tech Tip: Budget reports have a third possibility in the Organization drop-down list box: Supercategory. This choice organizes all items in the report according to the budget supercategories. The only other choices you might see are Net worth and Balance sheet, which appear for the Net Worth and Balance Sheet reports. These two choices determine whether the net worth appears as the net total or as an Equity balance sheet item.

On a report showing my checking account balance, the balance is higher than in that account's Register window. What happened to the numbers?

When you exclude the transfers from an account balance, Quicken doesn't include transfers in and out of the account. This can result in a balance that is different from your account's true balance. To fix this problem, show all transfers. To do this, customize the report and select the Show Rows button. Select Include All from the Transfers drop-down list box.

Graphs

Can I make a graph that will show me how much I've saved this year?

You can get a picture of what you have saved over the year with an Income and Expense graph. This graph has two parts to it: a Monthly Income and Expenses bar chart and a Net Savings and Expense Comparison pie chart. To create this graph:

1. Choose Graphs from the Reports menu and choose Income and Expense.

2. Enter the time period you want covered in the From and To boxes.

3. Select Create to create a graph like the one in Figure 9-7.

   This graph shows the income and expenses for twelve months. The bottom graph is a pie chart showing the categories in which you have spent money. To prevent the pie from having too many slices, the pie only shows ten categories at a time. Ideally, your savings are one of the first ten, but if not, click Next 10 until you see a Net Savings slice.

4. Double-click the Net Savings slice or its label on the right side of the pie. Quicken creates another graph focusing just on the Net Savings. This graph is labeled Net Income by Month but it shows how much you have saved through the year as you can see on this graph here:

   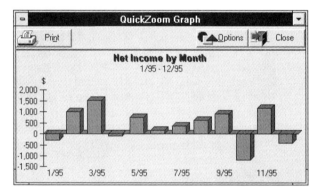

5. Select Close in both Graph windows to put them away.

How do I know the value of a bar or slice in a graph?

When you point to any slice or bar in a Graph window, the pointer turns to a QuickZoom magnifying glass that shows the small Z in the magnifier. When the pointer looks like this, you can see any slice's or bar's value by holding down the mouse on that slice or bar. With the slices, you can also hold down the mouse on the slice to see a label.

Chapter 9 *Reports and Graphs*

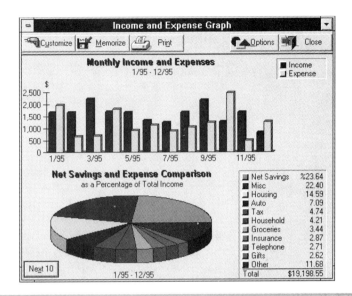

FIGURE 9-7 Income and Expenses Graph window showing what you have spent and earned

How can I create a report that shows the same numbers that appear in my graphs?

You can create a report that shows the same numbers that the graph presents. The report you create depends on the graph that you use. The following list describes the graph types and the reports you can create.

- For an Income and Expense graph, create a Cash Flow Report. You may need to modify the report to include the same accounts that appear on the graph. If you display the percentages as well as the actual amounts, the percentages on the report will be different from the ones in the graph. In a Cash Flow Report, the expense percentages are calculated according to the total expense. The percentages in the Net Savings and Expense Comparison graph show the percentages using total expenses and savings. When you want to see the expenses and income divided by month, show month columns in the Cash Flow Report. As an example, the Cash Flow Report in Figure 9-8 shows the year's worth of expenses. These are the same expenses that appear in the pie chart in Figure 9-7.

- For a Budget Variances graph, create a Monthly Budget Report. Make sure that the dates in the Monthly Budget Report include the entire month. You will want to organize the report by supercategories if the graph shows supercategories. The Diff column in the report shows the monthly over or under budget amounts that are graphed in the Annual vs. Budgeted Net Income. The Monthly Budget Report's final actual and budget column shows the same numbers as the Budget Variances graph. You may have a discrepancy if the Budget Variances graph includes the opening balance transaction in its amount.

- For a Net Worth graph, create a Net Worth report. You will want to change the Interval drop-down list box in the Customize Report dialog box to Month and set the From date to begin the first day of the month that the graph starts. The value of the graph's yellow bars is represented by the numbers in the Total Assets row. The value of the graph's blue bars is represented by the numbers in the Total Liabilities row. The value of the red dots in the graph is represented by the numbers in the Overall Total or Equity row.

- For the Investment Performance graph, you can create a Portfolio Value report for each month in the graph to show the balances in the investment accounts. The Average Annual Total Return graph shows the IRR or average annual total return calculated for the selected account's securities. You can choose to subtotal by account or by security, to select how to present the data.

12/20/95
BARNEY-Selected Accounts

Page 1

Cash Flow Report
1/1/95 Through 12/20/95

Category Description	1/1/95–12/20/95	
INFLOWS		
Int Inc		33.33
Salary		18,916.65
_DivInc		193.84
_LT CapGnDst		46.31
_ST CapGnDst		8.42
TOTAL INFLOWS		19,198.55
OUTFLOWS		
Auto:		
Fuel	120.34	
Service	240.93	
Auto - Other	1,000.00	
Total Auto		1,361.27
Bank Chrg		7.50
Charity		20.00
Clothing		99.00
Dining		123.20
Dues		226.00
Entertain		94.00
Gifts		502.97
Groceries		660.56
Hobbies		244.91
Household		807.52
Housing		2,801.00
Insurance		551.00
Laundry		0.50
Medical		430.00
Misc		4,300.75
Photography		129.02
Tax:		
Fed	557.00	
Local	353.00	
Total Tax		910.00
Telephone		521.10
Utilities:		
Gas & Electric	395.31	
Total Utilities		395.31
Vacation		422.11
Outflows - Other		51.43
TO Savings goal account		1,000.00
TO Savings goal account		150.00
TOTAL OUTFLOWS		15,809.15
OVERALL TOTAL		3,389.40

FIGURE 9-8   Cash Flow Report showing the numbers graphed in an Income and Expense graph

Changing Graphs

 Can I hide a category in a graph?

You can hide categories in a graph by filtering out the categories that you do not want. To select which categories appear in a graph:

1. Select Customize in the button bar.
2. Select Categories.
3. Click the categories you do not want in the graph so that they do not have a check mark.
4. Select OK twice to create the graph without the chosen categories.

Hiding a category only leaves out its pie slice from the pie. The Subtotal number remains the same.

Tech Tip: You can also temporarily hide categories by holding down the SHIFT key and clicking them. Hiding the category this way doesn't change the numbers that the graph shows. Hiding the category just removes it from the graph until that category is in the pie that is redrawn. This means that if you want to show the category that you have hidden, keep selecting Next 10 until you cycle through all the pies.

 How do I change which accounts are in an Income and Expense graph?

The Income and Expense graph initially includes all accounts but you can change which ones Quicken includes. For example, you may only want to focus on your credit card and checking accounts. You can select which accounts appear in a graph by following these steps:

1. Select Customize in the button bar.
2. Select the Accounts option button.

Chapter 9 *Reports and Graphs*

3. Click the accounts you do not want in the graph so that they do not have a check mark.
4. Select OK twice to create a graph with only the chosen accounts.

How can I view more detail in a pie chart or bar graph?

You can show more information about a particular bar or pie slice by creating a QuickZoom graph. Just point to any bar or pie slice, and you will see the mouse pointer showing a magnifying glass with a Z. Double-click the mouse and Quicken shows a QuickZoom graph. The contents of the QuickZoom graph depend on the original graph type and which part of the graph you double-click. For example, double-click a bar for a category in the Actual vs. Budgeted Categories and the QuickZoom graph shows a monthly breakdown for the budget and actual amounts for that category as you can see here:

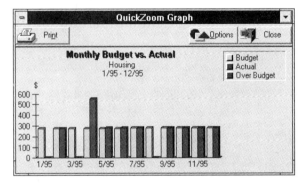

With a graph type such as a Net Worth graph, double-clicking the asset or liability bar displays a QuickZoom with a pie graph that illustrates the percentages of your different assets or liabilities for that month.

Can I put the different graphs Quicken has created into separate windows?

Most types of Quicken's graphs contain two parts. You can put each part in its own Graph window. To make the change:

1. Open a Graph window.
2. Select <u>O</u>ptions in the button bar.
3. Select the <u>C</u>reate All Graphs in Separate Windows check box and select OK.

Now, every time you tell Quicken to create a graph that has two parts, Quicken creates two Graph windows with each part appearing in its own window.

Tech Tip: Quicken closes any open Graph windows before it creates a new one. You cannot leave the Graph window from one graph type open while you create another one.

How do I make graphs faster?

If your system is slow, you can change how Quicken draws graphs, in order to draw them faster. To make the change:

1. Open a Graph window.
2. Select <u>O</u>ptions in the button bar.
3. Select the D<u>r</u>aw in 2D check box and then select OK.

Now, Quicken's graphs are flat bar and pie graphs instead of the three-dimensional ones. Quicken draws these graph types faster.

Printing Graphs

Can I print my graphs so that the bars are distinguished by patterns, rather than colors?

When your printer only prints in one color, Quicken can print the bars and pie slices in graphs using different patterns, rather than colors, to distinguish them. You can show the same patterns in the Graph window to see how the patterns will look when printed.

Chapter 9 *Reports and Graphs*

1. Open a Graph window.
2. Select <u>O</u>ptions in the button bar.
3. Select the <u>D</u>isplay Patterns on Screen check box and select OK.

Now, Quicken's graphs show patterns to mark the different slices instead of different colors.

My graphs take forever to print on my printer. What can I do?

The steps you can take to make printing graphs faster depend on your printer. All of these steps involve changing the printer setup. To make graphs print faster, follow these steps:

1. Choose Printer <u>S</u>etup from the <u>F</u>ile menu and then <u>R</u>eport/Graph Printer Setup.
2. Make the change that is appropriate for your printer:

Tech Terror: Some of the changes may have more far-reaching effects. Changing the print resolution here changes it for all applications, not just Quicken. The font changes you make for a dot-matrix printer will also affect your reports.

- Postscript Printer   Select the Print reports and graphs in <u>c</u>olor check box. This applies even if your printer does not print colors.
- Laser Printer   Select <u>S</u>ettings to go to the Control Panel's Setup dialog box for your printer. From here or from one of the dialog boxes available from here, you can change the dpi or graphics resolution to a lower number. Different laser printers have different Setup dialog boxes so your setting may be in the Setup dialog box or you may need to select a button or two. Select OK until you return to Quicken's Report Printer Setup dialog box.
- Dot-matrix printer   Select <u>H</u>ead Font and change the font Quicken uses for your reports and graphs to a font that is built into your printer. You want to choose a font that has cpi in its name or a printer next to its name. Select OK. Select <u>B</u>ody Font and change the font Quicken uses for your reports and graphs to the font that is built into your printer. Select OK.

3. Select OK to finish your printer setup changes.

Why don't my graphs print in color?

You can set Quicken to print graphs in several colors or in one color. To set Quicken to print in color:

1. Choose Printer Setup from the File menu and then Report/Graph Printer Setup.
2. Select the Print reports and graphs in color check box.
3. Select OK to finish your printer setup changes.

Now when you print the graph, your color printer will print the different bars and pie sections with different colors.

Something is wrong every time I print from Quicken but it doesn't happen when I print from other programs. How do I fix this problem?

The first change you want to make is to rename the WPR.DAT file. This file stores Quicken's settings for the printers you use. To rename the WPR.DAT file:

1. Open Windows' File Manager. This program's icon is in the Main program group in the Program Manager.
2. Find and highlight the WPR.DAT file, which is in the same drive and directory as your other Quicken program files.
3. Choose Rename from the File menu.
4. Type a new name for this file in the To text box and then select OK.
5. Choose Exit from the File menu to leave the File Manager.

Doing these steps, then restarting Quicken re-creates a new WPR.DAT file. Later when you are done, you can rename the old print settings file back to WPR.DAT to return to your previous settings. Be aware that you will lose your font and check alignment settings. If this doesn't work, the WPR.DAT file is not the problem and you should try printing directly to the printer following the steps below.

Disable the Print Manager. Disabling the Print Manager creates a "direct line" from Quicken to the printer. Under some

Chapter 9 *Reports and Graphs*

circumstances, this corrects printing problems by allotting the system resources to one job at a time. To disable the Print Manager:

1. Open the Windows Control Panel program. This program's icon is in the Main program group in the Program Manager.
2. Double-click the Printers icon to open the Printers dialog box.
3. Clear the Use Print Manager check box.
4. Select OK.
5. Choose Exit from the Settings menu to close the Control Panel.

Financial Planning

Careful financial planning can help you to realize your financial goals. We've already taken a look at Quicken's budgeting features and the Financial Calendar. Quicken has many additional financial planning tools that can help you put together a plan tailored for your individual needs. Many people will find that these tools provide them with everything they need, without any assistance from a personal planning professional. Even if you do decide to seek outside expertise to get your financial house in order, you will find that these tools provide a better understanding and perspective of what you need to do to realize your financial goals. If you have not used Forecasting or Quicken's planners, look at the Frustration Busters box for a brief description of what you can expect.

FRUSTRATION BUSTERS!

Quicken has several features that help you make financial plans. These features include:

- **Savings Planner** This planner can calculate how much you earn from investing money—as a fixed sum, a series of payments, or both. It can also work backward to calculate how much you must invest to earn a predetermined amount.

- **Retirement Planner** This planner can calculate your future retirement income, how much you have saved, and how much you need to set aside yearly.

- **Refinance Planner** This planner calculates how much you save when you refinance a loan. The return calculations show how the payment changes and how long it takes to recover what you pay in closing costs and points.

- **College Planner** This planner calculates how much you need to save in order to pay for rising tuition costs. This planner assumes that nothing is withdrawn for many years but that once you start withdrawing, you will withdraw for several years.

- **Loan Planner** This planner can calculate the monthly payment on a loan or how much you can borrow.

- **Savings Goals** Savings goals set aside money from an account that you earmark for a special purpose. By hiding money here, it is available for your goal and safe from impulse spending.

- **Forecasting Feature** This feature uses what you spend and earn to show how your account balances change over time. It can show you whether you can afford your spending habits.

Savings Planner

 How can I estimate what my CD will earn?

Quicken's Savings Planner can estimate what a certificate of deposit (CD) will yield. For example, to estimate what an $8,000 five-year CD earning 7% interest will return:

1. Choose Financial <u>P</u>lanners from the Pl<u>a</u>n menu and select <u>S</u>avings.

2. Enter the following information in the Investment Savings Planner dialog box.

   - <u>O</u>pening Savings Balance   Enter **8000** for the $8,000 initially deposited.
   - Annual <u>Y</u>ield   Enter **7%** for the 7% interest rate.
   - <u>N</u>umber of   Enter **Years** in the drop-down list box and **5** in the text box next to it.

3. Clear the Ending Balance in <u>T</u>oday's $ check box. Savings can be stated in today's dollars or in tomorrow's. Clearing this check box shows what the ending balance will be in 5 years. If you want to understand why checking or clearing the Ending Balance in <u>T</u>oday's $ check box makes such a difference in the ending balance, look at the question, "Why does the Savings Planner focus on today's dollars?"

   Quicken takes your entries and calculates the result after <u>E</u>nding Savings Balance. The completed dialog box looks like the one in Figure 10-1.

4. Select <u>S</u>chedule. The Deposit Schedule dialog box lists each year's ending balance, as you can see here. You can select <u>P</u>rint to print this schedule. Then, you can use the calculator to compute each year's interest income so you can include it in your financial forecasts. Select Close to put this dialog box away.

5. Select Done.

Tech Acct: Remember that when a CD matures and you renew it, it renews at a new interest rate. Also, you recognize the interest income from the CD each year even though you do not redeem it until it matures.

FIGURE 10-1 Investment Savings Planner dialog box for a CD

How can I find out what the mutual fund that I contribute to each year will be worth?

Calculating the value of an investment that you contribute to over several years is similar to estimating what a CD will earn. To give you an example of how to calculate an investment's value, suppose that you will add $2,000 yearly to your mutual fund and you plan to contribute to it for the next 40 years. To calculate how much the investment will be worth:

1. Choose Financial Planners from the Plan menu and select Savings.

2. Enter the following information in the Investment Savings Planner dialog box:

   - Annual Yield   Enter **7%** for a 7% interest rate. You don't know what the actual rate will be so you make a reasonable guess.
   - Number of   Enter **Years** in the drop-down list box and **40** in the text box next to it.
   - Contribution Each   Enter **Year** in the drop-down list box and **2000** in the text box next to it.

   Quicken calculates the value of your investment in today's dollars after Ending Savings Balance. The completed dialog box looks like the one in Figure 10-2.

3. Clear the Ending Balance in Today's $ check box. Now the dialog box shows what the final balance of your investment will be. If you want to understand why checking or clearing the Ending Balance in Today's $ check box makes such a difference in the ending balance, look at the question, "Why does the Savings Planner focus on today's dollars?"

4. Select Done to put the dialog box away.

Tech Tip: When you calculate an investment's value and you have already begun putting money into that investment, enter the amount you have already invested in the Opening Savings Balance text box.

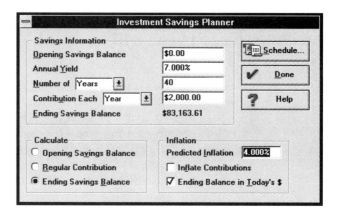

FIGURE 10-2   Investment Savings Planner dialog box for an investment

Why does the Savings Planner focus on today's dollars?

The Investment Savings Planner dialog box shows two separate numbers depending on whether you select or clear the Ending Balance in Today's $ check box. For example, the investment value calculated in the previous question shows $399,270.22 if the check box is not selected or $83,163.61 if the check box is selected.

The difference is created by inflation. Inflation strips away the buying power of money. For example, if yearly inflation is 8%, you will need $1.08 next year to buy what you currently buy with $1. Knowing the amount in today's dollars provides an idea of how much your savings or investments are worth using today's prices. So the value of the investment equals $83,163.61 of today's dollars. However, when you redeem your investment, you will have more dollars, each of which are worth less. The same investment in tomorrow's dollars is $399,270.22, for the example shown here. This is the value Quicken shows when you clear the Ending Balance in Today's $ check box. You can change the assumed inflation rate by entering a new percentage in the Predicted Inflation text box.

Retirement Planner

 How much I can withdraw yearly from my IRA for the next 20 years, now that I have retired?

The Retirement Planner can show you how much you can withdraw in today's dollars from an IRA or any other annuity for a set period of years. To see this feature, you can work with these assumptions:

- $100,000 for the current value of the IRA
- 8% annual interest
- 4% inflation
- A current age of 65

The steps that you perform are as follows.

1. Choose Financial Planners from the Plan menu and select Retirement to display the Retirement Planner dialog box.
2. Select the Annual Retirement Income option button so this dialog box will show the amount in today's dollars that you will be spending.
3. Enter the following information in the dialog box:

    - Current Savings   Enter **100000** as the current value of the IRA.
    - Annual Yield   Enter **8%** for the 8% interest rate that your IRA earns on the amount that you do not withdraw.
    - Annual Contribution   Enter **0** because you will not add anything to the account.
    - Current Age   Enter **65**.
    - Retirement Age   Enter **65**.
    - Withdraw Until Age   Enter **85**.

4. Move to another part of the dialog box so Quicken updates the calculation after A<u>n</u>nual Income After Taxes. The result of $5,941.04 tells you that you can withdraw this much yearly, adjusted for 4% inflation and the IRA will last for 20 years. If you want to see this information broken down to a yearly basis, select <u>S</u>chedule to see the following table:

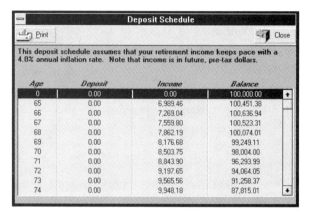

Tech Acct: The IRS has its own rules for minimum and maximum withdrawals. Make sure you check that what you withdraw is within the amount allowed.

Each year, you withdraw $5,941.04 adjusted for inflation. This decreases how much remains in your IRA earning interest, but you can continue withdrawing. In the last year, your final withdrawal of $14,725.77 removes all that remains in the account.

5. Select Close and then <u>D</u>one to put the table and dialog box away.

Refinance Planner

I'm thinking about refinancing my home. How do I enter the loan calculations to know if I want to refinance?

Quicken has its own Refinance Planner that can run through the numbers for you. Suppose that you are thinking of refinancing your $37,000 30-year mortgage that you have had for six years with an 11% interest rate. Your local bank will refinance the loan at 7.5% with 1% closing costs if it is shortened to a 15-year loan. To run through these calculations:

1. Choose Financial Planners from the Plan menu and select Refinance to display the Refinance dialog box.

2. Enter the following information in the dialog box:

   - Current payment   Enter **407.36**, which includes the $352.36 loan payment and the $55 taxes and insurance. You can determine this amount from your check register.

   - Impound/escrow account   Enter **55** for the taxes and insurance that are due with the mortgage payment.

   - Principal amount   Enter **$35,663.02** for the amount still due on the first mortgage. If you set up the loan in Quicken, Quicken allocates each payment between interest and principal; you can see this amount before you perform these steps by looking at the View Loans dialog box.

   - Years   Enter **15** for the term of the new loan.

   - Interest rate   Enter **7.5** for the interest rate of the new loan.

   - Mortgage points   Enter **1** for 1% of the loan amount for closing costs.

   Quicken reports the new principal and interest payment of $330.60 and monthly savings of $21.76. After your refinancing, your new payment will be 385.60, which includes the new payment plus insurance and taxes. The break-even analysis shows that you will recoup your closing costs in a little over 16 months.

3. Select Print if you want a printed copy of this or select Done to put this dialog box away.

Savings Goals

 I'm saving up for something special. How do I earmark what I've saved?

You can create a savings goal that separates money you have saved for this purpose from other money in the account. This money can be hidden so that the account looks as if you withdrew the money and put it into a separate account.
To try out this feature:

1. Choose Savings Goals from the Plan menu to open the Savings Goals dialog box.
2. Select New to create the new savings goal.
3. Enter the following information in the dialog box:

   - Goal Name   Enter a name for your goal, like **Trip to Germany**.
   - Goal Amount   Enter the amount you want saved in the text box.
   - Finish Date   Enter a date for when you expect to have all the savings set aside for this goal.

4. Select OK. You now have a savings goal. Also notice how Quicken has calculated a suggested monthly contribution based on how much you want saved and when you want it saved by.
5. Select Close to put this Savings Goal window away.

Now that you have the savings goal created, you can make contributions to it. You may notice that Quicken has created an account for the savings goal. Contributions appear as transfers to this account. To make a contribution:

1. Choose Savings Goals from the Plan menu.
2. Select the Contribute button.
3. Select the checking account or other account from which you want to contribute money in the From Account drop-down list box.

Chapter 10 *Financial Planning*

4. Enter the amount set aside for the savings goal in the text box after the $ sign and select OK. Now, the Savings Goals dialog box updates the progress you have made toward your savings. You can also show a progress report like this using Quicken's Progress Bars.
5. Select Close to put the Savings Goals window away.
6. Return to the account's Register window. The transaction you have made looks like this:

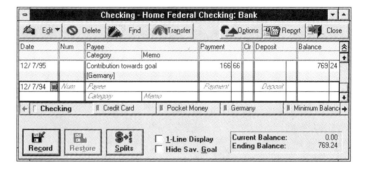

Remember that your bank balance does not include what you have set aside for the savings goal. If you need to see what the balance really is, select the Hide Sav. Goal check box. Then Quicken treats the account as though you had no savings goals. What you have set aside is included in the account's balance.

Tech Tip: You can set aside money for your savings goal from multiple bank accounts. Each account that has money set aside will show the Hide Sav. Goal check box in its Register window.

 ## How can I see how close I am to my savings goal?

Once you open the Savings Goals window, Quicken shows information about the highlighted savings goal. You can highlight the savings goal you are interested in and the window shows what you have set aside, as you can see in Figure 10-3.

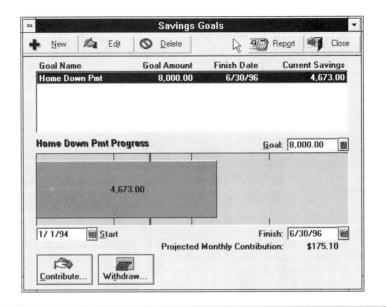

FIGURE 10-3   Savings Goals window showing what is set aside for a goal

I'm ready to spend what I've saved in one of my savings goals. How do I record it?

You can close out a savings goal with one of three methods, depending on whether you still want the savings goal to continue and what kind of records you want to leave behind.

The first method works when you are using part of what you have set aside for the savings goal and you still want to use the savings goal. An example is paying part of a child's tuition. You will still need the savings goal in order to pay the remaining tuition. For this case, follow these steps:

1. Choose Savings Goals from the Plan menu to display the Savings Goals dialog box.
2. Highlight the savings goal that you are spending from.
3. Select Withdraw in the window's button bar.
4. Select the account into which you want the money returned in the Put funds back in drop-down list box.

Chapter 10 *Financial Planning*

5. Select the amount to return in the text box after the $ sign.
6. Select OK.
7. Select Close to put the Savings Goals window away.

The amount you withdrew is now available in the chosen account. You are ready to pay for whatever you have saved for. You still have the savings goal and all of its transactions.

The second method works when you spend all of what you have set aside for the savings goal or when anything left returns to the account from which it was set aside. An example is a house down payment. For this case, follow these steps:

1. Choose Savings Goals from the Plan menu to display the Savings Goals dialog box.
2. Highlight the savings goal that you are finished using.
3. Select Delete in the window's button bar.
4. Select Yes, that you want to keep the asset account.
5. Select Close to put the Savings Goals window away.

You still have the savings goal, and the transactions for contributions that you made continue to appear in the register.

The third method works for removing the savings goal and all the transactions for the contributions that you made. For example, suppose that you are saving for a vacation in the Bahamas and you win a trip there. In this case, you can just delete the savings goal because you no longer need to reserve what you have set aside. To remove the savings goal for this reason:

1. Choose Savings Goals from the Plan menu to display the Savings Goals dialog box.
2. Highlight the savings goal that you no longer want.
3. Select Delete in the window's button bar.
4. Select No, that you do not want to keep the asset account.
5. Select Close to put the Savings Goals window away.

You no longer have an account for your savings goal and when you look at the register where you made savings goal contributions, you will see that these transactions no longer appear.

Forecasting

Can Quicken tell me how much I will save if I continue to earn and spend as I have been doing?

Quicken's forecasting feature takes what you spend and earn and projects how much you can save. When you choose Forecasting from the Plan menu, Quicken looks at the data you have and estimates what your income and expenses will be. These totals appear in the Forecasting window, like the one in Figure 10-4, after Income and Expense.

Are forecasting and budgeting identical activities?

Both forecasting and budgeting help you plan your financial future by looking at what you plan to spend and earn. They perform a what-if analysis for possible changes in your finances.

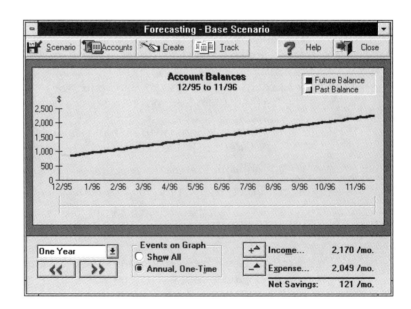

FIGURE 10-4   Forecasting window

A budget lets you to compare what you actually did versus what you had planned to do. Forecasting projects your cash flows. As an example, if you spend too much money dining out, the budget can compare what you spent to what you had planned to spend. A forecast shows you that if you keep spending as you have been, that you will run out of money. Budgets and forecasts are not unrelated since you can create a budget out of a forecast and a forecast out of budget.

Where do my forecasted income and expenses come from?

Quicken creates a forecast by assembling the income and expense items. These items are further divided into known and estimated items. Estimated items are like the estimates that Quicken can prepare for a budget. Quicken looks at the amount you have assigned to one of these categories and averages them for the entire time period. Known items include scheduled transactions as well as recurring register transactions. Known and estimated items don't overlap because Quicken doesn't calculate estimates for categories in which Quicken finds known items.

How do I adjust my forecast for buying a house?

When you buy a house, or move from one to another, you have one set of numbers in your forecast that ends and another that starts. For instance, you probably have an old housing expense that needs to end at a specific date and you need to add a new one. The following steps assume that it is December and that your $300 a month rent payments end in June and a mortgage payment of $450 starts in June. The steps from the Forecasting window are:

1. Select the Expense button to modify the expenses you have recorded.
2. Highlight the Housing category that includes the rent and select Edit.
3. Double-check the number in the Amount text box.
4. Select the Next Scheduled option button and then enter the next rent payment's due date in the adjoining text box.

5. Select Mo_re, then enter the number of remaining payments and select OK. As an example, if it is December, you would enter **6** for January through June's rent.

6. Select _New to create a new expense item in your forecast.

7. Enter the new information for the expense category. For the example of the mortgage payment, you make these entries:

    - Description   Enter **Mortgage Payment.**
    - Amount   Enter **450**.
    - Frequency   Enter **Monthly**.
    - Next Scheduled Date   Enter **6/1** of the next year.

8. Select OK to record the new expense and return to the Forecast Expense Items dialog box. You can see these expense items at the top of this dialog box in Figure 10-5.

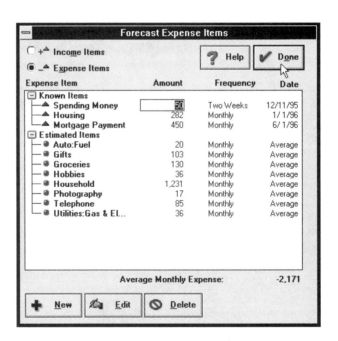

FIGURE 10-5   Forecast Expense Items dialog box

Chapter 10 *Financial Planning*

Tech Tip: If you make the rent and the mortgage payments scheduled payments, these steps are already done for you because Quicken entered these payments as known items rather than as estimates in the forecast.

Tech Acct: Remember to include moving expenses and new purchases for your new home in both your forecast and your budget.

How do I adjust my forecast for an expense that will change in the future?

The steps in the preceding question are the same steps that you perform for any other category that has changed in amount during the year. The only differences are the expense item that you modify and the name of the new one that you create.

I'm creating a forecast and Quicken wants to use the data from last year. I only have this year's data so how do I create my forecast with just this data?

Select Create from the Forecasting window and you can enter new dates in the From and To text boxes. You can even select a portion of a year's transactions when you only have complete records for a portion of the year. Once you select OK, Quicken re-creates the forecast using the dates you give it.

How do I change the time period in the Forecast window?

You can display your forecast for the period of one month, six months, one year, or two years. To change the forecast time period, select a different one from the drop-down list box at the bottom of the Forecasting window. You can change which time period the Forecasting window shows by clicking the << or >> button to see the previous or next time period.

Can I create a forecast out of my budget's numbers?

You can use your budget entries to create a forecast quickly. To create a forecast out of a budget:

1. Show the Forecasting window by select Forecasting from the Plan menu.
2. Select Create in the window's button bar.
3. Select Advanced to see more budget options.
4. Select the From Budget Data option button and then select Done.
5. Select OK to create the forecast.

The expense and income items for the forecast will be the same ones that you have entered into the Budget window.

Tech Tip: If you want to keep another forecast besides the one you create with the budget, save the first forecast before creating the one with a budget. Create this scenario by selecting Scenario from the button bar. Then select New, type a name for the scenario, select OK, and select Done. For more information on scenarios, read the next question.

Tech Terror: When you have Quicken create a forecast from budget entries, it does not replace income and expense items for categories that have scheduled transactions. The only way to do this is to edit the income and expense items before requesting the use of budget entries and deleting those listed under Known Items.

How can I compare my forecast to the budget?

You can create scenarios for your forecast and for a forecast created with your budget. Then you can compare the two scenarios. These steps are:

1. Create the forecast you want to compare to the forecast created with your budget.

2. Select Scenario from the button bar.
3. Select New, type a name for the scenario, and select OK.
4. Select <Base Scenario> from the Scenario Name drop-down list box and then select Done.
5. Select Create in the window's button bar.
6. Select Advanced to see more budget options.
7. Select the From Budget Data option button and then select Done.
8. Select OK to create the forecast based on the budget.
9. Select Scenario from the button bar.
10. Select New, type a name for the scenario, and select OK.
11. Select the Compare Current Scenario With option button in the Manage Forecast Scenarios dialog box.
12. Select the scenario name you entered in step 3 in the adjoining text box.
13. Select Done to put the dialog box away and show the two forecasts, like the two that you can see in Figure 10-6.

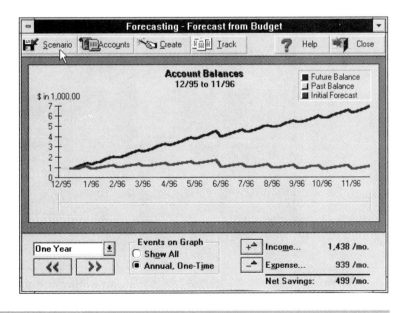

FIGURE 10-6   Forecasting window comparing two scenarios

After creating the perfect forecast, how do I use these numbers for my budget?

You can easily create a budget out of the income and expense items entered in the Forecasting window. Just select Track and then select OK when you see the confirmation about overwriting the existing budget. Quicken creates the budget. Quicken also creates a snapshot page for some of your spending items. You can select Done to return to the Forecasting window or select Snapshot to show the Snapshot page, like the one in Figure 10-7.

Tech Terror: The Track button in the Forecasting window destroys any budget information that you have already entered. Make sure that you do not want what currently appears in the Budget window before selecting Track.

FIGURE 10-7 Snapshot page created by updating the budget with the forecast

Index

A

Account balances, hiding, 63-64
Account reconciliation. *See* Reconciliation
Account register. *See* Register
Account selectors, showing, 47
Accounting methods (business), 198
Accounts
    vs. categories, 48-49
    for payroll, 202-203
    switching between, 51
    tax-deferred, 176
    transferring transactions between, 59-60
Accounts payable, 221, 223-224
Accounts receivable, 218-222
Accounts receivable report, 220-222
Accrual system of accounting, 198
Addresses
    showing, 88
    storing, 60
Aligning checks in the printer, 91-95
Alphabetizing in the Portfolio View window, 6
Archiving last year's transactions, 42-43
Assign Transaction to Group dialog box, 81
ATM transactions, entering, 60-61
AUTOEXEC.BAT file, 21

B

BACKUP directory, 19-20
Bank statements, errors in, 101
Basic transactions, 51-62
BillMinder program, 68-70
BILLMNDW.EXE file, 4
Bonds, 146, 177-181
    recording, 177-179
    redeeming, 179
    Series EE, 181
    zero-coupon, 180-181
Brokerage accounts, 184-186
Budget reports, 227-244
    amounts in, 238-240
    printing sideways, 229
    supercategories in, 236-238
    titling, 228
Budget Variances graph, 274
Budget window, 233, 238
    deleted accounts in, 240
    subcategories in, 240-241
    viewing subcategories in, 6
Budgets (and budgeting), 12, 225-244
    for a business, 200
    comparing with forecasts, 300-301
    creating entries for, 229-235
    creating multiple, 243-244
    exporting data from, 241-242
    and forecasts, 296-297, 300, 302
    hiding, 235-236
    for savings, 232-234
Business applications, 197-224
    accounting methods, 198
    accounts payable, 221-224
    accounts receivable, 218-222
    budgeting, 200
    categories, 199
    depreciation, 213-214
    job costing, 210-212
    meals and entertainment, 218
    mileage deduction, 216-218
    owner withdrawals, 214-215
    payroll accounting, 202-209
    vs. personal finances, 200-202
    recording expenses, 201-202
    reports, 252-253
    sales tax, 210
    setting up for, 199-200

Business deductions, 216-218
Buttons, investment register, 2
Buy vs. BuyX transactions, 5
Buy Shares dialog box, 173
Buyouts (share), 170-171

C

Calendars, 56, 254-255
Call waiting, modems and, 25
Capital gains, 182-183
Capital Gains report, 183
Cash basis accounting, 198
Cash Flow report, 66-67, 252, 256, 275
Cash monitoring, 66-68
Categories. (*See also* Subcategories)
 vs. accounts, 48-49
 adding, 28-29
 allocating sales tax to, 67-68
 business, 199
 copying between files, 37
 creating, 34-35
 credit card purchases in, 65
 custom, 34-37
 hiding in graphs, 276
 for payroll, 202-203
 printing transactions by, 57-58
 reassigning, 50-51
 removing, 29
 switching between, 50-51
 table of business, 29
 table of home use, 26-28
 tax features of, 35-36
 tax form assignments for, 117-119
 transactions without, 49
 with an underscore (_), 234-235
 using description in reports, 256-257
Category field, searching in, 52
CD earnings, estimating, 285-286
Check Printer Alignment dialog box, 92
Check register. *See* Register
Check style, setting default, 8-9
CheckFree, 102-111
 abbreviations used in, 107
 confirming payments made, 111
 contacting the company, 108
 listing transactions made, 107
 making payments with, 103-105
 paying a loan, 106-107
 setting up to use, 23-24
 using with OS/2, 111
Checks
 aligning in the printer, 91-95
 changing the background, 97-98
 changing the look of, 96-97
 correcting errors in, 87-88

investment account, 169-170
 printing, 17, 91-96
 printing logos on, 96-97
 recording partial payments, 86-87
 showing addresses for, 88
 voiding, 85-86
 writing, 83-88
 writing postdated, 86
Classes, Register Report with, 90
Clipboard, 264-265
Clr field, Xs in, 56
College Planner, 284
Color graphs, printing, 280
Communications links, setting up, 23-26
Comparison report, 250-251
Continuous-feed printers, 91, 93-94
Copying categories between files, 37
Copying data between files, 32-34
Create Scheduled Transaction dialog box, 77
Create Transaction Group dialog box, 80
Credit card accounts, reconciling, 62
Credit card expenses, business, 198
Credit card interest rate, tracking, 64
Credit card limit, tracking, 65
Credit card purchases, categories of, 65
Custom categories, 34-37
Customize Report dialog box, 246, 258

D

Data files
 accessing old, 15-16
 business and personal, 200-201
 copying categories between, 37
 renaming, 22-23
 switching between open, 21-22
 transferring between computers, 17-18
 transferring data between, 30-34
 using files from older version software, 14
Dates
 entering, 55-56
 in memorized reports, 266-267
 setting for reports, 253-254
Deleted accounts in budget window, 240
Deleting subcategories, 36
Deleting transactions, 51
Depreciation, 213-214
Desktop, saving, 17
Dividends, stock, 175-176

E

Earned Income Credit (EIC), 139
Electronic funds transfers, 108
Electronic Payment Account Settings
 window, 103

Index

Electronic payments, 103-105
  explained, 108
  stopping, 109-110
Employee stock options, 159-164
Employee wages, 202-209
Employee withholdings and taxes, 203-209
Employee W-2s, 126-127, 208
Error messages
  Cannot find BILLMNDW.EXE, 4
  Unable to decompress..., 5
Estimated taxes, 140-141
Excel, budget copied to, 242

F

File extensions, table of, 23
File options, 21-23
Files. *See* Data files
Filtering reports, 267-270
Financial Calendar, 13
Financial planning, 283-302
Find dialog box, 2
Find and Replace feature, 54-55
Find window, 53
Fiscal year, using in reports, 254-255
Fonts, setting for reports, 258-259
Forecast, comparing with budget, 300-301
Forecast numbers, using in a budget, 302
Forecast window, 296-302
Forecasting, 12, 284, 296-302
  from budget numbers, 300
  and budgeting, 296-297
401(k) retirement plans, 165-169

G

Gifts of stock, 176-177
Graphs, 245, 271-281
  hiding categories, 276
  investment, 191-192
  memorized, 13
  printing, 278-281
  printing in color, 280
  in separate windows, 277-278
  speeding up, 278-279

H

Hardware requirements, 13-14
Hide/Show button, 46-47
Hiding account balances, 63-64
Hiding budget numbers, 235-236
Hiding categories in graphs, 276
Hiding text in a Payee field, 87
Historical data, 37-43
Historical prices, storing, 194

Home improvements, and tax planning, 134-135
Home loan forecasting, 297-299
Home loan refinancing, 290-291
Home mortgages in Tax Planner, 133-134
HomeBase, 12

I

Income and Expense graphs, 271-274, 276-277
Inherited investments, 177
Installing Quicken, 11
IntelliCharge, 25-26
Interest charges, and reconciliation, 97-98
Interest checks, 179-180
Interest income, 179-180
Investment accounts
  negative balance in, 5
  transferring funds to checking, 7-8
  setting up, 147-149
  writing checks from, 169-170
Investment actions, table of, 148-149
Investment goals, 150-154
Investment graphs, 191-192
Investment Income report, 153-154
Investment Performance graph, 274
Investment register buttons, 2
Investment Savings Planner dialog box, 286-288
Investment transactions, scheduled, 193
Investments, 145-195 (*see also* Stock options; Stocks)
  account types for, 147
  bonds, 177-181
  brokerage accounts, 184-186
  and capital gains, 182-183
  common, 146
  401(k) plans, 165-169
  inherited, 177
  IRAs, 130-131, 146, 164-165, 289-290
  portfolio viewing, 188-191
  return of capital, 172-174
  showing, 151-153
  valuing, 183-184
IRAs (individual retirement accounts), 130-131, 146, 164-165, 289-290
IRR (internal rate of return), 191-192
IRS tax assistance, 114
Itemized Category Report, 57-58
Itemizing deductions on 1040 Schedule A, 131-135

J

Job costing, 210-212

Job/Project report, 212
Joint checking accounts, 89-90

K
Keogh contributions, 215

L
Last year's transactions, archiving, 42-43
Limited partnerships, 146, 182
Listing register transactions, 57
Loan calculations (home loan), 290-291
Loan forecasting (home loan), 297-299
Loan payments, 91, 106-107
Loan Planner, 284
Locked transactions, 75-76
Logos, printing on checks, 96-97

M
Mac files, on IBM computers, 18
Margins, changing for reports, 259
Memorized graphs, 13
Memorized reports, 266-267
Memorized Transaction window, 73
Memorized transactions, 46, 70-76
　automatic, 72
　as dollar amounts, 72-74
　errors in, 74
　locked, 75-76
　as percentages, 72-73
　recalling, 71
　removing, 74-75
　and scheduled transactions, 79
　selecting, 71
Memory requirements, 13-14
Messages (error)
　Cannot find BILLMNDW.EXE, 4
　Unable to decompress..., 5
Mileage deduction (business taxes), 216-218
Minimum account balances, hiding, 63-64
Modems
　and call waiting, 25
　setting up, 23-24
Modified-cash-basis accounting, 198
Monthly Budget report, 268
Monthly reports, 255
Mortgage forecasting, 297-299
Mortgage refinancing, 290-291
Moving an account between files, 30-32
Mutual funds, 146, 287-288

N
Naming a security, 150

Negative balance in investment account, 5
Net Worth graph, 274
New features of Quicken 4 for Windows, 12-13
New User Setup dialog box, 15-16
940 and 941 forms, 209

O
Online services, 13
OS/2, using CheckFree with, 111

P
Page printers, 91-93
Paper size for reports, 262
Partial pages of checks, printing, 95
Partial payments, recording, 86-87
Partnerships, limited, 146, 182
Password protection, using, 43-44
Payee field, hiding text in, 87
Payee Report, 48-49, 54
Payments, electronic, 103-105, 108-110
Payments, loan, 91, 106-107
Payments, scheduled, 90-91
Payroll, 202-209
Payroll report, 208
Percentage Split dialog box, 73
Portfolio Price Update, 194-195
Portfolio Value report, 152
Portfolio View window, 3-4, 6, 151-153, 188-191
Postdated checks, writing, 86
Previewing a report, 261
Print button, 261
Print Checks icon, 95-96
Printer setup options, 8-9
Printers, types of, 91
Printing
　aligning checks in printer, 91-95
　checks, 17, 91-96
　graphs, 278-281
　logos on checks, 96-97
　partial pages of checks, 95
　problems with, 94
　register transactions, 56-57
　reports, 260-262
　transactions by category, 57-58
Program Item Properties dialog box (Windows), 22
Progress bar, 12
Protecting data, 43-44

Q
QIF Export dialog box, 30

Index

Quicken 4 for Windows, new features of, 12-13
QuickFill, 79
QuickZoom reports, 262-264

R

Real estate investment trust (REIT), 146
Reconcile Bank Statement dialog box, 99
Reconciliation, 62, 83-111
    adding interest and service charges, 97-98
    canceling, 101
    of credit card accounts, 62
    and opening balance, 100
    problems with, 97-102
Recording transactions, 45
Refinance Planner, 284, 290-291
Register
    changing the look of, 46-47
    new features of, 12-13
    showing more entries, 46-47
Register buttons, 2
Register Reports, 56-57, 90. *See also* Reports
Register window, 45
Reminders, 68-70
    eliminating, 16
    new features of, 13
Renaming data files, 22-23
Rental income and expenses, 211-212
Repetitive transactions, 40-41, 76-78
Report windows, 260-261, 265-267
Reports, 245
    account balances on, 271
    with categories, 49
    without categories, 48
    category descriptions in, 256-257
    changing margins for, 259
    exporting to word processors, 264-265
    filtering, 267-270
    fitting columns on, 260
    layout and format of, 256-259
    limiting to business, 252-253
    memorized, 266-267
    with missing entries, 255
    monthly, 255
    new features of, 13
    previewing, 261
    printing, 260-262
    QuickZoom, 262-264
    setting dates for, 253-254
    setting fonts for, 258-259
    shortened entries in, 257
    types of, 247-252
    uncategorized transactions in, 269-270
Retirement Planner, 284, 289-290

Retirement plans—401(k), 165-169
Return of capital, 172-174
Return of Capital dialog box, 172

S

Sales tax, 67-69, 210
Saving an empty desktop, 17
Savings, budgeting for, 232-234
Savings Goals, 12, 63, 284, 292-295
Savings Goals window, 292-295
Savings Planner, 284-288
Schedule K-1 (Form 1065), 182
Scheduled investment transactions, 193
Scheduled payments, 90-91
Scheduled transaction groups, 79-82
Scheduled transactions, 40-41, 46, 76-79, 90-91
Searching
    in the Category field, 52
    for a company or person, 52-54
Section 179 deductions, 214
Securities. *See* Investments; Stocks
Security symbols, 7
Self-employment taxes, 138-139
Series EE bonds, 181
Service charges, and reconciliation, 97-98
Set Up Category dialog box, 35
Set Up Loan dialog box, 106
Setting up Quicken, 11-44
Setup requirements, 13-17
Shares, 170-176 (*see also* Stock options)
    buyouts of, 170-171
    spin-offs, 171-174
ShrsIn transactions, 5
Snapshot page (budget forecasting), 12, 302
Spelling errors, correcting, 54-55
Spending, monitoring, 66-68
Spin-offs (share), 171-174
Split Adjustment dialog box, 73
Split transactions, changing, 60
Splits window, 65, 87
Spreadsheet, exporting budget data to, 241-242
Standard categories for business, table of, 29
Standard categories for home use, table of, 26-28
Standard check style, setting, 8-9
Start New Year dialog box, 42
Starting Quicken, 11-44
Startup options, 21-23
Stock dividends, 175-176
Stock gifts, 176-177
Stock options, 146, 154-164
    buying and selling, 154-157

employee, 159-164
exercising, 155
expired, 157-158
writing off, 157
Stock prices, storing historical, 194
Stock rights, 158
Stock splits, 146
Stock symbols, 149-150
Stocks, 146 (*see also* Investments; Shares; Stock options)
inherited, 177
updating prices, 7
Stopping electronic payments, 109-110
Storing addresses, 60
Storing prices, 194
Subcategories
in the Budget window, 240-241
creating, 50
deleting, 36
viewing in Budget window, 6
Summary report, 248-249
Supercategories, in budget report, 236-238

T

Tax credits, 139
Tax features of categories, 35-36
Tax form assignments, 117-119
Tax Planner, 12, 113-143
entering income, 126-130
estimated taxes in, 140-141
home improvements in, 134-135
home mortgages in, 133-134
importing Quicken data into, 120-121
IRA deductions in, 130-131
local income taxes in, 133
planning with, 142-143
reports, 122-125
Schedule A, 131-135
Schedule B, 135-137
Schedule C, 137
Schedule D, 137-138
self-employment taxes in, 138-139
tax credits in, 139
tax form assignments, 117-119
tax projections report, 124-125
and tax refund checks, 133
vs. TurboTax, 117
updating, 142
withholdings, 140
W-2s, 126-127, 208
Tax Planner window, 115, 125
Tax reports, 122-125
Tax Scenario Comparisons dialog box, 143

Tax Schedule report, 122-124
Tax Summary report, 122-123
Tax-deferred accounts, 130, 176
Taxes. *See* Tax Planner
Templates, using transactions as, 70-71
1040 Schedules, 131-136
1099-OID, 180-181
Text fonts, setting for reports, 258-259
Tranferring funds from investments to checking, 7-8
Transaction groups, scheduled, 79-82
Transaction reports, 247-248
Transactions, explained, 45
Transferring data between files, 30-34
Transferring files between computers, 17-18
Treasury bills, redeeming, 180
TurboTax, 117

U

Uncategorized transactions in report, 269-270
Unit trusts, 146
Updating stock prices, 7

V

Virus checker, disabling, 17
Voiding a check, 85-86

W

Wages, employee, 203
WIN.INI, 4
Word processors
exporting budget data to, 241-242
exporting reports to, 264-265
WPR.DAT file, 8-9, 280
Write Checks window background, 98
W-2s, employee, 126-127, 208

X

Xln transfers, 8

Y

Year's transactions, archiving, 42-43

Z

Zero-coupon bonds, 180-181

Learn From The CLASSICS

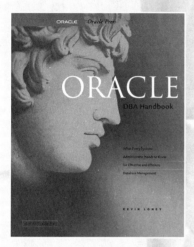

ORACLE DBA HANDBOOK

by Kevin Loney
Every DBA can learn to manage a networked Oracle database efficiently and effectively with this comprehensive guide. Oracle Magazine columnist Kevin Loney covers everything a DBA needs to manage Oracle, from architecture to layout considerations to supporting packages. A command reference and configuration guidelines are included as well as scripts and tips. The **Oracle DBA Handbook** is the ideal support and resource for all new and existing DBAs.

Price: $34.95
Available September 1994
ISBN: 0-07-881182-1
Pages: 608, paperback

TUNING ORACLE

by Michael J. Corey, Michael Abbey, and Daniel J. Dechichio, Jr.
Learn to customize Oracle for optimal performance and productivity with this focused guide. Michael Corey, president of the International Oracle Users Group, and Michael Abbey and Daniel Dechichio, recognized Oracle experts, teach strategies and systems to help administrators avoid problems, increase database speed, and ensure overall security. For a powerful and versatile database, **Tuning Oracle** is your ultimate resource for making Oracle reach its full potential.

Price: $29.95 U.S.A.
Available November, 1994
ISBN: 0-07-881181-3
Pages: 544, paperback

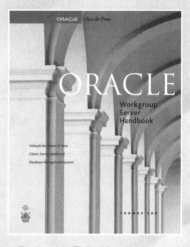

ORACLE WORKGROUP SERVER HANDBOOK

by Thomas B. Cox
Take full advantage of the power and flexibility of the new Oracle Workgroup Server with this comprehensive handbook. Thomas Cox helps users master the intricacies of this relational database management system, including creating a database, developing queries, and using SQL as well as explaining and defining declarations, referential integrity, and more. Perfect for both users and administrators, the **Oracle Workgroup Server Handbook** is the one authoritative book.

Price: $34.95
Available October 1994
ISBN: 0-07-881186-4
Pages: 448, paperback

 *Oracle Press*

Driving Your Information Systems for Optimal Performance

MAKE THE RIGHT CONNECTION

It's what you know that counts. With innovative books from LAN TIMES and Osborne/McGraw-Hill, you'll be the one in demand.

**LAN TIMES
ENCYCLOPEDIA OF
NETWORKING**
by Tom Sheldon
An authoritative reference on all networking facets and trends.
$39.95 U.S.A.
ISBN: 0-07-881965-2
Available now

**LAN TIMES
Guide to SQL**
by James R. Groff and Paul N. Weinberg
$29.95 U.S.A.
ISBN: 0-07-882026-X

**LAN TIMES E-Mail
Resource Guide**
by Rick Drummond and Nancy Cox
$29.95 U.S.A.
ISBN: 0-07-882052-9

**LAN TIMES Guide
To Interoperability**
by Tom Sheldon
$29.95 U.S.A.
ISBN: 0-07-882043-X

BC640SL

Revolutionary Information on the Information REVOLUTION

Alluring opportunities abound for the global investor. But avoiding investment land mines can be tricky business. The first release in the Business Week Library of Computing lets you master all the winning strategies. Everything is here—from analyzing and selecting the best companies, to tax planning, using investment software tools, and more. Disks include MetaStock, Windows On WallStreet, and Telescan, the leading investment analysis software.

The Business Week Guide to Global Investments Using Electronic Tools
by Robert Schwabach
Includes Three 3.5-Inch Disks
$39.95 U.S.A.   ISBN: 0-07-882055-3

The Business Week Guide to Multimedia Presentations Create Dynamic Presentations That Inspire
by Robert Lindstrom
Includes One CD-ROM
$39.95 U.S.A.
ISBN: 0-07-882057-X

The Internet Yellow Pages
by Harley Hahn and Rick Stout
$27.95 U.S.A.
ISBN: 0-07-882023-5

BYTE's Mac Programmer's Cookbook
by Rob Terrell
Includes
One 3.5-Inch Disk
$29.95 U.S.A.
ISBN: 0-07-882062-6

Multimedia: Making It Work, Second Edition
by Tay Vaughan
Includes
One CD-ROM
$34.95 U.S.A.
ISBN: 0-07-882035-9

BC640SL

When It Comes to CD-ROM...
We Wrote the Book

The Internet Yellow Pages
by Harley Hahn and Rick Stout
$27.95 U.S.A.
ISBN: 0-07-882098-7

The Internet Complete Reference
by Harley Hahn and Rick Stout
$29.95 U.S.A.
ISBN: 0-07-881980-6

CorelDRAW! 5 Made Easy
by Martin S. Matthews and Carole Boggs Matthews
$29.95 U.S.A.
ISBN: 0-07-882066-9

Teach Yourself C++, Second Edition
by Herbert Schildt
$24.95 U.S.A.
ISBN: 0-07-882025-1

Everything You Always Wanted to Know About CD-ROMs and More!

This Exclusive Book/CD-ROM Package Includes
- Sound and Clip Art
- Samples of CD-ROM Applications
- Multimedia Authoring Tools

Part buyer's guide, part standards guide, and part troubleshooter, the **BYTE Guide to CD-ROM** discusses all aspects of this proliferating technology so you can take full advantage.

BYTE Guide to CD-ROM
by
Michael Nadeau,
BYTE Senior Editor

Includes CD-ROM
$39.95 U.S.A.
ISBN: 0-07-881982-2

Osborne
Get Answers—Get Osborne
For Accuracy, Quality and Value

BC640SL

CORPORATE SOFTWARE

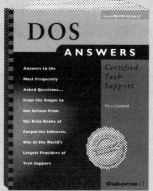

**DOS Answers:
Certified Tech Support**
by Mary Campbell
0-07-882030-8 $16.95 U.S.A.

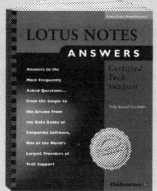

**LOTUS Notes Answers:
Certified Tech Support**
by Polly Russell Kornblith
0-07-882045-6 $16.95 U.S.A.

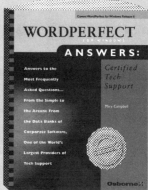

**WORDPERFECT for Windows
Answers: Certified Tech Support**
by Mary Campbell
0-07-882053-7 $16.95 U.S.A.

**NETWARE Answers:
Certified Tech Support**
by James Nadler and Donald Guarnieri
0-07-882044-8 $16.95 U.S.A.

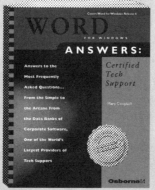

**WORD for Windows Answers:
Certified Tech Support**
by Mary Campbell
0-07-882031-6 $19.95 U.S.A.

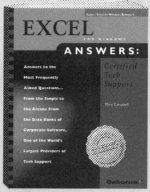

**EXCEL for Windows Answers:
Certified Tech Support**
by Mary Campbell
0-07-882045-5 $16.95 U.S.A.

Smart
ANSWERS

NOW, in conjunction with Corporate Software Inc., Osborne delivers the most authoritative new books that answer the most frequently asked tech support questions, all based on Corporate Software's comprehensive data banks. THE CERTIFIED TECH SUPPORT SERIES — the next best thing to having a tech support expert by your side.

BC640SL

Yo Unix!

INNOVATIVE BOOKS
from Open Computing and Osborne/McGraw-Hill

OPEN COMPUTING'S GUIDE TO THE BEST FREE UNIX UTILITIES
BY JIM KEOUGH AND REMON LAPID
INCLUDES ONE CD-ROM
$34.95 U.S.A.
ISBN: 0-07-882046-4
AVAILABLE NOW

OPEN COMPUTING'S BEST UNIX TIPS EVER
BY KENNETH H. ROSEN, RICHARD P. ROSINSKI, AND DOUGLAS A. HOST
$29.95 U.S.A.
ISBN: 0-07-881924-5
AVAILABLE NOW

OPEN COMPUTING'S UNIX UNBOUND
BY HARLEY HAHN
$27.95 U.S.A.
ISBN: 0-07-882050-2

OPEN COMPUTING'S STANDARD UNIX API FUNCTIONS
BY GARRETT LONG
$39.95 U.S.A.
ISBN: 0-07-882051-0

BC640SL

Think Fast
PASSING LANE AHEAD

Lotus Notes Answers: Certified Tech Support
by Polly Russell Kornblith
$16.95 U.S.A.
ISBN: 0-07-882055-3

What's the quickest route to tech support? Osborne's new Certified Tech Support series. Developed in conjunction with Corporate Software Inc., one of the largest providers of tech support fielding more than 200,000 calls a month, Osborne delivers the most authoritative question and answer books available anywhere. Speed up your computing and stay in the lead with answers to the most frequently asked end-user questions—from the simple to the arcane. And watch for more books in the series.

The Internet Yellow Pages
by Harley Hahn and Rick Stout
$27.95 U.S.A.
ISBN: 0-07-882023-5

Sound Blaster: The Official Book, Second Edition
by Peter M. Ridge, David Golden, Ivan Luk, Scott Sindorf, and Richard Heimlich
Includes One 3.5-Inch Disk
$34.95 U.S.A.
ISBN: 0-07-882000-6

Osborne Windows Programming Series
by Herbert Schildt, Chris H. Pappas, and William H. Murray, III
Vol. 1 - Programming Fundamentals
$39.95 U.S.A.
ISBN: 0-07-881990-3
Vol. 2 - General Purpose API Functions
$49.95 U.S.A.
ISBN: 0-07-881991-1
Vol. 3 - Special Purpose API Functions
$49.95 U.S.A.
ISBN: 0-07-881992-X

The Microsoft Access Handbook
by Mary Campbell
$27.95 U.S.A.
ISBN: 0-07-882014-6

ORDER BOOKS DIRECTLY FROM OSBORNE/McGRAW-HILL

For a complete catalog of Osborne's books, call 510-549-6600 or write to us at 2600 Tenth Street, Berkeley, CA 94710

Call Toll-Free: *1-800-822-8158*
24 hours a day, 7 days a week in U.S. and Canada

Mail this order form to:
McGraw-Hill, Inc.
Customer Service Dept.
P.O. Box 547
Blacklick, OH 43004

Fax this order form to:
1-614-759-3644

EMAIL
7007.1531@COMPUSERVE.COM
COMPUSERVE GO MH

Ship to:

Name _____

Company _____

Address _____

City / State / Zip _____

Daytime Telephone: _____
(We'll contact you if there's a question about your order.)

ISBN #	BOOK TITLE	Quantity	Price	Total
0-07-88				
0-07-88				
0-07-88				
0-07-88				
0-07-88				
0-07088				
0-07-88				
0-07-88				
0-07-88				
0-07-88				
0-07-88				
0-07-88				
0-07-88				
0-07-88				
	Shipping & Handling Charge from Chart Below			
	Subtotal			
	Please Add Applicable State & Local Sales Tax			
	TOTAL			

Shipping & Handling Charges

Order Amount	U.S.	Outside U.S.
Less than $15	$3.50	$5.50
$15.00 - $24.99	$4.00	$6.00
$25.00 - $49.99	$5.00	$7.00
$50.00 - $74.99	$6.00	$8.00
$75.00 - and up	$7.00	$9.00

Occasionally we allow other selected companies to use our mailing list. If you would prefer that we not include you in these extra mailings, please check here: ❏

METHOD OF PAYMENT

❏ Check or money order enclosed (payable to Osborne/McGraw-Hill)

❏ AMERICAN EXPRESS   ❏ DISCOVER   ❏ MasterCard   ❏ VISA

Account No. ☐☐☐☐☐☐☐☐☐☐☐☐☐☐

Expiration Date _____

Signature _____

In a hurry? Call 1-800-822-8158 anytime, day or night, or visit your local bookstore.

Thank you for your order   Code BC640SL